Mental Health and Deafness

Margaret du Feu and Cathy Chovaz

OXFORD
UNIVERSITY PRESS

OXFORD
UNIVERSITY PRESS

Oxford University Press is a department of the University of Oxford.
It furthers the University's objective of excellence in research, scholarship,
and education by publishing worldwide.

Oxford   New York
Auckland   Cape Town   Dar es Salaam   Hong Kong   Karachi
Kuala Lumpur   Madrid   Melbourne   Mexico City   Nairobi
New Delhi   Shanghai   Taipei   Toronto

With offices in
Argentina   Austria   Brazil   Chile   Czech Republic   France   Greece
Guatemala   Hungary   Italy   Japan   Poland   Portugal   Singapore
South Korea   Switzerland   Thailand   Turkey   Ukraine   Vietnam

Oxford is a registered trademark of Oxford University Press
in the UK and certain other countries.

Published in the United States of America by
Oxford University Press
198 Madison Avenue, New York, NY 10016

Library of Congress Cataloging-in-Publication Data
Du Feu, Margaret, author.
Mental health and deafness / Margaret du Feu and Cathy Chovaz.
pages cm.—(Professional perspectives on deafness)
Includes bibliographical references and index.
ISBN 978-0-19-986075-3
1. Deaf—Mental health.   2. Deafness—Psychological aspects.   I. Chovaz,
Cathy, author.   II. Title.
RC451.4.D4D83 2014
617.8—dc23
2014002932

9 8 7 6 5 4 3 2
Printed in the United States of America
on acid-free paper

Mental Health and Deafness

PROFESSIONAL PERSPECTIVES ON DEAFNESS: EVIDENCE AND APPLICATIONS

Series Editors

Particia Elizabeth Spencer

Marc Marschark

Mental Health and Deafness

Margaret du Feu and Cathy Chovaz

Literacy Instruction for Students who are Deaf and Hard of Hearing

Susan R. Easterbrooks and Jennifer Beal-Alvarez

Introduction to American Deaf Culture

Thomas K. Holcomb

Evidence-Based Practice in Educating Deaf and Hard-of-Hearing Students

Patricia Elizabeth Spencer and Marc Marschark

For my daughter, Frances
-Margaret du Feu

For my parents, Betty & Mickey, who travelled so faithfully with me into
deafness, and my husband, Scott, who is my soulmate on this journey.
-Cathy Chovaz

CONTENTS

ACKNOWLEDGMENTS

I would like to thank all my patients and colleagues, past and present, in the UK and the Republic of Ireland. I have learnt from them all I know. Special thanks are due to Dr George Milner, who inspired me to be a psychiatrist, Professor Ian Brockington, Robin Caley, Stuart Cumella and the late Dr John Beasley who laid the foundations for the Birmingham Mental Health and Deafness service, and the late Dr John Denmark who opened it. In Northern Ireland, Brian Symington, Professor Roy McClelland and Colin Wilmot were among the many people who enabled the service to develop. In the Republic of Ireland, Niall Keane and Sandra O'Brien and many others worked to set up the service, and President Mary McAleese formally opened the cross border initiative. They all deserve my gratitude.

Carol Carton, Barbara Rawlings, Bronagh Byrne, Gerasimos Chatzidamianos, Efthymia Karaouza, Peter McKenna and many others have given valuable advice for this book and I thank them all.

I cannot mention everyone individually, but my thanks go to my wonderful secretaries, past and present. Marcia Thornton, Andrea Harvey and Samantha Tyhuis deserve special mention, and extra thanks go to Rhonda Stitt for her invaluable help in preparing this book.

Margaret du Feu

I would like to thank Kings University College at Western University, London, Ontario, Canada for support on many different levels for writing this book.

Cathy Chovaz

INTRODUCTION

This book is written for clinicians such as family doctors, clinical psychologists, psychiatrists, and social workers who have relatively little experience working with D/deaf children and adults. Over the course of a career, a clinician working with the general population is very likely to meet at least one Deaf client/patient who is in need of a mental health assessment, diagnosis, treatment plan, or general support. It has been our experience that mainstream education in most health care disciplines does not provide adequate, if any, information related to deafness. The subject of deafness and mental health is not included in mainstream textbooks or standard course curriculums. As such, it is common for clinicians to feel ill-equipped to provide service, and perhaps even more important, the Deaf patient is often not well served. This, to us, is not acceptable, and it is for this need that we have written this book. We anticipate that this book may not be as helpful for those already well immersed in this field of mental health and deafness—rather, it is strictly an introductory text for mainstream clinicians.

Dr Margaret du Feu qualified in medicine in Cambridge and London, England, and began her training in psychiatry in 1984. Margaret was progressively deafened as an adult by cochlear otosclerosis. She uses British Sign Language and had a cochlear implant in 1999. In 1991 she was appointed in Birmingham to develop the third service for Mental Health and Deafness in England (after Manchester and London). In 2003 Margaret divided her time with continued work in Birmingham while also developing a Mental Health and Deafness service in Northern Ireland. In 2005 she relocated to Belfast to begin full-time work in Northern Ireland and the Republic of Ireland. In 2010 she retired from the UK National Health Service, but continues to work part time in the Republic of Ireland, in Irish Sign Language, with the help of an interpreter. Margaret was a guest lecturer on Deaf Children Australia's National Tour on the emotional and social well-being of deaf Australians in 2010.

Dr Cathy Chovaz was profoundly deafened as a young adult following her undergraduate degree in nursing. After learning American Sign Language, Cathy completed Master and Doctoral studies in clinical psychology at the University of Western Ontario (UWO) in London, Canada. Cathy was the first graduate student to attend Western using a sign language interpreter and went on to become the first Deaf clinical psychologist in Canada. Cathy consulted to a provincial school for the Deaf, following which she opened the first mental health clinic for deaf, deafened, and Deaf children in Canada. Cathy joined the faculty at Kings University College at UWO in 2009 where she holds a cross appointment in psychology and the Schulich School of Medicine in psychiatry. Her area of expertise is deaf children and mental health, and she continues to consult, lecture widely, and engage in research in this area. Cathy teaches at the university with an ASL interpreter and continues a private practice for Deaf children.

Together we bring 50 years of clinical experience to this book as well as personally walking the different roads of deafness. We have seen patients across the entire life span, many of whom have differed widely in clinical presentations and needs, yet have all been united by their deafness. As this book will share, deafness knows no boundaries, no race, and no social class. It is a fact of many lives and it is our hope that the descriptions, facts, and stories that we share in this book will fill a much needed gap in the literature for clinicians who are relatively unfamiliar with deafness. It is also our hope that this book will quickly become outdated as clinicians and academics alike learn more about deafness and incorporate it into mainstream practices of mental health.

The case examples described are drawn from the authors' experience, but details have been changed to preserve confidentiality.

Margaret du Feu is the author of Chapters 1 and 2 and 10 through 21. Cathy Chovaz is the author of Chapters 3 through 9.

Mental Health and Deafness

Mental Health and Disease

1 Deafness: The Facts

Deafness is a complex biological, social, and psychological construct that affects millions of people. Partial hearing loss affects 360 million people globally, 5% of the world's population. In developed countries such as the United Kingdom, if mild hearing losses are included, up to one in six of the population is affected. In regions such as Southeast Asia and Sub-Saharan Africa, the rate may be doubled (World Health Organization, 2013, Factsheet 300). The World Health Organization defines hearing loss greater than 40 decibels in the better ear in adults and greater than 30 decibels in the better ear in children as disabling. Approximately one-third of people over 65 years of age are affected by disabling hearing loss. Again the prevalence in this age group is greatest in South Asia, Asia Pacific, and Sub-Saharan Africa.

Hearing loss is measured in decibels, and the audiology awareness campaign defines decibel losses from normal to profound (see Tables 1.1 and 1.2).

Table 1.1 *Categories of Hearing Loss, Measured in Decibels (dB)*

−10 dB to 25 dB	Normal range
26 dB to 40 dB	Mild hearing loss
41 dB to 55 dB	Moderate hearing loss
56 dB to 70 dB	Moderately severe hearing loss
71 dB to 90 dB	Severe hearing loss
Over 90 dB	Profound hearing loss

(www.audiologyawareness.com)

Profound deafness from early life is much less common. Approximately one in a thousand of the world's population has been severely or profoundly Deaf from birth or early life. This is a total of approximately 7 million people, the equivalent of the population of Norway or New Zealand. These people are likely to use their national sign language and to identify themselves as "*Deaf*," as distinct from audiologically "*deaf*," and are likely to identify themselves with the Deaf community (Padden & Humphries, 1988). Sign languages have developed naturally in the same way as spoken languages in different countries. It is a common misconception that sign language is international. There is an International Sign Language, sometimes called Gestuno, which was developed by a committee of the World Federation of the Deaf (British Deaf Association, 1975) for use at international meetings, but like Esperanto it is not commonly used in everyday life. Sign languages are not based on spoken languages; for example, American Sign Language and British Sign Language

Table 1.2 *Everyday Equivalents of Decibel Levels*

0 dB	The lowest sound level a person with normal hearing can detect
20 dB	A quiet room at night
60 dB	A normal spoken conversation
80 dB	Shouting
90 dB	An underground railway
130 dB	An airplane taking off 100 meters away

(www.deafhear.ie)

are completely different. Sign languages are not gestures, though some signs are iconic in the same way that some speech is onomatopoeic (Emmorey, 2002). Much of this book is about profoundly Deaf people, particularly those who use sign language.

TYPES OF DEAFNESS

There are two main types of deafness, conductive and sensorineural, and there are also mixed types. Conductive hearing problems are in the outer or middle ear and can often be medically or surgically treated. Common examples would be so-called glue ear in childhood from fluid in the middle ear, or chronic middle ear infection at any age. Sensorineural hearing loss occurs in the inner ear in the cochlea or the auditory nerve. It is often progressive and is usually not treatable, though it may be alleviated by a cochlear or, more rarely, a brainstem implant.

Acquired hearing loss may be sudden or gradual, and its impact will vary with regard to both the speed of onset and the age at which it starts.

CAUSES

The most common cause of hearing loss is age-related damage to the cochlea. Other causes of deafness at any age include infectious diseases, chronic ear infections, ototoxic drugs, trauma, and excessive noise. Ménière's disease causes progressive inner ear deafness, with tinnitus and vertigo. There are also genetic causes of both early and late hearing loss.

More than 50% of early profound deafness is genetic (Arnos & Pandya, 2011). Most genetic causes are recessive, which means that the genes are carried by both parents but are not expressed in them. More than 70 genes have been mapped in association with hereditary deafness. Most cause deafness alone (Bitner-Glindzicz, 2002) but others are part of syndromes and have other effects. Sensitivity to the ototoxic effects of some antibiotics, the aminoglycosides, which are commonly used, can also be genetic (Bitner-Glindzicz & Rahman, 2007). More than 90% of people with early profound deafness are born into hearing families (Mitchell & Karchmer, 2004), and this has a major impact on the path through life for many Deaf people.

Non-genetic causes of early profound deafness include prematurity, neonatal hypoxia, low birth weight, fetal alcohol syndrome, severe neonatal jaundice, and prenatal infection with rubella and other pathogens such as syphilis, cytomegalovirus, and toxoplasmosis. Further causes of early profound deafness include exposure to ototoxic drugs during pregnancy and meningitis. Changes have been seen in the causes of deafness over time. Improved obstetric care and immunization against rubella have reduced profound deafness at birth. The improved survival of premature babies has formed a new cohort of deaf people, many with additional difficulties (Picard, 2004).

The prevalence of deafness can be marked in different populations. For example, a study in Italy (Bubbico et al., 2007) showed a higher rate of prelingual deafness in southern Italy than in northern Italy. The higher rate was thought to have been caused in part by an epidemic of maternal rubella that occurred in the 1940s and 1950s and in part by the practice of consanguineous marriage. Records held by churches showed that in some small villages these accounted for over 40% of marriages.

In populations with reduced access to health care, there are high rates of childhood deafness. For example, a survey in Nigeria (Oblako, 1987) showed high rates of childhood deafness, and the reasons included measles, seizures, meningitis, and anti-malarial drugs, combined with a high rate of communicable disease and malnutrition. The indigenous population of Australia also has high rates of childhood deafness, mainly from chronic otitis media (Faye'herbe & Teuma, 2010).

ASSOCIATED DISABILITIES

Deaf people with additional sight problems face further difficulties in independence, mobility, and communication. In the United Kingdom, out of a total population of 62 million, there are an estimated 356,000 people with combined visual and hearing loss, nearly two-thirds of them over 70 years of age (Sense for Deafblind People, 2010).

Many people have hearing loss and additional disabilities. As many as 30% of deaf children have additional or complex needs (Hindley, 2005). About half of older people in the United Kingdom have additional disabilities or long-term health problems as well as hearing loss (Action on Hearing Loss, 2011).

From these outlined figures it is clear that deafness is extremely common and very varied. It can occur alone or with additional health problems or disabilities, which may or may not be associated with the cause of the deafness. All these issues will be explored in more detail in subsequent chapters.

MEDICAL AND SOCIAL MODELS OF DEAFNESS

Deafness can be regarded as a disability, but Deaf people who sign see themselves not as a disabled group, but as a cultural and linguistic minority. In recent decades there has been a paradigm shift away from the medical model for all disabilities, which in total affect over 1 billion people worldwide, 15% of the world's population (World Health Organization, 2011). This shift from a medical to a social understanding of disability indicates that it is increasingly recognized that society disables people as much as any sensory or physical differences. In addition, increasing recognition of bilingualism (Diamond, 2012), diversity, and the equality of cultural minority groups has brought about a more positive attitude toward Deaf people by the hearing majority and has given impetus to the Deaf community to be more assertive politically. In 1988 the Deaf students at Gallaudet University in Washington, D.C., staged a demonstration when the chairman of the board, Jane Bassett Spilman, said, after the appointment of a hearing candidate, Elisabeth Ann Zinser, as president, that deaf people were not ready to lead themselves. As a result of this demonstration, I. King Jordan was appointed as the first Deaf president of Gallaudet (Sacks, 1989).

There has been official recognition of many national sign languages around the world. The first was in Sweden on May 14, 1981. The European Union recognized sign languages in all its member states in 1998 (Timmermans, 2005). British Sign Language was recognized in 2003; in Northern Ireland,

British Sign Language and Irish Sign Language were recognized in 2004 (Symington & Carberry, 2006). At the time of writing, Irish Sign Language is not recognized as an official language in the Republic of Ireland.

At the same time, the United Nations Convention on the rights of people with disabilities has asserted the rights of all citizens for equality in society and the provision of reasonable adjustments (United Nations Convention on the Rights of Persons with Disabilities, 2006). For D/deaf people this means the right to environmental aids, communication support, and sign language interpreters. The Americans with Disabilities Act (1990) and the UK Equality Act (2010) define these rights.

LIVING WITH DEAFNESS

Whatever the cause, nature, or degree of their deafness, individuals do not regard their deafness in purely medical terms. Communicating and living in a hearing environment is a role that must be played, and what happens in an individual's life depends very much on the surrounding society's attitude toward people who function differently, whether they are signers or use speech and lip reading. Deaf people hear with their eyes and need to operate visually, even if they have some usable hearing.

TECHNOLOGY

People with partial or acquired deafness usually want and need ways to continue to function as if they could hear, though some deafened people also learn to sign and then participate in the Deaf world. Most people with hearing loss want hearing aids and other audiological and medical technology, such as bone-anchored hearing aids or cochlear or brainstem implants. None of these is perfect, and these devices do not give all the features of normal hearing. Background noise, speech discrimination, and speech localization are all problematic. Clarity and tone may be poor. Group situations are usually very difficult. Hearing aids give feedback when molds do not fit properly, and the resultant whistling can be painful. Receiving a hearing aid or an implant is a very different matter from putting on a pair of glasses. Hearing therapists, lip-reading training, and auditory rehabilitation courses do as much to help people as the aids themselves. People need instruction and practice in getting the most out of their hearing aids and associated technology, such as induction loops in telephone receivers or in public places. For meetings, FM systems using special microphones can be very helpful.

Methods of operating visually are also essential. Visual travel information, e-mailing and texting, speech-to-text technology, relay telephone services, and video communication with webcams are all a great help for all Deaf people. Remote video relay interpreting is a valuable tool that is being increasingly used. Telecommunication used to be a huge stumbling block for Deaf people, but this is no longer the obstacle it once was. Subtitling on DVDs and on television has opened up information and entertainment for Deaf people, though live television subtitling is not without its problems. The words can be delayed or distorted.

> A television program in 1981, before the marriage of Prince Charles to Diana Spencer, showed the stately home where "they were going to spend the first days of their honeymoon." However, these words only appeared on the screen below a picture of a large four-poster bed.

> At the funeral of Queen Elizabeth, the Queen's mother, in 2002, the request for a moment's silence was subtitled as "a moment's violence."

All deaf people need alerting technology, such as fire alarms, doorbells, and baby alarms, with flashing lights or vibrating pagers. At night, fire alarms and alarm clocks can be either visual or under-pillow vibrating pads.

> A 30-year-old Deaf woman and her hearing mother were together at an outpatient appointment. The deaf psychiatrist had her vibrating pager alarm clock on the desk, as there was no clock in the room. When asked about this, she explained its function. The mother turned to her daughter and said, "If you had one of those, you could leave home."

> A community nurse wanted to visit a Deaf man with depression. He asked to be visited in the evening, as he thought that his visual doorbell only worked by dimming the lights. He had not been told that he could change the setting to flash the lights during the day.

For people who are profoundly Deaf, the spoken language of their country can be their second language, as their first language is their national sign language. It therefore cannot be assumed that a signer has fluent literacy skills. Even Deaf people who are not signers may have had limited access to education, and it cannot be assumed that reading and writing are effective means of communication. Information can be conveyed in sign language with an interpreter, via video technology interpreting and through informational DVDs. The use of sign language interpreters (www.actiononhearingloss.org.uk) is discussed further in Chapter 10.

DEAF AWARENESS TRAINING

Deaf awareness training is an information package that is usually offered by Deaf community organizations (www.actiononhearingloss.org.uk) about appropriate ways to interact with and communicate with Deaf people (Middleton, 2009). It has been established that this training improves participants' attitudes toward Deaf people (Cooper et al., 2003). The training offers information about positive attitudes and the importance of appropriate communication for all Deaf people, whether they speak or sign. This involves appropriate eye contact and lighting and the realization that a Deaf person cannot understand someone whose face they cannot see (for example, a doctor who is wearing a surgical mask or examining a patient from behind). Speech is easier to follow at a normal pace. Shouting at hearing aid users is painful and also distorts lip patterns. Awareness trainers give advice about the use of visual and alerting technology and about interpreters.

> A young orally educated Deaf girl was asked at an ENT (ear, nose, and throat) appointment if she had any questions. She asked, "Why is my mother always angry?" Her mother was in the habit of shouting, which distorted her facial expression.

SUMMARY

Deafness is extremely common and is very varied. It can occur early or later in life, alone or with additional health problems or disabilities that may or may not be associated with the cause of deafness. Profoundly Deaf people who are likely to use sign language comprise one in a thousand of the population. Over 90% of them are born into hearing families. The personal family, educational, and social experiences of Deaf people have significant implications for their path through life. All these issues will be explored in subsequent chapters.

2 Deaf People in Society

BACKGROUND

People who have been profoundly Deaf from early life comprise, as described in Chapter 1, one in a thousand of the world's population. Many people use sign language although they have not always had access to this from early life, particularly if they were born into hearing families. Culturally deaf communities who use sign language are found all over the world, and their members have a strong cultural identity. Unlike other cultures, where the main transmission is from parent to the child, the Deaf community is mainly composed of people who have joined it, either from school years or in early adult life. Deaf people from Deaf families are often at the heart of these communities.

Deaf people have local, national, and worldwide networks and organizations. They have varied and successful family, social, and professional lives, in the same way as the general population. However, as a minority group, they have in the past been at risk of marginalization and social exclusion, particularly if geographically isolated. In order to understand the role of Deaf people and their communities in the modern world, it is necessary to look at their history, particularly with regard to sign languages and the educational controversy that persists to the present day.

DEAF PEOPLE IN HISTORY

Deaf people have appeared in history and literature since earliest times (Eriksson, 1993). In ancient Greece, Socrates (d. 399 B.C.E.) referred to someone using sign language, and Aristotle (384–322 B.C.E.) thought that Deaf people could not be educated. This view was accepted for many centuries. In medieval times, Deaf people were considered to be incomplete humans, as it was thought that what separated men from the animals was the power of speech. St. Augustine (354–430) recognized that signs could be used to learn the gospel (Lang, 2011), but also wrote that "innocence is sometimes born blind and sometimes born deaf which blemish indeed hinders faith as witness the apostle who says that faith comes by hearing" (Dimmock, 1993). In many societies, Deaf people were not recognized as full citizens and could not marry, own property, or make a will.

SIGN LANGUAGES AND THE EDUCATIONAL CONTROVERSY

In modern times, it is accepted that there is a critical period for language development in children. It is also acknowledged that at least half of the world's population is bilingual in the sense that they have more than one language that they can use in everyday life (Grosjeàn, 1996, cited in Parasnis, pp. 20–21). It is also well established that the national sign languages of the world are full languages (Poizner, Klima, & Bellugi, 1987). They have vocabulary, grammar, and syntax and can fill all the roles of any spoken language. Sign languages are in fact "as complex and useful and beautiful as any spoken or written language" (Crystal, 2010, p. 116). However, there has been a fierce controversy for centuries about the best ways to communicate with and educate a profoundly Deaf child; as controversies continue, many Deaf children are still denied access to sign in early life in an effort to make them speak.

As more than 90% of profoundly Deaf children are born into hearing families (Mitchell & Karchmer, 2004) their parents are strongly influenced by the beliefs, attitudes, and policies of their time. The linguist Steven Pinker has described language deprivation in the following terms. Among the humans mind's magnificent faculties, "pride of place must go to language, ubiquitous across the species, unique in the animal kingdom, inextricable from social life and from the mastery of civilization and technology, devastating when lost or impaired" (Pinker, 2007, p. 28). He also notes that "because the Deaf are virtually the only neurologically normal people who make it to adulthood without having acquired a language, their difficulties offer particularly good evidence that successful language acquisition must take place during a critical window of opportunity in childhood" (Pinker, 1994, pp. 37–38).

Ree (1999, p. 87) stated that the "story of deaf education has three great lessons to teach us: the banality of ignorant cruelty, the tenuousness of scientific progress and—last but not least—the stubborn persistence of folk metaphysics." In sixteenth-century Spain there was a high rate of hereditary deafness in the intermarried aristocracy, and as Roman law required a person to speak in order to inherit property, great efforts were made to teach these individuals to speak. Ponce de León (c. 1520–1584), a Benedictine monk, was one of those employed for this purpose. He never divulged the secret of his method, but it is thought that he used monastic sign language in his teaching. At the time, monasteries used sign languages within orders during periods of silence imposed for religious reasons. There are many other isolated examples in the sixteenth and seventeeth centuries of individual teachers of the Deaf, and many finger-spelling alphabets were developed. However, the real breakthrough in education was in pre-revolutionary Paris when Abbé de l'Épée (1712–1789) saw two Deaf sisters signing to each other. He believed they could not receive the word of God to save their souls, so he made the intellectual leap of teaching them in their own language. At first he devised a complicated system of signed grammatical French, but this was abandoned by his successor, Abbé Sicard, who realized that in fact sign was a complete language. De l'Épée founded a school that became famous throughout Europe, and many public schools for Deaf children were created, using national sign languages, in Europe (Lane, 1984).

At the same time, there were initiatives to teach more Deaf children by speech. Heinecke in Germany and the Braidwoods in England and Scotland were at the forefront of this trend. The Scottish Braidwood school was visited by Dr. Samuel Johnson in 1775 when he described deafness as "one of the most desperate of human calamities" (Grant, 1987, p. 15).

In 1815 Mason Cogswell, a surgeon in Hartford, Connecticut, asked Thomas Gallaudet (1787–1851) to educate his Deaf daughter, Alice. Gallaudet went to the Braidwood schools in England for advice but was informed that their method was secret. He therefore went on to the Paris school, where he met a Deaf sign language teacher, Laurent Clerc, and brought him back to America. It was in this way that the foundation of American Sign Language was French Sign Language, mixed with the sign of Martha's Vineyard, where there was a high level of genetic deafness and Deaf and hearing people all used sign language (Groce, 1985).

In the 1840s French Sign Language spread to Ireland as nuns and Christian brothers from Dublin trained in Paris in order to instruct Deaf children in Catholicism (Matthews, 1996). The Claremont School, already established in Dublin, was educating the children as Protestants using British Sign Language (Pollard, 2006). In the 1860s Deaf teachers from England and Scotland established schools in Australia, in Sydney and Melbourne, and thus British Sign Language developed into Auslan, the modern Australian Sign Language.

The Milan Resolution

The century until 1880 was seen as the golden age of deaf education, and the schools created the foundations for flourishing Deaf communities with national networks for sports, social, and cultural events. However, in the United States, Alexander Graham Bell was at the forefront of advocating strict oral methods for educating Deaf children (Bell, 1883; Lane, 1984).

In Europe the controversy between signing and strict oralism was also coming to a head. In 1880 an International Congress of Educators of the Deaf was held in Milan, organized and attended by those who advocated oralism. Few Deaf people were invited; one of the few supporters of sign language in attendance was Edward Gallaudet, the son of Thomas Gallaudet. The arguments for speech instead of sign included a presentation by Dr. Symes-Thompson of Brompton Chest Hospital in London, to the effect that signing instead of speaking made Deaf people breathe in a way that made them more susceptible to tuberculosis and other illnesses (Dimmock, 1993). Guilo Tarra, one of the conference organizers, gave a speech that included such statements as "signs are not sufficient to express the fullness of thought" and "the fantastic language of signs magnifies the senses and inflames the passions, whereas speech elevates the mind much more naturally" (Lane, 1991, p. 119). A vote was passed to ban the use of sign language for the education of Deaf children, and this was strictly applied in Europe and America. The number of Deaf teachers declined, and the Deaf community had to fend for itself to protect its language. The British Deaf Association was founded the following year. In the United States, the National Association of the Deaf was founded soon after. Lane (1991, p. 120) quotes an American Deaf leader: "1880 was the year that saw the birth of the infamous Milan Resolution that paved the way for foisting upon the Deaf everywhere a loathed method, hypocritical in its claims, unnatural in its application, mind deadening and soul killing in its ultimate results."

The Twentieth Century

Social work with Deaf people developed, often as part of church pastoral services. The British sign for social worker indicates the collar of these "missioners." Lane (1992) writes of the paternalism of these workers, who worked hard to support Deaf people, but also perpetuated the concept of Deaf people as less capable than hearing people. It was only in the late twentieth century that the roles of social worker and interpreter formally separated. Modern social work has now developed a much more enabling role.

Meanwhile, with the advent of amplification and hearing aids, the oral movement advanced, spearheaded by the Ewings in Manchester in the 1940s and 1950s. Professor A. W. G. Ewing's book *Educational Guidance and the Deaf Child* does not even list sign language in the index. It also contains such statements as "hearing mindedness is more readily achieved by Deaf children when they are very young" (Ewing, 1957, p. 325). He recommended that parents should be taught to carry out auditory training at home so that Deaf children, except in exceptional circumstances, should not have to go to school before the age of two. The majority of Deaf children at that time went to residential schools. Giving evidence to the Lewis Committee on the education of Deaf children in 1968, Ewing stated that he would "regard combined methods as a last resort for children failing to achieve any score in language after all that was possible had been done for them." He went on to say that an appropriate age to change to such methods would be 12 years (Denmark, 1994, p. 16).

The oral method spread eventually to Ireland, where sign language had been retained in schools until the 1960s. It was found necessary to strictly separate the oral streams from those who still needed sign in order to create "an oral atmosphere" (Griffey, 1994, p. 47). Lady Irene Ewing wrote approvingly of this arrangement: "There is an entirely separate school for pupils... who have not proved suitable for oral methods of teaching. The welfare of these children is just as dear to the hearts of their Teachers as that of the oral children but at no time do they mix" (Griffey, 1994, p. 159). Signing in the "oral" school was strictly punished. Even siblings were separated if one was more "oral" than the other.

> A 40-year-old Deaf woman described how they were not allowed to use sign language at school. They would be hit on the hand or made to stand and face the wall. She explained that as the pupils' literacy was so poor they were encouraged to do crafts, sewing, art, and so on. She signed "we were encouraged to use our hands for everything except what we needed them for, to communicate."

By the end of the 1960s, Bangkok had the only Deaf school officially using sign language (Brelje, 1999). Sacks (1991, p. 28) comments, "None of this would have mattered had oralism worked. But the effect, unhappily, was the reverse of what was desired—an intolerable price was exacted for the acquisition of speech."

The late twentieth century saw significant changes. The recognition of the linguistics of sign languages was given huge impetus by the publications of Stokoe and colleagues, including the first dictionary of American Sign Language (Stokoe et al., 1976). Neurological researchers showed that signed languages are processed in the same parts of the brain as spoken languages (Poinzer et al., 1987). The shortcomings of a strictly oral education for children who had always been profoundly Deaf were exposed. Conrad (1979) studied every Deaf child of school-leaving age in the United Kingdom in 1974–1976 and found that they had an average reading level of age 9. Only 14% of them had wholly intelligible speech, and their lip reading was no better than untutored hearing children. Psychiatrists including Dr. John Denmark wrote of attitudes that were based on ignorance and superstition, and identified the cause of many of his patients' mental health problems as the denigration of the use of sign language by the teachers of Deaf children (Denmark, 1994). Susan Gregory and colleagues showed that a cohort of Deaf children from the 1970s who were brought up orally were, when re-interviewed in the 1990s, far from being a totally oral group (Gregory, 1976; Gregory et al., 1996). Furthermore, 17% of her cohort (14 of 82) were not able to complete an interview in either speech or sign, as they had insufficient language development of any sort. This was a group who had been screened to exclude intellectual disability. Deaf people can be "trapped in a vacuum of inexperience with our school years lying fallow behind us" (Ladd, 1978, p. 49).

MODERN DEVELOPMENTS

In the twenty-first century, recognition of sign languages has continued, with a positive effect for Deaf communities everywhere. There is now a sign language translation on the United Nations website of the Universal Declaration of Human Rights (www.signworldlearn.com).

This first British Sign Language translation has led to the creation of a completely new category of translations of the declaration in the world's sign languages.

Terminology about deafness is changing in the same way as terminology that refers to races, ethnicities, and disabilities. The terms "deaf mute" and "deaf and dumb" are at last going out of use. Deaf people perceive these words as offensive, implying that they are stupid or inarticulate, and object to their use.

The advent of cochlear implants and the new policy trends toward mainstream education have had a major impact on Deaf children. The educational controversy between oral and bilingual approaches has continued and is starting earlier as universal neonatal screening is being introduced (Young & Tattersall, 2007). Many cochlear implant programs oppose the use of sign, even though many researchers have concluded that sign does not detract from implant use (Watson et al., 2008).

The controversy rests upon a myth that allowing deaf children to use sign language will prevent them from speaking (Marschark, 2007). It is known that the bilingual brain develops well; in Wales, which is officially a bilingual country, new parents are given a card that states "two languages from day one, give your children the best start, they will thank you for it." Hearing parents are using baby sign so they can communicate with their hearing babies before the vocal apparatus is mature enough for speech (Garcia, 2005). It is ironic that the children who really need a bilingual approach, deaf children, are so often denied it. The Deaf children of Deaf parents who grow up with sign as their first and family language are often those who become high achievers and live their lives bilingually and biculturally (Schlesinger, 1969).

Unenlightened attitudes unfortunately still persist.

The author was asked by an oralist teacher if "she thought more slowly as she was deaf."

"His parents were deaf and dumb, he never went to a play until he was seventeen. But now at sixty four, Richard Griffith's career has hit a peak." *The Times London*, April 25, 2012.

> A card with communication tips for Deaf or deafened people to show people had on the reverse side "This card should not be used to ask for money."
>
> At a conference a Deaf professional was looking at the speech to text translation on a screen on her table. Later someone asked her why she had been checking her e-mails during the presentation.
>
> A Deaf man had an interview for a job in a supermarket. The following week when he was shopping there, he was told that he should have reported for work. He has been offered the job by voice mail.

HEARING CHILDREN OF DEAF ADULTS (CODAS)

An account of Deaf people and their families would be incomplete without a description of CoDAs and their roles and experiences in the Deaf world. Just as most Deaf people have hearing parents, they also usually have hearing children. The exceptions occur when at least one parent has a dominant genetic cause of deafness or when both parents have the same recessive cause. Many hearing children from Deaf families are bicultural and bilingual in the same way that children of first generation immigrant families are bicultural and are often more fluent in the majority language than their parents (Sanghera, 2008). In the same way, children can become interpreters for their parents and an intermediary between them and the majority culture. This can be both a difficult and a rewarding situation. In the past, when there were few or no interpreters, no subtitling, and only spoken telecommunication, Deaf people could become dependent on their hearing children.

> Before there were subtitles or remote controls, a 12-year-old hearing girl interpreted television dramas for her Deaf parents. Her mother would leap from her seat and switch off the television if there was any sexual content, wait a little while before switching it on again, and then resume the program after the sexual episodes were finished.

Many hearing children would go with their Deaf parents to the Deaf club and have good social networks, both with Deaf people and other hearing children. It was only occasionally that they would feel different from children with hearing parents.

> The hearing children of Deaf parents who played outside the apartment build-
> ing where they lived were the only ones whose parents would not hear the ice
> cream van and throw money down for them.

Sometimes, the hearing children of deaf parents would not realize that other people had hearing parents and would only find this out when they went to school. It would be hard for the Deaf parents to go to parent-teacher meetings as there was no interpreter. If the child was used as the interpreter, he or she could moderate the teacher's report.

> A hearing son of Deaf parents had forgotten that he had told his school friends
> that his parents spoke differently because they were French and was surprised
> to be asked years later what part of France his parents were from.
>   The hearing daughter of Deaf parents was not allowed to go on a foreign
> exchange school visit, as the school principal believed that her parents were
> not suitable to host a foreign student for the return visit.

The grown-up hearing children of Deaf adults may realize in retro-spect that their parents were often quite institutionalized in some of their behaviors, like always setting the table the previous night for breakfast, because this is what they always had to do at school.

Sometimes CoDAs can have painful memories. In the days before baby alarms, they could be left to cry at night in their cribs because their parents could not hear them. Some Deaf mothers would sleep near or with their babies or have a ribbon tied from the baby's wrist to their own so they could respond when the baby woke.

Many CoDAs, when they reach adulthood, continue to participate in the deaf community. They are truly bilingual, with sign as their first lan-guage. They may become interpreters or work in other professional roles with Deaf people.

SUMMARY

The history of Deaf people, particularly the educational controversy, which continues to this day, reveals the marginalization of Deaf people and their sign languages in many societies. Progress has been very varied in different parts of the world, as in the case for racial equality and the emancipation of women. What has been consigned to history in some countries is very much a present reality in others. In many countries, sign language is recognized as a national language and Deaf people are treated as equal citizens, while in other countries the battle has hardly started. There are often great contrasts. In a single city there may be a university department of Deaf Studies, staffed by Deaf professionals, while a few miles away a Deaf person of normal intelligence with minimal language is a long-term patient in a psychiatric hospital, with no communication and no diagnosis.

> A 65-year-old man who was born in a psychiatric hospital to a schizophrenic mother was removed at birth but remained in institutional care. His profound deafness was not diagnosed and he never developed any language. He was found by a religious deaf organization at the age of 30 but the consulting psychiatrist did not agree to his transfer to a signing residential home. He was found again, 30 years later, by a social worker, and he is now learning some rudimentary sign. He is of apparently normal intelligence and there is no evidence of any psychiatric illness.

Although modern developments and the increased political awareness of Deaf communities worldwide are bringing many changes, any individual Deaf adult's path through life has depended greatly on where and when he or she was born, whether into a Deaf or hearing family, the age of recognition of deafness, and communication and educational decisions made on his or her behalf. Deaf adults still live with the consequences of past attitudes and policies.

3 Deaf Children: The Beginning

PREVALENCE OF DEAFNESS

The prevalence of deafness varies among countries and is likely influenced by socioeconomic and cultural factors. Deafness is considered to be a low incidence condition (Mitchell & Karchmer, 2004); however, the implications can be life defining, life changing, and in some regard perhaps immeasurable (in both positive and negative ways). The profound impacts on individuals' lives seem out of balance with the difficulties in establishing accurate rates of prevalence, although this is indeed the case with children with hearing loss in any country. Typically, these rates are hard to accurately establish due to the heterogeneity of the group whereby children with mild hearing loss may be considered "hearing," and children with severe disabilities in addition to some degree of hearing loss may be included in categories other than deafness, and finally, those with any degree of hearing loss who function well in mainstream settings may simply not be counted at all (Marschark & Spencer, 2009). Regardless, then, of the actual prevalence of deafness, the identification of hearing loss is an important and complicated construct.

IDENTIFICATION OF DEAFNESS

In past times, the birth of a deaf child may have been an unremarkable event. For example, in the twentieth century Martha's Vineyard, an island off the coast of Massachusetts, had an unusually high percentage of deaf island-ers, and most residents had both deaf and hearing siblings. As such, deaf-ness itself was unremarkable and was not viewed as atypical. The islanders were largely all bilingual in both Martha's Vineyard Sign Language (MVSL) and spoken English, and deafness was viewed neither positively nor nega-tively—it's just the way it was (Groce, 1985). From this worldview, there was no formal or specific identification of deafness, no more than there was a formal or specific identification of a child's hair color.

This worldview, however, was not the norm for most Western or European countries. Earlier societies tended to judge social or biologi-cal differences as deviancy. Any research devoted to children with hear-ing loss was primitive, with recommendations focused on how to "cure" deafness, often by forcing deaf children to use oral speech. Identification of hearing loss in children was not systematic and tended to follow obser-vations that the child was "slow" or not developing similarly to siblings. Deafness was frequently confirmed through crude homemade measures such as banging pots together and seeing if the child responded.

Prior to the 1990s, the average age of identification in the United States was typically 3 years (Early Identification of Hearing Impairment in Infants and Young Children, 1993).

Similarly, the age of identification of hearing loss in the general popu-lation in Canada historically has been between 2½ to 3 years and in some cases much later. This meant that a significant number of children navi-gated their first important years of childhood in relative degrees of silence and unrecognized isolation. There are extreme cases in which children were misdiagnosed with mental retardation and were institutionalized for a number of years until professionals realized that it was the hearing

sense that was different, rather than intellectual capacity. Interested read-
ers are referred to American accounts of these tragic mistakes, such as
*I Was #87: A Deaf Woman's Ordeal of Misdiagnosis, Institutionalization,
and Abuse* by Anne Bolander and Adair Renning (2000) or *Kids with
Courage: True Stories about Young People Making a Difference* by Barbara
A. Lewis (1992).

Referrals to one author of this book have included children with hearing loss also diagnosed with a developmental delay (mental retardation).
Careful and accessible testing and review of some of these youngsters
has shown significant hearing loss, frequently impoverished language,
delayed adaptive functioning across selected domains, yet nonverbal
intelligence *within* the borderline-to-average range of ability. In these
instances, missed, late, or misdiagnosis of deafness has likely contributed
to factors that have led mainstream professionals to incorrectly diagnose
developmental delay.

There was a paradigm shift in the identification of deafness in the
United States in 1990. At this time, the Joint Committee on Infant Hearing
(JCIH) issued a position statement recommending that high-risk infants
be screened prior to their discharge from the hospital and no later than
3 months after their birth (Joint Committee on Infant Hearing, 1990).
The importance of early identification of hearing loss was also well documented in Canada (Joint Committee on Infant Hearing, 2007; Canadian
Working Group on Childhood Hearing, 2005), the United Kingdom
(Young & Tattersall, 2007), and Ireland (Marschark & Spencer, 2009).
The original overall goal of identifying early hearing loss was to enable
early interventions for communication and language development. The
premise was that babies identified accurately and early with a hearing loss
would be afforded parental awareness as well as early professional intervention to optimize language development in the early years.

For the following decade, however, only babies with high-risk factors
were routinely screened for hearing loss. Although this screening adequately identified at-risk babies, it became apparent that there were limited
measures to effectively identify hearing loss in the well-baby population
(Canadian Association of Speech-Language Pathologists and Audiologists,
2010). Similar observations were being made in other countries such as

New Zealand, which in 1996 reported that children who were at high risk for deafness were identified on average eight months earlier (22 months of age) than those with no risk factor (29 months of age) (Greville, 1996).

To address the inadequacies in the identification of children not known to be at risk of deafness, universal newborn hearing screening (UNHS) programs were developed. This screening procedure used an inexpensive and non-invasive test to quickly and accurately screen for hearing loss in newborns. Within the decade in the United States, The American Academy of Pediatrics (American Academy of Pediatrics Newborn and Infant Hearing Loss: Detection and Intervention, 1999) endorsed:

- Universal newborn hearing screening;
- Detection of hearing loss before 3 months of age;
- Intervention services initiated by 6 months of age.

While research continued to emphasize the benefits of early intervention, the UNHS continued to improve physiological hearing screening techniques, enabling easier and more cost-effective identifications. These two factors have resulted in UNHS becoming a standard of care in many different countries, using a variety of screening methods and protocols housed within existing health care, social and educational systems Furthermore, the research data appear to significantly support improved language development, assuming the child has access to high-quality multidisciplinary services (Young & Tattersall, 2005).

PARENTAL REACTIONS TO THE IDENTIFICATION OF DEAFNESS

One's worldview is often the lens through which we frame experiences. Thus, the identification of deafness may be processed differently, depending on factors such as previous life experiences and level of awareness, as well as hearing status. The emotional response to the identification of deafness is multifaceted. It is of interest to note that we are unable to assess the infant or young child's response to the identification unless we question d/Deaf children and adolescents retroactively, once they have acquired language. However, researchers have studied and documented parental reactions (Young & Tattersall, 2007).

Parents' responses may often be defined by their own hearing status, given that the identification of deafness is not as foreign to a Deaf adult as it may be to a hearing adult. The reaction of many hearing parents has been described in negative terms, recognizing that there are highly individual, varied, and extremely complex experiences, personal resources, social support, social status indicators, and comorbid disability factors that shape a parent's perception and response to their child's deafness. Some parental reactions have been likened to a grief process, following Kübler-Ross's (1969) stages of denial, anger, bargaining, depression, and acceptance. There is a difference, however, from an adaptive grief process, as some parents remain in the stages of denial and anger. Consider the parents who insist that the child remove his or her hearing aids for every family photograph, rather than accepting the child for who he or she is, or the parents who devote their lives (often giving up their jobs or distancing themselves from other children in the family) to "helping" their child to the point where the child is completely dependent. Sadly, some parents never see the strengths, the beauty, or the potential in their child as they remain angry at their perceived injustice of raising a child with deafness.

There are many hearing parents who are able to travel through the necessary stages toward a healthy acceptance of their child as deaf and themselves as hearing. This might include periods of time when a parent is supported unconditionally through overwhelming feelings of loss and confusion. This is not specific only to having a deaf child and is a fact and reality of living a human life.

PROFESSIONAL REACTIONS TO THE IDENTIFICATION OF DEAFNESS

Similar to parental reactions, the reactions of professionals to the identification of deafness may reflect biases and faulty thinking. Consider this hypothetical example, which highlights different true scenarios recounted to the author over years of practice.

A culturally Deaf couple (both had generations of Deaf family members) took their infant son to the family doctor for his first well-baby routine check. The family doctor nervously asked the young couple to sit down as he had bad news to share with them. The couple immediately became nervous and somewhat alarmed. The family doctor wrote on a piece of paper (his first mistake) that he was upset to share this with them but felt fairly confident that their son was also deaf. To his amazement, the young couple smiled gratefully with the news and hugged each other tightly. The doctor assumed because of their deafness that they were not very bright (his second mistake) and wrote DEAF Λ in big letters, much like a Grade 1 student would write. The couple stood up and shook his hand enthusiastically while kissing their baby and took their leave. The doctor remarked to his nurse that she had better contact Children's Services (his third mistake) as this couple were likely not competent enough as parents to care for their deaf son.

Clearly, this well-meaning doctor failed to appreciate that the world-view of this couple celebrated the identification of deafness. How could this be? From the parents' perspective, one can understand that it meant that their child's first language would be the same as their own first language (sign rather than oral language), their child would likely understand and navigate through the hearing world in a similar fashion to them, and that there was a sense of solidarity or sameness between themselves and their child. From the doctor's perspective, it perhaps meant a lifetime of hardships for the child, an inability to ever function like a hearing person, and a hardship for both parents and child.

Two weeks later, this same family doctor completed another well-baby checkup and met with new parents who were both hearing. Remembering the earlier reaction of the Deaf couple, he smiled broadly and told the hearing parents that he was happy to tell them that he felt fairly confident their infant son was deaf (his fourth mistake). To his horror, the parents looked at him disbelievingly, hugged each other tightly, and holding their baby somewhat tentatively and at arm's length, left his office in tears. The doctor remarked to his nurse that clearly there was no appropriate way to handle this situation, as no matter what he did, it seemed wrong and he may as well avoid telling parents anything (his fifth mistake!).

Again, this well-meaning doctor failed to appreciate the worldview of this hearing couple, who likely had never encountered deafness before in any capacity. Suddenly, their future with this new baby became one of extreme uncertainty, negativity, and confusion. How would they use their spoken language in the home? What would their family members think? How would they ever teach their child? How could they ever effectively parent a child so different from them?

This example serves to remind professionals and parents alike that interpretation of any life event will be unique to and shaped by individual and collective worldviews and beliefs. What is a celebration to some may be a tragedy to others. There can be no right or wrong interpretation, yet there are certainly adaptive and maladaptive ways of responding and coping.

Let us briefly revisit the family doctor's five errors:

1. It somehow seems intuitive for hearing professionals to assume that writing notes to Deaf individuals replaces meaningful dialogue. For some Deaf people this may be acceptable. For many it is not, as it requires fluency in the written word of what is often their second (or third) language. The rule of thumb is to inquire of the Deaf individual regarding the best mode of communication. For Deaf individuals, it is likely best to book a sign language interpreter until the parameters of accessible and meaningful language have been established.

2. It is a wrong and dangerous assumption to assume cognitive capacity based on language choices, ethnicity, mental health status, or any other factor. Cognitive ability can be determined only through accessible and appropriate intellectual functioning and is not a construct to be assumed. "Dumbing down the writing" is just dumb.

3. Parenting capacity can also not be assessed or assumed by virtue of an individual's language choice, hearing status, or worldviews. Legitimate concerns for the well-being and care of children can best be evaluated by a formal psychological parenting capacity assessment.

4. Basing professional decisions on faulty premises is negligent. Each professional interaction requires critical examination and accurate appraisal of presenting factors as well as symptoms.

5. Although it may seem easiest for frustrated professionals to choose not to repeat or engage in difficult situations, effective work with individuals with differences from the majority requires thoughtful assessment and reassessment of one's own skill and experiential set.

DEAF CHILDREN OF DEAF PARENTS

The development of deaf children of Deaf parents parallels the development of hearing children of hearing parents (Lieberman, Volding, & Winnick, 2004). This may be reflected in the fact that Deaf parents often seem to have less of an adjustment to their child's identification of deafness, presumably because it is familiar territory. There are few reports of Deaf parents of deaf children experiencing the same degree of complex constellation reactions as described by hearing parents. Deaf parents are more likely than hearing parents to communicate effectively with their deaf children (Calderon, 2000; Courtin, 2000); furthermore, Stinson (1994) observed that interactions between deaf children and their Deaf parents are more natural perhaps because the dyad shares the same language.

There has been a more recent move away from the medical model of describing a child's deafness toward a cultural-linguistic model. In this approach, a child's deafness is not framed as a tragedy but rather as a difference, and perhaps more important, a difference that can be supported and nurtured. It is acknowledged that language development will likely occur along different timelines and patterns, yet it will still occur. The child may literally not hear the drummer but likely walks to an entirely different tune. This approach allows professional interventions to wrap effective and accessible resources around receptive parents such as d/Deaf mentors, language models, cultural experiences, and an overall degree of acceptance. Andrew Solomon's book *Far from the Tree: Parents, Children and the Search for Identity* (Solomon, 2012) focuses on the topic of differences in children from their parents. Chapter 2 of Solomon's book is devoted to deafness, and parents and professionals alike may find the author's descriptions of parents' progression toward acceptance and comfort level with difference to be useful reading.

ATTACHMENT

Perhaps one of the most important relationships we ever establish in our lives is that of the attachment relationship, which typically begins immediately at birth with the primary caregiver (most often the biological mother). The construct of attachment, as first described in ethological evolutionary terms by John Bowlby, has evolved into an entire field of study engaging the notable minds of many scholars. Basically, the essence of this first human relationship is predicated on the following four core hypotheses, as summarized by van Ijzendoorn & Sagi-Schwartz (2008):

1. Attachment is universal: all infants (with the exception of those with severe neurophysiological impairments) become attached in some manner to one or more individuals.
2. Attachment security is normative.
3. Attachment security is dependent on maternal sensitivity.
4. Attachment security is predictive of later competencies such as emotion regulation, the development of peer relationships, self-reliance, self-confidence, and greater empathic concerns for others (Bohlin, Hagekull, & Rydell, 2000; Sroufe, Egeland, Carlson, & Collins, 2005; Pederson & Moran, 1995).

The attachment relationship has been well studied across many different cultures, languages, disabilities, and situations. The attachment relationship is a dyad (existing between two individuals) with both partners contributing in different ways. There are many well-designed longitudinal studies suggesting that the effects of specific socioemotional constructs may influence the attachment classification as secure or insecure.

However, inconsistencies in findings reported in the literature suggest that caution is advised when considering attachment classification and developmental outcomes; clearly, more studies are needed before decisive outcomes can be predicted.

There is a danger in assuming that individual differences in either maternal or infant contributions (i.e., a hearing parent and deaf infant) result in a disruption in the attachment relationship. Although that may well be the outcome, a careful review of the constructs by Thomson, Kennedy, and Kuebli (2011) summarizes the following important points:

1. Theoretical and empirical evidence suggests that deaf infants are likely to be just as prepared at birth as their hearing counterparts to form secure attachments with their caregivers (p. 43). This suggests that the deaf infant's ability to signal needs including babbling, grasping, clinging, smiling, crying, and reaching is comparable to that of hearing infants. In addition, there is some evidence that deaf infants respond even more effectively to other forms of communication, such as visual and tactile modalities (gaze seeking, sustained eye contact, touching).

2. Research findings are inconsistent in terms of the interactional style/quality of the hearing mother/deaf infant dyad. Some studies indicate that there is no difference from a hearing mother/hearing infant dyad, whereas others have suggested that there are differences in interactional styles (i.e., more intrusive and less sensitive mothers). However as Thomson et al. (2011) point out "virtually nothing is known about whether and how hearing mother/deaf infant interactions, even if different or somewhat lower in quality compared to interactions with hearing infants, ultimately have any adverse impact on attachment security" (p. 51).

A review of the current literature suggests that there do not appear to be compelling reasons to assume that the deafness of an infant results in an insecure attachment relationship. However, it could well be that individual differences such as infant deafness *do* introduce profound differences into the relationship and that these differences may require mothers to develop a qualitatively different type of maternal sensitivity, such as one characteristic of more tactile and visual strategies. This also supports the important need for early identification of infant deafness such that mothers are fully aware of the nature of the relationship with their baby, thus perhaps empowering mothers to then fine-tune their mothering skills to better fit the relationship.

The attachment relationship is a template for all other future relationship representations. We do not formally teach all new mothers how to interact with their hearing babies and instead hopefully assume that maternal instincts will kick in effectively. As one hearing mother recounted:

> My baby was screened at birth and we were told she was deaf. On one level this threw my husband and I into chaos—How will we communicate? What do we tell her grandparents? How could this have happened? And yet on another level, I felt strangely calm and mobilized all my internal resources to enter into this fascinating, strange and yet so lovely relationship with my baby. I have always sung to my babies yet this time found myself singing while turning the baby's head to look at me. I have always loved to touch my children yet with this baby I found myself always touching her or tapping her to get her eye contact before I even changed her diaper. I put my other two kids down for naps on their tummies. I did the same with this daughter but found myself crouching down to her eye level in the crib until she fell asleep so she knew I was there. How did I know this stuff? Nobody told me yet I seemed to intuitively know what to do....If I had not known I hate to think of how much she and I would have missed together.

DEVELOPMENT

Child development generally refers to the time period between birth and the end of adolescence. This time period is markedly different from any other stage of human development for it encompasses tremendous biological, psychological, social, and emotional changes. These developmental changes are different from growth, which simply refers to the change in the physical size of the child over time. Rather, developmental changes represent a progression from dependency toward increasing autonomy and are thus marked by the achievement of developmental milestones.

Developmental milestones are functional skills or age-specific tasks that most children can perform within a certain age range. Each milestone that a child reaches is like a stepping-stone and is typically built upon to support the next phase of change. Child development typically progresses through four major skill areas which are:

1. *Language:* Expressing needs, wants and thoughts, using body language and gestures, and understanding what others say/sign;
2. *Movement and muscle coordination:* Using the body's large muscles (sitting, standing, walking, running, keeping balance, and changing positions) as well as small muscles (eating, drawing, playing, dressing, colouring) and developing hand-eye coordination;
3. *Play and social:* Having relationships with others, cooperating, and responding to the feelings of others;
4. *Thinking and reasoning:* Learning, understanding, problem-solving and remembering.

Parents are often encouraged to learn about and track their child's progress through the use of charts such as the one depicted in Table 3.1.

Clinicians should encourage parents to remember that each child develops in a unique way and that charts are meant to serve as guides, not as a source of concern. There are clearly wide variations of what is considered "normal," influenced by factors such as genetics, intellectual stimulation, family history, parenting skills, physical and mental health, culture, nutrition, as well as environmental and educational factors.

Recognizing that each child develops differently, a general knowledge of developmental milestones may alert parents and/or clinicians to children who may be achieving developmental milestones early or later than typically expected. Children who are late in achieving developmental milestones may be showing delays in one or more areas of development. As developmental changes in one area are often related to changes in another, delays in one area are often likely to influence development in other areas.

DEAF CHILDREN AND DEVELOPMENT

Does deafness affect a child's successful acquisition of developmental milestones? This is a complex question and needs to be considered carefully. Risk factors influencing a child potentially not acquiring the skill set necessary to achieve a developmental milestone (this is termed a developmental delay) generally are either related to

- Genetic factors or
- Environmental factors.

A baby is considered to be at genetic risk if he or she is born with either a genetic or chromosomal abnormality (errors in the number or structure of genes or chromosomes). A common example is Down syndrome, which is a genetic condition in which an individual has 47 chromosomes instead of the usual 46, causing developmental delays and physical problems. A baby is considered to be at environmental risk following inadequate prenatal care such as poor nutrition or maternal illness (i.e., measles, HIV) or exposure to toxins (i.e., lead or drugs). A child is considered to be at environmental risk from such factors as lack of care in the postnatal period, being born prematurely, abusive or neglectful homes, having a mother with severe mental health issues, or severe poverty. All of these factors place a baby at increased risk for not meeting developmental milestones or having a developmental delay.

The complexity arises when one considers that deafness also may be caused by or be associated with genetic factors or environmental factors. Genetic factors account for at least half of all individuals with deafness (see Figure 3.1).

Scientists studying genetics classify genetic hearing loss into two general categories of non-syndromic (which means that the child has hearing loss without other clinical issues) and syndromic (meaning

Table 3.1 Child Development Chart: First Five Years
Copyright ©2004, 1994 Ireton Harold, PhD. Reprinted with permission.

CHILD DEVELOPMENT CHART – FIRST FIVE YEARS
Harold Ireton, Ph.D.

Age	SOCIAL	SELF-HELP	GROSS MOTOR	FINE MOTOR	LANGUAGE	Age
5-0 yrs.	Shows leadership among children.	Goes to the toilet without help.	Swings on swing, pumping by self.	Prints first name (four letters).	When asked, for example, "What is an orange?" answers, "A fruit."	5-0 yrs.
4-6		Usually looks both ways before crossing street.	Skips or makes running "broad jumps."	Draws a person that has at least three parts - head, eyes, nose, mouth, etc.	Reads a few letters (five+).	4-6
	Follows simple rules in board or card games.	Buttons one or more buttons.	Hops around on one foot, without support.	Draws recognizable pictures.	Prints a few letters or numbers.	
4-0 yrs.	Protective toward younger children.	Dresses and undresses without help, except for tying shoelaces.			Counts ten or more objects.	4-0 yrs.
					Follows a series of three simple instructions in order.	
3-6	Plays cooperatively with minimum conflict and supervision.	Washes face without help.	Hops on one foot, without support.	Cuts across paper with small scissors.	Talks in long, complex sentences (10 or more words).	3-6
				Draws or copies a complete circle.	Answers questions like, "What do you do with your eyes? ears?"	
	Gives directions to other children.	Toilet trained.	Rides around on a tricycle, using pedals.		Identifies at least four colors by name correctly.	
3-0 yrs.	Plays games like tag, hide and seek.	Dresses self with help.	Walks up and down stairs - one foot per step.	Cuts with small scissors.	Asks questions beginning with "Why? When? How?"	3-0 yrs.
	Plays a role in "pretend" games like house or school - mom, dad, teacher.				Answers questions like, "What do you do with a cracker? a hat?"	
2-6		Washes and dries hands.	Stands on one foot without support.	Draws or copies vertical (	) lines.	Speaks clearly - is understandable most of the time.	2-6
	Plays with other children - cars, dolls, building.				Talks in sentences at least four words long.	
	"Helps" with simple household tasks.	Opens door by turning knob.	Climbs on play equipment - ladders, slides.	Scribbles with circular motion.	Has a vocabulary of at least 20 words.	
2-0 yrs.	Usually responds to correction - stops.	Takes off open coat or shirt without help.	Walks up and down stairs alone.	Turns pages of picture books, one at a time.	Follows two-part instructions.	2-0 yrs.
	Shows sympathy to other children, tries to comfort them.	Eats with spoon, spilling little.	Runs well, seldom falls.		Names a few familiar objects in picture books.	
	Sometimes says "No" when interfered with.	Eats with fork.		Builds towers of four or more blocks.	Asks for a drink or food, using words or sounds.	
18 mos.	Greets people with "Hi" or similar.		Kicks a ball forward.		Uses at least ten words.	18 mos.
	Gives kisses or hugs.	Feeds self with spoon.	Runs.	Scribbles with crayon.	Talks in single words.	
		Insists on doing things by self such as feeding.	Walks without help.	Picks up two small toys in one hand.		
12 mos.	Waves "Bye-bye."	Lifts cup to mouth and drinks.	Stands without support.	Stacks two or more blocks.	Says "Mama" or "Dada" for parent, or similar.	12 mos.
		Picks up a spoon by the handle.	Walks around furniture or crib while holding on.	Picks up small objects - precise thumb and finger grasp.	Understands phrases like "No-no" and "All gone."	
9 mos.	Plays social games, "peek-a-boo," "patty-cake."		Crawls around on hands and knees.			9 mos.
	Pushes things away he/she doesn't want.		Sits alone . . . steady, without support.	Uses two hands to pick up large objects.	Makes sounds like da-da, ma-ma, ba-ba.	
	Reaches for familiar people.	Feeds self cracker.	Rolls over from back to stomach.	Transfers toy from one hand to the other.	Responds to name - turns and looks.	
6 mos.	Distinguishes mother from others.	Comforts self with thumb or pacifier.	Turns around when lying on stomach.	Picks up toy with one hand.	Babbles.	6 mos.
		Reacts to sight of bottle or breast.	Lifts head and chest when lying on stomach.	Looks at and reaches for faces and toys.	Laughs out loud.	
Birth	Social smile.				Makes sounds - ah, eh, ugh. Cries in a special way when hungry.	Birth

hearing loss with other clinical findings). By far, the more common is non-syndromic hearing loss, which includes two-thirds of all genetic hearing losses (Boystown, http://www.babyhearing.org/hearingamplification/causes/genetics.asp). Figure 3.1 shows that 50% of deaf children have a hearing loss due to a genetic factor. Of that 50%, it is expected that only 17% of children with hearing loss will have a syndromic genetic

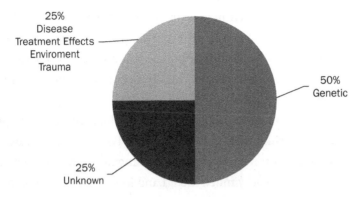

Figure 3.1 Overview Causes for Hearing Loss

deafness thereby increasing their risk of developmental delay. Therefore it is the minority of children who are deaf from genetic causes who can be predicted to show developmental delays associated with their syndromic deafness.

Figure 3.1 also indicates that 25% of children have unknown causes for their deafness, while the remaining 25% of deaf children have etiologies related to disease, treatment effects, environment, and trauma. These causal factors of deafness make it much more difficult to predict with any degree of accuracy if developmental delays may occur. It is imperative that both parents and clinicians be diligent in observing the developmental milestones as they occur, as well as being mindful of which developmental areas may be at most risk due to deafness. By far, the area of development that seems to be impacted the greatest in deaf children is their development of language.

The implications of language decisions are discussed in Chapter 4. The critical point is the fundamental importance of language to the child's overall development, including social-emotional status, development and maintenance of relationships, theory of mind, and sophistication of receptive/expressive linguistic abilities. Language decisions must be made thoughtfully in terms of the accessibility of the language and the "goodness of fit" with the child. Furthermore, language decisions must be assessed and reassessed to determine developmental progression. If delays in language development are detected, parents and clinicians *must* remediate immediately with increased exposure and/or a different language modality. The profound impact of language development is a risk factor across all etiologies of deafness and may potentially occur with and/or influence other developmental areas.

The development of fine and gross motor skills and muscle coordination needs consideration in deaf children. For example, studies have shown that fine motor development and language development (especially expressive) are very much linked and in fact may depend on common areas of the brain. This suggests that fine motor development may be adversely affected if the child's language development is delayed due to inaccessibility or lack of exposure. This is a good example of the interconnectedness between developmental areas and how delays in one area may have influential effects on other areas. This again highlights the importance of early and accessible language development in deaf children.

In some children, sensorineural deafness is caused by the absence or degeneration of sensory hair cells in the cochlea, which essentially severs the connection between the peripheral and central auditory system (Gheysen, Loots, & van Waelvelde, 2008). This absence of hair cells can result in disturbances of vestibular function, including balance, thereby adversely affecting gross motor development. Some studies have concluded, therefore, that Deaf children lag in motor skills (Brunt & Broadhead, 1982; Wiegersma & Van der Velde, 1983) although these studies have been criticized for not distinguishing Deaf children from Deaf children with vestibular damage. Conversely, other studies have concluded that Deaf children develop similarly to their same age hearing peers in motor skills (Butterfield, Van der Mars & Chase, 1993; Dummer, Haubenstricker & Stewart, 1996).

Lieberman et al. (2004) compared the gross motor development of Deaf children of Deaf parents and Deaf children of hearing parents, given that earlier studies have consistently shown improved academic (Ritter-Brinton & Stewart, 1992), linguistic (Courtin, 2000; Harris, 2001; Vaccari & Marschark, 1997), and social (Hadadian & Rose, 1991; Harris, 2001) abilities in Deaf children with Deaf rather than hearing parents.

Lieberman et al.'s study showed no significant difference between the motor development by parental status and they furthermore stressed the fact that environmental factors, such as type of schooling and parental involvement in physical activity, were more influential factors on motor development.

One of the wonderful aspects of many of the residential Deaf schools in Canada has been the focus on sports. Although perhaps initially started as a way for school children to have fun with their peers, the benefits of motor development are invaluable. The Deaf community in Canada, recognizing the worth of Deaf sports, founded the Canadian Deaf Sports Association (CDSA) in 1964. The CDSA is a pan-Canadian nonprofit organization aiming to support the development of the practice of sports within the Deaf community, and in particular among Deaf youth. Their mission statement recognizes that sport is a source of well-being, values, and self-esteem for people who practice it. Many other countries have developed similar organizations.

A focus on sports will improve movement and muscle development but will potentially also have an effect on play and social development. Engaging in play encourages children to increase their understanding of themselves and others. Young infants typically engage in sensorimotor play (Piaget, 1962) where they experiment with bodily sensation and motor movements, and with objects and people. As toddlers play, they develop a growing awareness of the functions of objects in the social world. Older children around the age of 3–4 years engage in play, developing the ability to represent experience symbolically. An example of this is pretend play in which children carry out action plans, take on roles, and transform objects as they express their ideas and feelings about the social world (Youngblade & Dunn, 1995).

While children are playing, their social worlds are constantly expanding to include others, from siblings to their preschool and kindergarten classes, and neighborhood children and siblings. An important element of play includes the development and use of language. Developing language skills through play encourages the child to interact with others and also to form his or her own thoughts and mental processes. A child who is deaf faces challenges in these developmental areas. There is first the enormous challenge of accessible language development, but there are also often difficulties finding playmates who share the same language.

Consider Marty, who became deaf as an infant from meningitis. His parents decided on a sign-supported oral approach and placed Marty in a preschool classroom where Marty had an educational assistant (EA) and was the only deaf child. By the age of 4 years, Marty was able to express himself adequately to his EA, yet none of the other children understood his utterances, nor did they know any signs to support their own communication. As a result, recesses and lunch hours were very lonely times for Marty, as he was excluded from any play activities with the other children.

Consider also Joanne, who was deaf from unknown reasons. Joanne's parents chose an auditory-verbal approach, and Joanne was placed in a preschool program with hearing aids and a looped classroom where the teacher wore an FM system. Joanne progressed well academically and appeared to function fairly autonomously during instructional times. Yet similar to Marty, Joanne was a loner on the playground, where the auditory world became inaccessible to her. When the other children were engaged in pretend play involving cops and robbers, Joanne maintained her solitary play at a much younger developmental level.

And finally consider Lucille, who was also deaf from birth with an unknown etiology. Lucille's parents immersed their daughter and themselves in American Sign Language (ASL) at a very young age and also enrolled Lucille in the local residential school. By preschool age, Lucille was showing normative language development in sign and loved to play with four other little girls at recess, all sharing the same sign language.

SUMMARY

This chapter has examined the prevalence and identification of deafness, followed by common reactions of parents and family members. The early development of the deaf infant and toddler was then conceptualized within the important tenet of attachment relationships and representations. One of the critical developmental tasks facing all children is the acquisition of language. The development of and exposure to language appears to be often delayed for deaf children of hearing parents. One of the many functions of language acquisition is the child's understanding of him or her as "the self," as well as parents, siblings, teachers, and friends being "the other." This emotional and cognitive representation, moving from a developmentally immature egocentricity of thought to an understanding of one's own and other's minds, is critical to the child's later understanding of the relation between people's minds and the world around them. Although this is a very complex developmental task likely involving more than language alone, deaf children of hearing parents tend to show difficulties and/or delays in their development of theory of mind which will be further explored in the next chapter. This may in part be responsible for some of the common descriptors commonly expressed by family and teachers attempting to relate to the deaf child and used to explain their behaviors.

4 Psychological Development of Deaf Children

LANGUAGE

The development of language in humans has been studied considerably and often with some controversy. For many years, Chomsky's nativist view described language as basically an accomplishment unique to humans and suggested that individuals are biologically programmed to gain knowledge through language. The nativist view postulated that children were able to develop language from infancy (unless severely neurophysiologically compromised) as babies were born equipped with a language acquisition device (LAD). The LAD was described as an instinctive mental capacity facilitating the development of expressive and receptive language. In direct contrast to the nativist theory, behaviorists such as B. F. Skinner hypothesized that language is learned solely through operant and classical conditioning (positive/negative reinforcement and imitation). Support for both these theories as absolute has been controversial throughout the past decades.

One of the more recent theories is the interactionist perspective, which embraces both the nativist view (biological) as well as the behaviorist view (social). Vygotsky largely developed the interactionist theory explaining it through his model of collaborative learning (Shaffer, Wood, & Willoughby, 2002). This model proposes that children's conversations with adults fundamentally support and are, in fact, the keystone to cognitive and linguistic development in children.

How does this theory include and/or explain the language development of deaf children? This question has been asked repeatedly and the answer is a complex one. In most families, the child is born into the language of the family. There are not other examples in the human condition where a baby is born into a family and a decision must then be made by the parents as to the linguistic modality of their child or, in fact, their child's "mother tongue." Yet hearing parents of deaf babies find themselves in that very situation, quickly having to decide critical issues shortly after and more likely while still experiencing and processing the myriad emotions that accompany the identification of deafness.

Are there "correct" answers to the language questions that parents ask of themselves and professionals regarding their baby? For example:

- Should my baby learn to speak?
- Will my child be more hearing than deaf?
- Should my baby learn to sign?
- Will my child be more deaf than hearing?
- How will I communicate with my child if she signs and I speak?
- If she speaks, will she speak clearly so that others can understand her?
- If he signs, how will he ever communicate with his brothers and sisters who speak?

The answers are both yes and no. Fundamentally, our brains are hardwired for language. Even before we are born, we are programmed to learn language. The assumption, however, which has been made by many and which has in fact driven and defined the lives of the vast majority of deaf children has been that our brains are hardwired for *oral* language or speech. In one sense, perhaps this assumption was reasonable, given that it has long been recognized that spoken language has been a defining feature that separates humans from less complex forms of life. As often seems to happen, though, this biological difference became a value, and the ability to speak became somehow synonymous with the ability to communicate.

Pettito, in her groundbreaking neuropsychological studies in Canada, clearly challenged this assumption (Petitto, Katerelos, Levy, Gauna, Tetreault, & Ferraro, 2001). Pettito's research has made significant discoveries about the linguistic structure, acquisition, and representation in the brain of the world's natural signed languages, especially American Sign Language (ASL). For decades, babbling was viewed as inextricably tied to sound and speech. However, Petitto's research clearly showed that deaf children babble with their hands rather than their voices and on a similar developmental timeline as hearing babies. The conclusion drawn from this research was rather than *sound* being inherently necessary and important, manual and voice babbling reflects the infant's biologically given sensitivity to highly specific *patterns* that are part of language structure.

Previously, neurobiological studies of spoken language had demonstrated that phonological processing was found to occur in the left hemisphere's (LH) superior temporal gyrus of the brain. The human brain's ability to search and retrieve information about word meanings was clearly established in the left inferior frontal cortex. Based on these and other more sophisticated findings, language was long assumed to be located in the left hemisphere in 95% of right-handed dominant individuals; even in 60–70% of left-handers, the left side of the brain was predominantly used for language.

Petitto and her team, through groundbreaking research, clearly showed that the same brain tissue recruitment is used when processing the same parts of language, *regardless* of whether the language was on the hands in signed language or the tongue in spoken language. In other words, Petitto's team (based on findings that other teams have since replicated) proposed a new hypothesis that the left hemisphere brain tissue is not neurally set to *sound* but rather to specific *patterns* that are part of language structure. This finding corroborated her earlier infant manual babbling discoveries, moving beyond "where" language processing occurs in the human brain to explain the nature of its underlying neural basis.

These findings shattered earlier beliefs that speech was somehow superior to signed languages. Clearly, neither speech nor sign language are in of themselves at all special. Language patterns are special. The brain of a human baby is hardwired not to necessarily speak or to necessarily sign, but to develop language patterns; furthermore, the development and acquisition of these language patterns is somewhat time dependent. Lenneberg (1967) first proposed the critical period hypothesis, which states that the first few years of life constitute the time during which language develops readily and after which language acquisition is much more difficult and ultimately less successful. What then does this mean for deaf babies?

Pettito's research offers wonderful insights into the language development of deaf babies and children. Unless a child is severely neurobiologically compromised, it is reasonable to assume that his or her brain is seeking to develop a sophisticated language base. The task of parents and other professionals, then, is to structure the environment in terms of language such that the child is afforded the most accessible and rich linguistic opportunities. This returns to the complex question of making the best decisions for the child. It is noted that once again these decisions are being made for, rather than by, the child. Many Deaf adults reflect on the decisions made for them by parents especially when they have reversed those decisions later in life and sought to learn language many years after their brains were optimally primed for it (i.e., after their critical developmental period).

The reassuring and unequivocal assumption that parents can make is that their deaf child is capable of developing a rich, sophisticated and abstract receptive and expressive language. However, it is quite possible to place roadblocks to this development in terms of structuring linguistic environments that are in fact inaccessible or not wholly accessible to the child's cortical language structures. The controversy has long centered on the fact that speech has been greatly valued and many organizations and agencies have devoted tremendous efforts, funds, and lobbying to the goal of developing speech in a deaf child. Parents are often literally bombarded by well-meaning but perhaps uninformed professionals who advocate either speech or sign without a comprehensive knowledge of the roles of either. The key point here is that neither is necessarily "better," but one will be likely more accessible to the child.

Children who are placed in auditory-verbal programs that utilize all possible hearing aid technologies, as well as maximizing residual hearing, may potentially do well and develop some degree of spoken speech. Children may, however, not do well in an auditory-verbal program (and this may have some correlation with the extent of the hearing loss) and yet may remain within an inaccessible linguistic environment for their entire childhood. The end result is clearly disastrous, and it is these children who present to this author as language delayed or in some cases language impoverished. These are the children who are not able to communicate using spoken language yet who have been denied the opportunity to develop an accessible language such as sign. A child who is language delayed or language impoverished may develop mental health concerns stemming from frustration and isolation. Although the astute clinician will be able to identify these mental health disorders, the treatment interventions that may include the development of a sophisticated first language may be less attainable if the child has chronologically exceeded the innate temporal critical developmental period.

The essential point of this discussion is not to determine which language is the right or wrong choice, but to assert that there is a critical need for a thorough and timely language assessment to determine that the most effective language decision has been made. Placing a child in either an auditory-verbal or sign language environment must be reviewed thoroughly, and if linguistic milestones are not being met, the language environment should/must be modified to be accessible to both the child's cortical language patterns as well as the environmental influences. If a child is thriving linguistically in an auditory-verbal environment then the language is accessible (while recognizing that social and emotional issues of isolation and peer relationships may still need to be addressed). If the child is not thriving in such an environment, then the child needs to be as quickly as possible immersed in a sign language environment. Alternatively, logic may argue that the most accessible language is likely a visual one, which is why many professionals are currently advocating that deaf children should be exposed first and early on to a sign language environment. Many of these children may effectively establish first language sign fluency, only then to become bilingual in a second spoken language through literacy.

Environmental influences in the context of the social learning theory of language development imply that the child has access to adults fluently using the child's language. It has been this author's professional experience that the vast majority of hearing parents establish a goal early on of having their child learn to speak. Sadly, this may neither be possible or realistic, as directly related to the explanation of accessibility described above.

All too often and usually after a child is identified as lagging behind in spoken language development, hearing parents elect to send their child to a Deaf school, only to never learn or become fluent in the language themselves. Although admittedly a challenge, the relationship and healthy development of the child depends on open and meaningful dialogue with the parents and, in an ideal world, extended family members as well. This may mean utilizing Deaf role models for language instruction, watching DVDs of sign language tutorials, and seeking out Deaf members of the home society with which to socialize. The added bonus of this is that the parent will gain fluency through exposure and imitation as well as being exposed to the rich and wonderful Deaf culture.

THEORY OF MIND

We cannot see into other people's minds. How then can we know what another person is thinking or feeling? We imagine other people's thoughts or feelings and through this we then create a "theory" of their mind. This process starts off fairly young in a child's life, as it is thought that by the age of 2 to 3 years children begin to establish very rudimentary comprehensions of three mental states:

Perception: young children understand that Mommy sees what is in front of her, which may not necessarily be what the child is seeing.

Wants: young children understand that when someone wants something, he or she will make an effort to get it. Example: "John wants
a cookie!"

Emotions: young children can differentiate between happiness and
sadness in themselves and others. Example: "Mommy is sad."

Children who are 4 to 5 years of age have even more developed theories of mind. By this age, children start to understand that there are such
things as false beliefs. A false belief is the understanding that sometimes
people can believe things that turn out to be misleading or untrue. In one
study (Jenkins & Astington, 1996) children were shown a box of name
brand bandages. The children were then shown the contents of the box,
which were pencils, rather than the expected bandages. When the children were then asked what they thought a child who had never seen the
box might think was in it, 3-year-old children answered, "Pencils"; however, the 4- and 5-year-old children grinned and answered, "Bandages!"
This capacity to understand mental states such as beliefs, feelings, desires,
hopes, and intentions seems to be intimately tied to the acquisition of
language. If language development is delayed, how does theory of mind
develop?

Research studies have shown that deaf children of hearing parents
typically lag several years behind hearing children of hearing parents
regarding their development of theory of mind (Peterson & Siegel, 1995;
Lundy, 2002). However, Deaf children of Deaf parents or deaf children
of hearing parents immersed in a sign language–rich environment are
typically on par with their hearing peers in their development of a theory
of mind. This is compelling support for the value of creating a language
accessible and rich environment during critically important periods of a
deaf child's development.

Theory of mind, however, is likely not only related to language. Lundy
(2002) examined age and language skills of Deaf children in relation to
theory of mind development and found that although deaf children with
greater language delays did exhibit more difficulties acquiring a theory
of mind, language ability proved to be less important than the age of the
child. Her study found that by age 9 and 10 years, deaf children even

with relatively low-level expressive language skills demonstrated an age-appropriate theory of mind. Lundy (2002) queried that perhaps there is a minimum language competency that is critical for the development of theory of mind. Although this may suggest that deaf children will ultimately "catch up" in their acquisition of a theory of mind as they become older, this may happen in qualitatively different ways.

An example from my own clinical practice with hundreds of Deaf children are the frequent comments by teachers and family members that the Deaf child is "selfish," "thinks only of himself," and shows "a lack of regard for his classmates in terms of their feelings." These behavioral and emotional expressions of egocentricity may be intimately tied to a delay in theory of mind acquisition such that social skills, turn-taking, and dialogue (many rooted in understanding the states of minds of others) are not achieved at normal developmental ages but are delayed. Although it is encouraging that deaf children seem to ultimately acquire a theory of mind, albeit at a much later age than a typically developing child, the concern arises that maladaptive behavioral and social patterns of interacting with others may be well established.

Consider Matthew a 12-year-old deaf boy of hearing parents referred for a psychological evaluation. His parents shared that Matthew was a "failure at speaking" and that they were disappointed after attending many years of auditory verbal therapy to admit that Matthew still could not talk with his classmates at his mainstreamed school, had not made any friends, did not follow the rules of any games well, and persistently preferred to play with younger children. An assessment of Matthew revealed a boy of average nonverbal intelligence and a profound delay in receptive and expressive language. Although testing suggested that Matthew had acquired some degree of theory of mind, his maladaptive manner of interacting and engaging with others was so well entrenched that almost invariably his first response to any kind of social overture was to respond with egocentricism.

This example highlights the importance of developing a theory of mind at normative ages. When children are delayed or impoverished in linguisitic skills, the behavior of people around them must be baffling if it cannot be linked to inner feeling states. How can a deaf child with delayed or absent theory of mind make sense of the behavior of their classmates or teachers or parents if he or she does not understand that someone is sad or angry or frustrated? How can a cause-effect be established (i.e., Mommy is mad because I broke her vase) if deaf children are unable to link their own behavior to the feelings of others and furthermore may be unable to anticipate or predict the responses of others toward them? These and other questions are currently being studied, yielding invaluable understanding into the minds of these children. In addition, active teaching strategies to promote the development of a sense of the "other" in children's lives are being promoted for use with deaf children with some promising results.

SOCIAL AND EMOTIONAL DEVELOPMENT

In addition to theory of mind, the social and emotional lives of deaf children may develop differently from typical hearing trajectories. Conceptualizing social-emotional development is complex given that individuals, families, and communities may differ as to what is considered typical and/or expected based on culture, language, and mores. Furthermore, clinicians are limited by a lack of assessment tools developed for and standardized on deaf children.

The older literature presents a mixed review, with some researchers describing deaf children as generally leading emotionally troubled and isolated lives (Myklebust, 1960) and with more contemporary research delineating more explicitly the difficulties observed in social-emotional development. For example, Peterson and Siegal (2000) described the close link between deaf children's well-documented theory-of-mind difficulties and a relative lack of emotional competence. The same authors also describe how deaf children frequently have difficulties acknowledging that different people can hold different mental states regarding the same situation. Rieffe and Terwogt (2006) reported that Deaf children use the communicative function of anger expression differently from hearing children. Whereas hearing children used anger expression to reflect on the anguish that another child caused them, deaf children used it rather bluntly, explained less, and expected less empathic responses from the peer causing them harm.

It seems quite likely that at the core of the social-emotional development of many deaf children lays a language problem. But as Rieffe's (2012) research from the Netherlands points out, the issue is much more complex than that. Her research with Dutch Deaf children shows that deaf children clearly exhibit different emotional development from hearing children, yet all cannot be explained by delays in language acquisition.

It should be remembered that deaf and hard of hearing children are a very heterogeneous group, differing on constructs such as etiology, degree and type of loss of hearing, age of identification, accessible exposure to language, use of technical devices, type of school attended, and hearing status of family members. Given all these factors, it is erroneous to make general assumptions or statements regarding the social-emotional development of deaf children. In addition to language and theory of mind as discussed earlier, the following constructs of identity, family relationship and peer relationships are likely useful in assessing and better understanding the social and emotional development of deaf and hard of hearing children.

IDENTITY

The formation of an identity at the most basic level involves representation of the self. This usually includes both self-identity (Who am I?) as well as social identity (How do others see me?). How do deaf and hard of hearing children internalize these two forms of identity?

> Consider Sarah, a signing deaf child of hearing parents attending a mainstreamed school. At the age of 7 years, she tearfully signed to her mother, "I am different from everybody else in my school because nobody else knows they have hands!"
>
> Matthew, a Deaf child of Deaf parents attending a Deaf school, at the age of 7 years signed to his Dad, "Why don't those people who live beside us know how to sign like everybody else in the world?"

Finally, Celeste, a 7-year-old deaf child of hearing parents who had bilateral hearing aids and an EA in a mainstreamed school, said to her mother that she refused to go to her grandparent's house without her EA to "help" her not look stupid.

Obviously, these three scenarios will result in very different understandings of the self and place of belonging in the world.

The fact that a child is deaf or hard of hearing will not usually and singularly determine their sense of identity (Corker, 1996). The determination will be made by the emphasis placed on their deafness within their daily living (i.e., Matthew's understanding was much different from that of Celeste), the reactions of parents, family members, and teachers (i.e., "No, Cindy cannot take physical education class in case she damages her hearing aids"), whether the prevailing family worldview is a medical/disability vs difference model, and finally, the difficulties, obstacles, and barriers personally experienced by the child (i.e., a child who is deaf and in a wheelchair may face additional and cumulative challenges).

Much of the research specifically examining identity formation in a deaf child concludes that healthy identity formation and social-emotional development are usually experienced by children comfortable in both hearing and Deaf culture (bicultural) with a Deaf identity (Weinberg & Sterritt, 1986; Glickman, 1996; Jambor & Elliot, 2005; Hintermair, 2008).

FAMILY RELATIONSHIPS

Few would disagree that the family is an important factor in the overall healthy development of a child. Regardless of gender, social class, age, or culture, the concept of family is integral to children and youth feeling loved, accepted, and supported. Although recognizing the enormous benefits that a healthy family has to offer, many families face formidable and at times insurmountable challenges affecting their functioning and enduring influence on their children. Examples might include families stressed by poverty, warfare, divorce, physical and/or mental health issues of parent or child, trauma, or catastrophic environmental disasters. In all of these situations, a stressed family may be less able or less likely to nurture, love, and support their children through normative developmental changes.

Hearing families with a deaf child are no different from other families in terms of the aspired outcome of raising healthy, competent, and happy children. The inclusion of a deaf child within a hearing family, however, tends to change family dynamics (Meadow-Orlans, Mertens, & Sass-Lehrer, 2003) as mediated by factors such as reactions to the identification of deafness, attachment, development of theory of mind, and language choices. These different dynamics often seem to impose greater complexity on family and parenting issues, requiring more thought and greater care (Luterman, 1987). In the past there was a belief that these different family dynamics as a result of membership of a deaf child within a hearing family resulted in more negative family affect, such as sorrow, depression, and emotional turmoil (Luckner & Velaski, 2004). Yet this causal claim has been rejected by more contemporary thought with a move away from deafness as a pathology toward deafness as a difference. Inclusion of a deaf child within a hearing family likely requires some reorganization of the family's inner resources, yet there is little empirical evidence to claim that this shift needs to be negative.

In a parallel shift, there are more studies now than in the past supporting the concept that families are not necessarily adversely affected by parenting a child with a disability (Powell & Gallagher, 1993; Dunst, 2000; Turnbull, Turnbull, & Wehmeyer, 2010). In fact, some studies are describing how families of children with disabilities may be strengthened and as well adjusted as families with able-bodied children. It is evident from the preceding discussions of attachment, language and theory of mind that parenting a deaf child is likely different from parenting a hearing child. In an effort to better understand this within the paradigm of deaf children within hearing families, and especially in considering how these family dynamics may be strengthed, professionals have been interested in better understanding the dynamics of healthy families with deaf children.

One such study by Luckner and Velaski (2004) specifically identified and interviewed hearing families of children who were deaf. They summarized their results within the following overarching themes:

- Families indicated that support was essential. This support included strong understanding and open dialogue with inner and extended family members as well as helpful interactions with professionals.
- Families indicated that they were proactive in terms of an earlier understanding of the implications of deafness, as well as what best practices indicated in terms of language choices and educational placements.
- The majority of families decided to immediately learn sign language to ensure open and meaningful communication with their child from an early age.
- The families made the point that this was not necessarily to replace spoken language but was clearly the most accessible route to early two-way dialogue with their children.
- Families emphasized the importance of family involvement in the education of their children.

Parents of a deaf child often have other hearing sons and/or daughters. Studies suggest that the relationships of deaf children and their hearing siblings are generally positive, yet there are often areas where sibling relationships might benefit from consultation with a mental health professional (Bat-Chava & Martin, 2002).

> Susan was the 14-year-old hearing sister of a deaf 8-year-old boy, Jared. Susan eloquently shared during a family therapy session that she felt she was expected by her parents to take on a protective role with Jared while at school, as well as on the bus to and from school. Susan described how she felt she missed out on being "a kid" as she always had to be "a mother" to her brother.

This may put undue stress on the older child, potentially leading to resentment and an unhealthy dependence of the parent to obtain school and/or peer information through the hearing child. Hearing siblings have also, however, described repeatedly the special bond they have with their deaf brother or sister. In these situations, it has been evident how the deafness has been framed as "just Joey" rather than as a pathological family stressor. And in yet other families, older hearing siblings have described how detached and emotionally distant they felt from their deaf sibling, especially if he or she attended a Deaf school. Clearly, the dynamics of the family in terms of framing the deaf child as either a "family member" or a "family stressor" or a "family vistor" may potentially lead to strikingly different sibling relationships.

PEER RELATIONSHIPS

Childhood friendships start to become evident in toddlerhood when young children begin to interact with other children through play. At this stage of development, toddlers do not perceive language as important as the attention to and time spent in a common play activity. Observations of hearing and deaf toddlers playing together are instructive, as one begins to appreciate the minimal role that language plays at this stage and the invaluable opportunities that play time provides for socialization. Parents of deaf toddlers often wonder if it is appropriate for their child to be in a hearing toddler play group, and the answer is yes—whether it is a hearing, deaf, or mixed group, as developmentally the play at this age tends to operate on behavioral rather than linguistic principles. In this sense, the deaf child is on equal playing ground with the hearing child.

There is a developmental shift in the preschool years, when language has a more central role in friendships. Preschoolers begin to pick specific children with whom they want to play and also begin to behave differently around children whom they have not selected as friends. Parents may be teaching their preschool children rhymes and songs, which the children will often recite and sing repeatedly while engaged in a play activity. Observations of this developmental age typically show both linguistic and behavioral elements involved in play. It is likely at this early and vulnerable stage of development that deaf children may be observed to maintain more solitary than group play. As children of this age generally still engage in both solitary play and play with friends, this subtle shift may go somewhat unnoticed by parents.

During the elementary school years, children establish, develop, and maintain friendships with children who are generally perceived as similar to themselves. Clearly, at this stage language is utilized for determining likes, dislikes, similarities and differences. It is not hard to imagine how a child with a different language from the mainstream language may begin to feel left out. A child's exclusion from friendships is a concern and is often rightly worrisome for parents. Friendships provide children with road maps for healthy social and emotional navigation. School-age friendships provide a place where different ways of relating can be tried, where social dilemmas can be experienced and resolved, as well as where intimacy can be experienced outside the family. Friendships at this stage teach a child how to lose, how to win, how to be aggressive, how to be forgiving, how to understand power, how to comfort, how to deal with frustration, how to enjoy company, and how to deal with anger. The school-age years provide a fertile learning ground for children to build on their theory of mind in terms of understanding themselves in relation to the larger social world around them. These years can be instrumental for establishing a strong sense of self-esteem, which reflects how one feels about oneself as a person.

Bat-Chava (1993) conducted a meta-analysis study of self-esteem examining the effects of family and school factors as well as the influence of Deaf group identification. Her results found overall that deaf children of deaf parents had higher self-esteem than deaf children of hearing parents. The study also found that self-esteem was higher among deaf people who used sign language, as opposed to those who used oral language. And finally, the study also found that the more strongly one identified with being a member of the Deaf community, the higher the self-esteem scores. These are important conclusions for parents and teachers to consider when making language and educational choices as well as perhaps understanding the behavior and emotional regulation of the deaf child.

SUMMARY

This chapter has explored the development of language in deaf children. The brain of any child is hardwired for language, and there is no preference for modality. The responsibility of the parents and professionals is to make wise informed language choices with frequent and meaningful assessments of those choices.

Language plays an important role in the development of a theory of mind. Theory of mind is often thought to be delayed in deaf children, and this is likely due to host of factors including compromised language acquisition. A working theory of mind positions the deaf child well in his or her understanding of family and peer relationships, and it behooves both parents and professionals to augment the deaf child's experiences toward a healthy and normative sense of self and other.

The social-emotional development of the deaf child needs to be understood within the context of being deaf, as does the development of self and social identity. Family and peer relationships play an important role and can be influenced by many different factors.

It is important to remember that many deaf children navigate through childhood showing healthy and resilient psychological development. Study of these children may serve us well in understanding specific protective and adaptive constructs.

5 Education of Deaf Children

EDUCATION: PHILOSOPHIES AND BEST PRACTICES

Views and opinions on how to educate deaf children are long-standing, confusing, and controversial. As a clinician who teaches in a university, I encourage my students to search the literature to support their claims. Although this is a good practice, it can also leave one feeling confused, as there seems to be references to support almost any position, any claim, and any option. I therefore also remind my students that not all research is good research and not all claims are adequately supported. The literature surrounding education and deaf children unfortunately falls into this category. For a thorough review of evidence-based practice in educating deaf and hard of hearing students, the reader is best directed to Spencer and Marschark's (2010) book, which provides a comprehensive evaluation of what we know, what we think we know, and what we don't know about best practices.

Educational practices for deaf students have tended to be diametrical in nature. For example, parents have had the choice to educate their child in a residential versus day program, a sign based versus an oral program, or a mainstreamed versus segregated. What is what?

RESIDENTIAL DEAF SCHOOLS

In many countries, including Canada, there was no formal Deaf culture or Deaf community prior to the establishment of residential schools for deaf students. Deaf children were often quite isolated from each other, and the majority did not receive any formal education. Abbé Charles Michel de l'Épée is credited with the establishment of the first school for the deaf in 1760 in Paris, France. The first school for deaf students in the United States followed in 1817 in the state of Connecticut, and the first school for deaf students in Canada opened in 1831 in the province of Quebec. These residential schools were developed specifically for deaf students, and the teachers and staff were trained to teach and interact with the deaf children in an environment that was more discussion based as opposed to didactic, in classrooms that were physically constructed in a least restrictive manner to ensure that all students were able to communicate and interpret information freely, and in direct communication with the students without the use of educational interpreters (Garay, 2003).

The benefits of the residential schools are access to an accessible and visual language, access to Deaf role models and mentors, camaraderie with Deaf friends, Deaf sports and social clubs, and finally, the transmission of Deaf heritage, traditions, and identities. It was often at the residential Deaf school where the deaf child felt he or she belonged and often thrived. However, attendance at a Deaf residential school also meant separation from the family and reduced opportunity for the family members to learn sign language if the child was only home on the weekends or holidays.

The residential schools have changed their language of instruction over time. At one point when oralism was strongly supported, deaf children were not allowed to sign, and children were forced to manually finger-spell all words in the spoken language. More recently, some of these schools for the Deaf have adopted a bilingual bicultural (bi–bi) philosophy to education, which in Canada includes using American Sign Language (ASL) and written English (or Langue des Signes Québécoise [LSQ], and written French) as the classroom languages and introducing subjects such as Deaf Studies into the curriculum with the goal of students gaining appreciation of both Deaf and hearing cultures. The residential schools gradually changed to also incorporate day programs, which allow a child to remain at home with his or her family while also partaking in the opportunities the residential schools have to offer.

Mariam is a 13 year-old Deaf child of Deaf parents. Mariam was voted by her peers to be the Grade 8 president of the student council. The most pressing issue that Mariam and her student council faced was to lobby for the government not to close the residential Deaf school. Mariam engaged her classmates, who launched a well-planned and organized strategy to educate both the general public and the politicians about their school. In their presentation, the students described how they were children first, and like all other children deserved the best education that adults could offer. In their view, the best education included having Deaf adults as role models, learning about their Deaf culture, sharing pride with others in their language, and feeling a strong sense of community.

Many Deaf adults look back at their time in residential Deaf schools as the time when they developed a sense of identity and belonging.

Marsha, now 55 years old, shared that when her parents first left her at the age of 5 years at the residential school she felt confused and bewildered. Her parents did not sign, and they had no way of really explaining that they were leaving her there. Instead, they told her "you good girl goodbye." She remembers crying those first few weeks, feeling homesick for her family. With time she began to feel more comfortable, and by the time she graduated from high school Marsha had developed close relationships with her classmates that continue today. Marsha shared that it was at the school that she really came to understand "who I was and that more importantly I was a good person, a normal person and could have a happy life."

MAINSTREAMED PROGRAMS

Although there are several variations, mainstreamed educational programs all integrate the deaf child into a classroom or school with hearing children. Some programs use interpreters, some rely on maximizing residual hearing through technology, or some may create small classrooms of only deaf children within the larger school. These programs vary in their use of an oral approach, a Total Communication approach, artificial signed representations of a language (i.e., Signed Exact English) or a mixture of a few approaches. Some classrooms have adopted co-teachers, with one teacher specializing in the education of deaf and hard of hearing students. In addition, technological advances have meant that classrooms can be looped with inductive devices, teachers use FM systems, and children utilize advanced digital hearing aids as well as cochlear implantation. Mainstreamed programs are not residential programs.

The benefits of mainstreamed programs are that the child continues to live at home with his or her family, may attend the same school as his or her sibling(s), and may have a greater access to academic programs, as the school is usually larger than a residential school. The disadvantages of such programs can be the frustration and potential isolation that a deaf child may feel in trying to interact with hearing peers, fatigue from constantly trying to navigate in a hearing world, expectations to take "hearing-centric" courses like music, little exposure to Deaf role models and mentors, lack of standardization in teaching strategies as well as qualifications of interpreters, and finally, confusion regarding the development of an identity or an understanding of Deaf culture.

Jack was a 9-year-old child with a cochlear implant. Jack had the implant at the age of 4 years and had made impressive gains in his auditory ability since then. In his current Grade 4 mainstreamed classroom, Jack's receptive language skills exceeded his expressive language skills. He was a bright, inquisitive child and the teachers in his school recognized his strengths and supported his weaknesses. As Jack's classmates often had trouble understanding his spoken speech, the school purchased computer software trained to Jack's speech such that what he said was immediately transcribed onto a computer screen that all the students could easily see. With this acceptance and technology, Jack felt and was included in all academic activities. He excelled in his academic subjects and quickly mastered reading.

Jonathan, now 42 years old, is a Deaf man who attended all of his school years in a mainstreamed program. Upon reflection, he thinks he may have received a better education than if he attended a residential school as "I was forced to figure school out fast or be left behind." He grew up in an oral program where he was the only deaf child, and thinks it was the best educational choice for him in term of reading and writing. He does recall, however, how he felt very left out and confused on the playground. He remembers not being invited to any birthday parties and secretly feeling glad of it, as he did not know how he would have communicated with his peers. At the conclusion of high school Jonathan attended Gallaudet University in Washington, D.C. As he had not been exposed to sign language before, Jonathan was required to add an extra year to his degree to obtain some sign language fluency. Jonathan excelled at university and feels that for him he had the best of both worlds—a strong educational start, followed by immersion in a program where he felt a sense of "sameness" with his classmates in terms of their deafness. Today, Jonathan is a successful lawyer who uses spoken language as well as sign language interpretation. In his words, "I use everything that might help to be successful."

All of these educational practices have been likely founded on good intentions, strong emotions, and perhaps even in some theoretical basis. Somewhat surprisingly, though, and with some disappointment, it is becoming clear that these different approaches have not been rigorously studied to evaluate academic outcomes. Among their key findings, Spencer and Marschark (2010) conclude, "there is little empirical evidence that either mainstreaming or separate education generally is better for deaf and hard of hearing students" (p. 8). Recognizing that each deaf child is unique and deserves individualized assessments of needs, the current state of deaf education lacks overall systematic directives regarding best practices for education. Without these directives, deaf children will not benefit from evidence-based practices, and educational decisions will continue to be made perhaps with emotion rather than logic and reasoned thought.

DEVELOPMENT OF LITERACY SKILLS

> There is no such thing as a child who hates to read; there are only children who have not found the right book.

> — Frank Serafini

Finding the "right book" for deaf and hard of hearing children has been perhaps one of the most long-standing and frustrating challenges for parents, educators, researchers, and deaf children themselves. Although some deaf and hard of hearing children demonstrate excellent reading skills, the majority tend to show significant lags as compared to their hearing same-aged peers (Padden & Ramsey, 2000). These lags mean that 50% of deaf students in the United States graduate from secondary school with a fourth-grade reading level or less (Traxler, 2000), and 30% leave school functionally illiterate (Marschark, Lang, & Albertini, 2002). These lower literacy levels are also observed in other countries such as Canada, the United Kingdom, and Europe.

Deaf children of Deaf parents tend to fare better in terms of literacy skills than deaf children of hearing parents, although there still remains a lag behind hearing same-aged peers (Strong & Prinz, 1997). This improvement has been attributed to factors such as deaf children of deaf parents being better adjusted emotionally because of more positive parental attitudes, early exposure to sign language in the home, and the fact that the cause of deafness is likely to be genetic and not from infection, rubella, anoxia, or trauma, which in themselves may be associated with cognitive compromises. Braden (1994) summarized that the advantage Deaf parents offer their Deaf child is the early development of an internal language base, which better supports their acquisition, storage, and application of academic knowledge. However, despite this apparent protection afforded deaf children by virtue of having Deaf parents, there still remains a substantial discrepancy between hearing and deaf children regarding the acquisition of reading and writing skills.

The reasons for this lag is not clearly understood, and it has been suggested that these delays in reading and writing acquisition may be related to any or all of the following factors:

- Delays in early language acquisition;
- Paucity of incidental and environmental learning;
- Lack of shared reading activities with parents;
- Inadequate teaching strategies;
- Lower teacher and parent expectations;
- Etiology of deafness.

One of the most intriguing and challenging aspects is that deaf children appear to follow similar trajectories as those of their same-aged hearing peers (Mayer, 2007). Williams (2004) reviewed the relevant literature and wrote that "deaf children's emergent reading reflected the developmental sequence of hearing children described in the research literature" (p. 356) and that "young deaf children's emergent writing development may be similar to that of hearing children" (p. 361). Further complicating the issue is that evidence of delays in literacy are still observed today, despite earlier identification of hearing loss, language modality, advanced multimedia and computer technology, sophisticated hearing aids, and cochlear implants. What is/are the cause(s) of delays in literacy levels? Clearly, further research is needed to establish specific methods of developing literacy skills in deaf children in spite of, rather than due to, differences in language choices and parental hearing status.

MENTAL HEALTH AND EDUCATION

It is not possible to separate mental health from education. A child who is in good mental health is likely in a better position to learn from didactic instruction as well as from school experience. A child who experiences distressed mental health is less likely to learn in terms of motivation, concentration, as well as fewer available internal resources.

Consider the deaf child who is placed in a less than optimal educational placement. In Chapter 4, the premise was made that deaf children of hearing parents are often at a linguistic disadvantage and that wise choices coupled with ongoing assessments are crucial to a "goodness of fit" situation regarding the acquisition of language. That same model also holds true for educational placement, although now the situation has expanded to include not only the child and their family but the wider school community as well.

In terms of the child, the educational setting should ideally compliment and build upon the linguistic foundation set during the preschool years.

Consider Tabitha, whose parents embraced the auditory verbal method from infancy. Born with a congenital bilateral severe-to-profound hearing loss, Tabitha was identified at the early infant screening while still in the hospital with her mother. Within one month, Tabitha wore bilateral hearing aids and the parents positively reinforced every coo and babble the baby made. By the age of 4 years, Tabitha was an inquisitive and energetic child who still had not spoken her first words. Her parents remained encouraged that she did make many non-linguistic vocalizations, ensured that her hearing aids were functioning well, and exposed her to a wide variety of auditory stimuli. At age 5 years, Tabitha was enrolled in the local school in the kindergarten program. The teacher did not have any experience or training with deaf children and as such found it cumbersome when Tabitha pulled the hearing aids out to have to continually replace them, as well as ensuring that the FM system was functioning properly. The teacher had a class of 22 active children and felt she did not have time to stop and check that Tabitha's hearing aids were in place and turned on, nor was it feasible for the teacher to always wear the FM system when she at times engaged in active play with the children. As such, during the school hours and unbeknownst to her parents, Tabitha often did not receive any auditory input through her hearing aid and FM system. By the end of kindergarten, Tabitha's report card indicated that she was a lovely child who preferred to play on her own and did not follow simple instructions well. The truth of the situation was that Tabitha was indeed a lovely child but was unable to interact appropriately with her hearing peers and as such withdrew out of necessity. She did not follow instructions, as she did not hear them.

In this example, which has occurred all too frequently across classrooms, the teacher was ill prepared and was unable to manage the extra demands imposed by the hearing aids and FM system. Sadly, in these cases it is the child who is marginalized, as Tabitha began Grade 1 far behind her peers linguistically and with a frightened shy demeanor when asked to take part in group activities.

By Grade 3, Tabitha's parents were perplexed. Their audiologist continued to assure them that Tabitha's hearing aids were functioning well mechanically, yet Tabitha had a very small vocabulary compared to her peers and was difficult to understand. Her teacher ensured that Tabitha always had preferential seating at the front of the room and used the FM system as much as she could. Yet Tabitha was performing academically far behind her peers, often cried without an apparent reason, and usually stood alone on the playground at recess. Tabitha failed the Grade 4 curriculum demands and at that point the parents decided to withdraw her from the local school and transferred her to the residential school for the Deaf located one hour from their home. Tabitha had never been to sleepovers as she did not have any friends, and at the age of 10 suddenly found herself separated from her parents and living in the residential dorm. Tabitha had never seen any sign language before and was clearly bewildered by the gestures of her peers and her teacher. Tabitha withdrew even more until one day, near the end of Grade 5, she was found sobbing uncontrollably under her desk in an empty classroom. When a teacher attempted to remove her from under the desk, Tabitha screamed and bit her hand. Tabitha was suspended from the school and subsequently refused to return to school again. A subsequent psychological assessment suggested that Tabitha was suffering from an Axis I major depressive episode, social anxiety, school phobia, and had a learning disability.

A diathesis-stress model of child psychopathology emphasizes how a child's vulnerability or disposition—be that genetic, inherited, environmental, or emotional—may in combination with specific stressors result in an abnormal condition. In this case, the initial diathesis or vulnerability arising out of early child development was Tabitha's delayed language acquisition. The complex combination of inaccessible language decisions, inappropriate educational placements, and lack of socialization experiences were all likely stressors that may in themselves have no causal bearing but certainly contributed to or brought about the onset of Tabitha's mental health disorders.

In contrast, consider Roger, who was also born with a congenital deafness to hearing parents.

Roger, similar to Tabitha, was also identified early on and was bilaterally aided with amplification. Roger's parents also elected to enroll him in the local school, but Roger was placed in a classroom that was co-taught by one teacher who had training as a teacher of the deaf. In the kindergarten class, the teacher of the deaf ensured that Roger's hearing aids were always inserted correctly and were turned on prior to any teaching. She also wore the FM system continuously, and the other children were also encouraged to speak into the FM microphone during any group discussions. The teacher utilized a variety of visual and auditory teaching strategies to engage and maximize Roger's learning. Roger thrived in this setting and began Grade 1 with a slight language delay as compared to his peers. By the end of the first term in Grade 1, Roger continued to lag behind, and it was decided that supplemental signs would be used to support Roger's expressive and receptive language. The teacher ensured that the parents had a DVD of the sign vocabulary, and they were encouraged to utilize a Deaf mentor to increase their own sign vocabulary. Roger's progress was reassessed again at the spring break of Grade 1 and it became evident that Roger was making conceptual, developmental, and linguistic gains with the use of sign-supported speech. At that point, the school board decided to create a self-contained classroom of children with similar needs, and Roger was placed in a Grade 2 classroom with 10 other deaf children within the local school. This class was again co-taught with a regular teacher as well as a teacher of the Deaf, and Roger continued to thrive, making normative gains in all areas. Roger appeared to be happy, was engaged in school, and was popular with his friends.

These two scenarios illustrate the importance of deciding educational placements based on meaningful assessments. It also highlights the idea of multifinality, which is an important concept in deaf education. This refers to situations in which similar initial conditions (i.e., both children were born deaf) lead to different end effects as defined by the educational placements. This is different from equifinality, which suggests that different conditions (i.e., different educational choices) all lead to the same outcome. There is no place for equifinality in deaf education. Each deaf child is unique, and it is our responsibility as professionals to ensure that outcomes are defined by measured and thoughtful decisions.

SUMMARY

This chapter has discussed different philosophies and best practices regarding the education of the deaf child. There is not one clear reason that deaf children as a group tend to lag behind their same-aged hearing peers in the acquisition and development of literacy skills. Educational strategies have not kept up with research, and as such, there is little empirical evidence to support different philosophies. What is known to be important is early intervention and frequent assessment of gains to ensure that the child benefits from the placement. If gains are not present, changes need to be made. Finally, it is evident that there is likely no more to be gained by debating "which" educational practice is best, but rather research should be devoted to better understanding the specific processes by which a deaf child might best learn how to read and write.

6 Adolescence

Adolescence is a time of profound change. One parent shared that it was like putting her Grade 8 child on a train entering a tunnel for the next five or six years. As the train seemed to go at a breakneck pace, she and her husband wondered what would emerge at the end of the tunnel—a train wreck or an entirely different locomotive?

Most parents hope that the tunnel of adolescence does not end in a train wreck (although sadly some do), yet what does emerge can often seem to be a foreign and new set of wheels. During these years young people experience rapid and profound changes in their physical growth, sexual maturation, and social-emotional development. These changes are an inevitable part of growing up for each child, yet the process is uniquely individualized, as influenced by factors such as experience, culture, cognition, genetics, family, and temperament.

The period of adolescent development is often a challenging period for both children and their parents. A teenager's development can be divided into three stages: early, middle, and late adolescence. The age at which each stage is reached, however, varies greatly from child to child. Different rates of maturation can be influenced by many things, some of which are not under either the control of the parent or child, such as outward physical development and hormone balance. Other influential factors, such as language development and educational experience, can be directly influenced by either the parent and/or the environment. It is these types of influences that seem to have an even greater significance for deaf teenagers. Adolescent developmental stages can be generally understood as including the elements listed in Table 6.1.

DEAF ADOLESCENTS

The general developmental stages through which a deaf teenager travels will be fundamentally similar to those of a hearing adolescent. However, the deaf adolescent potentially faces a much more complex route than the hearing teenager, and this road map is often directly dependent upon and in some sense predetermined by the language and educational decisions made on their behalf. In her book entitled *Inner Lives of Deaf Children: Interviews and Analysis*, Sheridan (2001) used qualitative research techniques to write about the individual and collective aspects of the lives of seven deaf children. In her follow-up book, *Deaf Adolescents: Inner Lives and Lifeworld Development* (2008) Sheridan catches up with the seven children, who are now all deaf adolescents, with an eloquent description of all the positive and negative interrelating factors profoundly influencing their lives and development. Of considerable interest is their resiliency in the face of adversity. These two books provide the reader with a fascinating glimpse into the lives of deaf children who have grown into deaf adolescents. The interviews highlight both the joys and hardships inherent in the challenges of transition.

Consider the following developmental tasks with unique challenges as potentially experienced by a deaf adolescent.

Table 6.1 *Developmental Stages*

Developmental Task	Early Adolescence (11–14 years)	Middle Adolescence (15–16 years)	Late Adolescence (17–21 years)
Thinking	Emerging capacity for abstract thought	Continued capacity for abstract thought	Ability to think ideas through and exam inner thoughts
Identity Development	Forming sense of identity	Struggling with establishing sense of identity	Firmer sense of identity
Social-Emotional Functioning	Moodiness	Intense self thought and self-involvement	Increased emotional stability
Family Relationships	Less attention shown to parents	Complaints that parents interfere with independence	Peer relationships remain important with a greater tolerance for parental relationships
		Growing dependence on peers	
Independence	Increased influence of peer group	Strong reliance on peer group	Increased independence and self-reliance
Moral Thought	Beginning moral thinking	Greater interest in moral reasoning	More social and moral awareness

THINKING

As explained earlier in this book, the etiology of the deafness may potentially influence the thinking and reasoning abilities of the child's brain. For example, premature low birth weight babies may have disabilities including cerebral palsy, learning issues, sensory loss, attention deficits, psychological problems, behavioral difficulties, emotional disorders, and seizure disorders. Amidst this constellation of insults, the deaf child is likely to have compromised thinking and reasoning skills. As this child enters early adolescence, he or she may experience significant delays in the formation of abstract thought and moral reasoning.

If the child is deaf, however, from an unknown cause or non-syndromic genetic etiology, it is likely that reasoning and thinking skills are intact. This is a child who has the capacity to think, to reason, to feel, to experience—with perhaps the only fundamental difference being deafness. This is where the complexity of developmental progression is introduced. If this child has been denied adequate exposure to an accessible language and thus has experienced a delay in receptive and expressive language acquisition, both thinking and reasoning will be influenced, despite the fact that these psychological processes may be relatively intact. More simply said, how does a child without a language begin to be assertive toward developmental autonomy? Begin to try on different scenarios in terms of moral reasoning? Engage in a growing capacity for abstract thought? Generally expand his or her intellectual interests? Make sense of changing body parts in terms of an evolving sexuality? These examples make it evident that a child's language development holds importance for the successful resolution and mastery of developmental cognitive milestones.

Identity Development

The development of a deaf identity emerges as adolescents consciously reflect upon differences and similarities between themselves and others. As they observe and attach values to these similarities and differences, they begin to also reflect on how these are interpreted by significant others in their lives. Teenagers engage in this process actively with each other through social interactions, as well as more subtly as they observe the impacts of their behaviors on others.

A deaf child who has attended a Deaf school will have been exposed to deaf peers throughout her childhood development. This child likely shares the same sign language as his or her peers, leading to established friendships, peer groups, shared traditions, similar worldviews, and feelings of acceptance. This child will likely be well positioned to navigate through this particular developmental challenge of forming her own identity relative to her peers.

The difference, however, for these deaf teenagers compared to hearing teenagers may be related to the qualitatively different relationship with their parents. As the majority of hearing parents tend to never learn to sign fluently, their relationship with their deaf teenager will be different from a home where there is a shared language between parent and child. As can be seen in Table 6.1, the normative adolescent strategy involves a distancing from the parents in early to middle adolescence in favor of the peer group, with increasing independence and self-reliance. But if the deaf adolescent feels emotionally distant from his parent by the language barrier from a very early age, this developmental shift may be an even stronger alliance and allegiance to deaf peers or, in other words, a deeper relationship with Deaf culture.

A study examining the attachment representation of Deaf adults supports these powerful protective benefits afforded by Deaf culture (Chovaz McKinnon, Moran, & Pederson, 2004). Based on the culturally Deaf participants' descriptions of strained and distant parent-child relationships (i.e., not sharing the same language, as well as early placement in a residential school), the authors predicted that the distribution of attachment classification would differ from normative distributions in that there would likely be a higher number of insecure attachments. Somewhat surprisingly, the distribution of the classifications of the Deaf sample was not different from existing normative distributions. The authors speculated that powerful developmental peer experiences may allow many Deaf individuals to reconstruct an autonomous state of mind regarding attachment, despite a socially maladaptive early parental relationship.

In contrast to the deaf adolescent attending a Deaf school, deaf teenagers in a mainstreamed program may find themselves without deaf peers.

Depending on the type of educational program, a deaf mainstreamed student may be in a self-contained class with other deaf children or may be the sole deaf teenager in the school. Circumstances will yet again change depending on the language choice elected by the parent. For example, a self-contained classroom supporting the auditory verbal approach may foster a sense of peer kinship within the classroom where all students interact using the same communicative mode.

> Jonathan, an oral deaf teenager, shared that "I feel pretty good with my friends in the classroom as we all wear hearing aids and use an FM system, but when we go to an assembly, we are the odd men out and we know it. We are different from everybody else and they tend to stare at us and hardly ever try to talk to us."

A sole deaf child attending a mainstreamed program with a sign language interpreter may find the classroom to be accessible yet the cafeteria or hallways to be foreign places. As one deaf mainstreamed student told me "I just don't fit in with them. I can't talk like a normal teen-ager through my interpreter as she is an adult and just does not get it and the other kids don't want to say stuff in front of her either." The task of forming a self-identity for these deaf teenagers may be complicated by their educational placements as well as language choices.

As Sheridan writes, "identity development for deaf adolescents may necessitate a process of assessing and resolving these diverse perspectives on what and who they should be, where they fit in, and what this means in terms of choices for their futures" (2008, p. 10). This holds great importance from a mental health perspective, for it may be that some deaf adolescents feel overwhelmed, anxious, or resentful as they strive to meet the normative developmental milestones of adolescent self-identity.

Glickman and Harvey (1996) proposed that the deaf individual has four possible options through which to transition in developmental growth:

1. *Culturally hearing:* A hearing identity that mirrors the ways that hearing people behave and views deafness as a disability to be surmounted.

2. *Culturally marginal:* An identity that lacks social embedded-ness in either a hearing or deaf environment.
3. *Culturally deaf:* An awareness of and positive acceptance of one's deafness so that the deaf person pursues positive rela-tionships with a social group of deaf persons.
4. *Bicultural:* An identity that reflects comfort in both deaf and hearing environments.

From a psychological perspective, it is evident that the formation of a self-identify in a deaf teenager may be a complicated developmental task. The child already in turmoil by rapid and profound physical and hor-monal changes may not be well mobilized to deal with myriad confusing and negative feelings, ranging from "Who am I when there is nobody else similar to me?" to "Who can I possibly be when there are so many barriers around me?" to "Why should I even try to be anybody?" From a mental health perspective, the concern then regarding deaf adolescent self-identity is threefold:

1. It may be a painful, negative, and confusing experience.
2. It may lead to mental health issues such as anxiety and depression.
3. It may not be successfully resolved.

The following examples will illustrate all three possible outcomes.

Joshua was a 16-year-old deaf teenager who excelled at school. Joshua had a cochlear implant as an infant and had always been raised and educated in an oral environment. Joshua's parents were very involved, and his mother assisted in the classroom until Grade 8. Joshua loved the academic chal-lenges of high school but found it increasingly harder to "hang" out with his peers as he could not hear them well. In the past, his mother had always gone with him to his Scout club meetings and sports events so communication had been relatively easier. Joshua's group of male friends were all excited to take their first level of driver's education and attended the driving classes together. Joshua was adamant that his mother not attend as he wanted to "be like the guys." He worked very hard to understand all that was said and came home exhausted. The boys all wanted to go out for a burger following the driving class, but by that time Joshua was so tired from the effort of following the conversation he just went home. He was aware he was missing out on fun things and felt frustrated by it. When he went without his mother, Joshua said he felt more normal, but it was so much harder to cope. He felt conflicted that he was hurting his mother, who had helped him all his life, but he really just wanted to be like his friends and didn't know why everything seemed so confusing to him.

Sarah was a 15-year-old deaf teenager attending a mainstreamed program with an American Sign Language (ASL) interpreter. Sarah was deaf from a high fever as a young infant and initially attended school in an auditory verbal class. As her oral language did not progress, the school recommended in Grade 8, at the age of 14 years, that Sarah have an ASL interpreter. Neither Sarah nor her family knew any sign language and the sign language interpreter found that she was basically teaching Sarah signs, as well as trying to interpret class content. By Grade 11, Sarah had only a functional fluency in sign language and was unable to engage in sophisticated or age-appropriate conversation. While her hearing peers were distantly nice to her, Sarah felt herself becoming more and more isolated from the girls she knew in elementary school and had no idea how to act around boys. She ate lunch alone, as her interpreter took her break at that time and Sarah did not understand the students' speech around her. Sarah began to sleep in and miss her bus to school, which angered her parents, causing numerous fights. She began to eat enormous amounts of food and gained 40 pounds over 6 months. She tried to interact with her hearing friends online but her English literacy skills prevented her from understanding their shortened abbreviations and quick interactions. By the end of Grade 11, Sarah had failed four high school credits, did little for enjoyment, and subsequently took an overdose of sleeping pills. Although she physically recovered from this episode, Sarah continued to develop depressive symptoms.

Rochelle was a 27-year-old deaf woman who still lived at home. Rochelle had attended school with an ASL interpreter in a self-contained classroom of five students in a mainstream setting. Rochelle was deaf from the effects of prematurity and had a number of learning issues. Rochelle did not interact with any students other than the four individuals in her class and had limited English literacy skills. Upon high school graduation, Rochelle was invited to live in an apartment with two of her former classmates. None of the women obtained jobs, and they were quickly in financial trouble. Rochelle had never given much thought to living independently and after a few months felt overwhelmed by the responsibility, was unsure what to do all day, and preferred to move back home, feeling content to watch daytime soap operas. When her parents challenged her, Rochelle became very juvenile and weepy, asking them to never make her leave them again.

Social-Emotional Functioning

Adolescence is a time of emotional upheaval, as childhood feelings are replaced with feelings of awkwardness about one's self and one's body, worries about being "normal," and the realization that parents are not perfect. Deaf adolescents have the additional challenges of frequent communication barriers, prejudiced attitudes, and daily hassles of navigating through a world based on sound. Deaf teenagers who have limited contact with other deaf adolescents may have additional challenges of loneliness, isolation, and feeling left out.

The literature on the self-esteem of deaf people suggests that there is considerable variation in results (Bat-Chava, 1993; Crowe, 2003), with some studies reporting lower self-esteem among deaf people than among hearing individuals (Bat-Chava, 1994; Schlesinger, 2000) and other studies concluding that the self-esteem of deaf individuals does not vary from hearing individuals (Bat-Chava, 2000; Emerton, 1996; Crowe, 2003). Lukomski (2007) specifically examined deaf college students' perceptions of their social emotional adjustment. The students were all in the late developmental phase of adolescence and were administered the 16PF—Adolescent Personality Questionnaire, which covers many areas of social-emotional functioning known to be problematic for adolescents. The results suggested that although there are significant differences between deaf and hearing late adolescents in terms of their thoughts and feelings, there are more similarities than differences. The main differences related to the deaf students' perception of experiencing more home-related stress in terms of separation and coping with social-emotional difficulties than their hearing peers. Lukomski noted that this was consistent with Bat-Chava's (2000) study suggesting that deaf adolescents experience more challenges in the individuation process from parents than do hearing adolescents.

What about feelings related to a sense of self? As adolescents interpret their behavior in relation to others, more mature feelings evolve in
response. If a deaf adolescent does not engage in this type of self-analysis,
she may remain in an earlier developmental stage as related to thoughts
and feelings. This is problematic given that an adolescent's body, regardless of hearing status, will physically mature, with resulting sexual urges
and desires. An adolescent who responds with childlike feelings may be
compromised regarding normative social-emotional development.

Of particular interest are the studies which clearly show that the
social-emotional development of deaf adolescents of deaf parents parallels that of hearing adolescents of hearing parents. Deaf teenagers with
Deaf parents have likely experienced a broader range of social interactions, observed as well as experienced a greater range of emotions, and
experienced a greater sense of understanding and acceptance from family members than deaf teenagers living with hearing parents (Marschark
& Wauters, 2011). In families with Deaf parents, the deaf children learn
language through naturalistic modeling in the home (LaSasso & Metzger,
1998) and typically both parent and child share a similar deaf identity
that helps the child in the development of his own self-identity (Emerton,
1998). In addition, Deaf children with Deaf parents are more likely than
those with hearing parents to have grown up with more consistent parenting behaviors, more effective dialogue, and less stressful family social
interactions (Greenberg & Kusché, 1987). All of these factors likely facilitate better behavioral and emotional regulation in the deaf child, providing
a more stable foundation upon which to build developmental milestones.

Parental Relationships

The parent-child relationship through adolescence can function much
like a well-used and battered basketball backboard. Parents go from
being the center of their child's world to being barely tolerated bystand-
ers as the adolescent distances him- or herself from the parents in favor
of the peer group. With developmental maturity by the end of late adolescence, the parents have hopefully regained status as respected and
loved supports. However, the upheaval in changing dynamics as dictated

by the teenager requires a solid foundation in childhood to weather the adolescent storm. This foundation is rooted in meaningful and shared communication, mutual respect, and unconditional positive regard. The challenges of a child's deafness upon a family have already been discussed in earlier chapters and are widely documented in the literature (Foster, 1998; LaSasso & Metzger, 1998; Schlesinger, 2000). Unfortunately, these challenges often remain unresolved, weakening the parent-child bond through limited communication, different worldviews, and mutual feelings of non-acceptance. A chain is only as strong as its weakest link, and it may be this weakened link that does not withstand the tensions of adolescence.

Hearing parents have expressed concerns that if their child is part of the Deaf culture, he or she will not remain part of their family. Yet Deaf culture does not in any way suggest or advocate leaving one's family of origin, and it seems that separation from the family is done out of necessity in response to developmental demands rather than choice. The premise of families becoming bicultural (hearing and deaf) and bilingual (spoken and signed language) is perhaps the most psychologically sensible solution based on both the research and successful experiences of deaf children and deaf parents, as well as hearing children and hearing parents.

Society likes to embrace adages such as "love will conquer all." Although these are nice sentiments, love is a multifaceted construct built on tenets of effective communication, trust, loyalty, respect, and acceptance. These principles of a relationship need to be consciously considered and nurtured in order for love to be fully realized. It is not enough for a parent to claim to love her child (whether hearing or deaf) without engaging in the work needed to build that relationship. It is certainly more challenging for hearing parents to enter into a solid relationship with their deaf child given the demands of language, educational practices, and views of society and extended family members, yet that is simply what is required. The nature of development is dynamic and evolving requiring frequent tending and cultivating. It is tragic to see parents of an 18-year-old deaf child who has behavioral and emotional issues, along with limited language, reflect on what they "wish they had known to do."

It is the responsibility of professionals to utilize experience and research to empower parents early on with the necessary knowledge and tools for successful relationship building and sustaining.

Independence

Deaf children are often conceptualized as vulnerable in a hearing world. The legacy of abuse in the Deaf residential schools lends support to this premise. In fact, in a court case where a hearing teacher was charged with multiple counts of sexual assault of Deaf adolescent girls, the prosecutor asked each of the defendants why they ever chose to leave the school property with the teacher. All of the young women responded, independently of each other, "because he was hearing." This perceived power differential may be reflective of majority/minority dynamics yet is complicated by the simple fact that the hearing and deaf worlds remain divided on a mechanical wave that is simply an oscillation of pressure, or more simply put—sound.

There has been much written about socially constructed views that marginalize deaf people (Lane, 1992). Somewhat in line with this perjorative view of deaf people, there have been a number of older studies that sought to evaluate the "social maturity" of deaf children by measuring the "degree of independence or self-sufficiency" (Meadow, 2005). For example, Avery (1948), Myklebust (1960), Myklebust and Burchard (1945), and Streng and Kirk (1938) all reported significantly lower scores for deaf children than hearing children on these constructs. As such, it seems to have become common to characterize deaf children as being immature and more dependent than hearing children. It should be pointed out, however, that those researchers were working with what we now know were inappropriate assessment tools, thereby likely making the children overall look more challenged than they actually likely were.

Meadow (2005) challenged these findings in her landmark study of deaf signing children attending the California School for the Deaf in Berkeley. Among other variables, Meadow (2005) assessed the characteristics of immaturity of deaf children that had been well reported in earlier studies. Her results suggested "that there is nothing inherent in the condition of deafness itself—that is, in the lack of auditory contact with the environment—which produces characteristics of immaturity that so many have noted" (p. 326). More specifically, Meadow found that the differences were more pronounced with deaf children of deaf parents in terms of better social functioning regarding maturity and independence than measured in deaf children of hearing parents.

Why then have deaf children been characterized as more dependent and less mature than hearing children? As Meadow (2005) hypothesized, this may in fact be due more to conditions in the deaf child's environment, such as the presence or absence of early communication and the quality of family relationships, than due to conditions of deafness itself. In that regard it may be that socially constructed expectations based on decades of inaccessible language exposure and inferior family functioning have conditioned parents, educators, and perhaps even researchers to expect less mature and more dependent traits in deaf children. Given that Meadow's (2005) research shatters these expectations, it seems reasonable to expect that given accessible language exposure and positive family supportive traits, deaf adolescents should achieve a developmentally normative increase in independence and self-reliance.

Consider Joshua, who was the 14-year-old son of hearing parents. Joshua had two older hearing siblings and attended a self-contained classroom for deaf children. Following the identification of Joshua's deafness, his parents, grandparents, and two siblings hired a Deaf woman to come to the home on a weekly basis for instruction in sign language. They also sought out Deaf adults in their community and struck up friendships with them. The family decided early on that all communication in front of Joshua would be done in sign language, and over time the family evolved into speaking and signing at the same time. At 14 years of age, Joshua was in Grade 8, played on the school basketball and hockey team, and had a few neighborhood hearing friends he considered his buddies. Joshua appeared happy, content, and at ease with his identity within the family and the school. Joshua was voted by his classmates to be the valedictorian for the entire Grade 8 class (hearing and deaf), as his friends thought "Joshua taught them a lot about differences and always had a good attitude."

Consider also Patricia, who was 16 years of age and the daughter of Deaf parents. Patricia had two younger Deaf siblings and two older hearing siblings. The language in the home was ASL and Patricia attended the school for the Deaf as a day student. Patricia was strong-willed and was involved in many different activities. She excelled in school, played sports, and enjoyed family time and vacations. She entered and won the community Miss Deaf contest, where she demonstrated beauty as well as knowledge on factual tests.

Moral Thought

Adolescence is filled with new experiences often requiring reflection and decisions. The decisions made by adolescents are typically based on their participation in different activities with peers, the types of friends they choose, and behavior toward the world in general. These decisions are based on moral thought, which becomes more developed as a child progresses through the phases of adolescence.

Moral thought requires adolescents to internalize ideas and experiences as well as show self-control in their actions. Internalizing ideas and experiences means reflection on knowledge about human relationships as well as the mores of the society in which they live. Teenagers usually make conclusions based on their interactions with others and how relationships work within the boundaries and rules of their society's norms. Typically, adolescents learn about themselves in terms of moral thoughts as they experiment with various relationships, activities, and different roles. These are the times in an adolescent's life when a parent hopes that the solid foundation of childhood serves him or her well in deciding whether to partake in risky activities, in learning the worth of moral decisions, and in guiding life decisions.

Cognitive development and educational experience are both important for developing moral thought, as the reflection on moral dilemmas requires abstract thought and values. In order to make good decisions, an adolescent needs to try on all different options for size and to select the best option. Acting on moral thought requires both behavioral and emotional self-regulation.

Similar to the other developmental tasks of identity formation, social-emotional functioning, and family relationships, the actual construct of deafness should not make moral reasoning either easier or more difficult. Clearly, and once again, influential factors on the life of the deaf teenager, such as language, education, visual environments, and acceptance by family members, will either support or thwart the development of moral thought and reasoning.

Deafness can and does exclude adolescents from the world around them. It can require effort by the deaf adolescent, as well as her educators and parents, to ensure that the world remains within reach. A prime example is incidental learning, or that type of learning that almost happens by accident around a child, which often provides new information or in some instances fills in the gaps. Consider what a hearing adolescent might learn without effort from talk shows on the TV or the radio or from overheard conversations, all of which can remain inaccessible for the deaf adolescent. Incidental learning for a deaf adolescent almost needs to become intentional learning—that is, to ensure closed captioning is always available, to interpret audio radio shows for the deaf child, and to provide visual information to supplement auditory cues.

Delays in incidental learning may contribute to delays in moral reasoning simply because the deaf adolescent has not been able to access needed information with which to experiment and make decisions.

Consider Robert, who is a deaf 15-year-old, and his identical twin brother, Timothy, who is hearing. The parents shared their concerns about Robert in that comparison to his brother he seemed so "unworldly" and not "street smart." Further questioning revealed that Timothy had an iPOD® that he was using to constantly download new information from a show called "Between Teens" and listening to it throughout the day. Robert tried to gain the same information by asking his brother to interpret for him, which Timothy did with some irritation and short cuts. Clearly, Robert may be at a disadvantage in obtaining the same amount and quality of social information needed to make moral decisions compared to his hearing brother.

TRANSITIONS

At the beginning of this chapter, an analogy was used of a teenaged train going through a tunnel with eventual emergence as a somewhat changed entity. The tunnel represents a time of metaphorical transition from one place to the next physically, cognitively, emotionally, and morally. The transition itself is inevitable in that development continues no matter what the conditions (with the exception of profoundly neurocompromised children). However, it is the nature of the conditions that are somewhat modifiable throughout and prior to the transition. It is the failure to attend to these conditions—through knowledgeable mechanical work and occasional tune-ups—that results in breakdowns.

These breakdowns for adolescents through the transition developmental phases can have enduring effects. Fear and anxiety are prevalent phenomena among youths from the general population (Ollendick, King, & Muris, 2002) and even more worrisome research has found that these childhood fears and worries reflect significant underlying anxiety problems in more than 20% of healthy American school children (Muris, Merckelbach, Mayer, & Prins, 2000).

Within a diathesis-stress model of mental health disorders, the diathesis is considered to be the stressor, which when placed within certain environmental, genetic, and/or inherited conditions, may develop into a mental health disorder. Unsuccessful mastery of developmental milestones in deaf adolescents as a function of vulnerable conditions, such as lack of language or inadequate family functioning, in association with a genetic or inherited vulnerability may lead to either internalizing or externalizing symptoms. Internalizing or overcontrolled symptoms in adolescents may lead to subjective symptoms such as worry, tension, and sad thoughts, and somatic symptoms such as twitches, muscle aches, headaches, diarrhea, and sleep disturbances. These symptoms without treatment interventions may progress to panic, phobias, obsessive-compulsive, generalized anxiety, or depressive disorders. Externalizing or undercontrolled symptoms in an adolescent, such as aggression, violence, hyperactivity, inattention, and defiance, may lead to disorders such as oppositional defiant, conduct, and attention-deficit hyperactivity disorder.

Deaf adolescents are likely a more vulnerable group to transitional adolescent developmental stressors. If 20% of the American general adolescent population is experiencing mental health distress, it is not difficult to speculate how the added conditions of language delays and/or deficits, weak family relationships, and daily logistical hassles of navigating through a hearing world may heighten susceptibility to mental health disorders. Hale, Raaijmakers, Muris, Hoof, and Meeus (2008) prospectively examined the developmental trajectories of anxiety disorder symptoms in a large sample of adolescents from the general Dutch population. Their conclusions over a five-year span found that adolescent anxiety disorders continue into adulthood with slight variations between boys and girls. This is compelling evidence for preventing as well as recognizing and treating adolescent mental health disorders prior to their transition to adulthood. Given their added vulnerabilities, it would seem even more critical to do the same in a highly vulnerable sector such as deaf adolescents. In a British paper, Hindley (2005) wrote how deaf children and young people are more vulnerable to mental health problems than hearing children. His work reported that 40% of deaf children and adolescents in British community samples experienced clinical mental health disorders. Left unnoticed or untreated, these enduring issues arising from the adolescence phases of development may have a lasting effect on the mental health of deaf adults.

SUMMARY

This chapter has described the developmental challenges facing deaf adolescents. Developmental tasks include changes in thinking, identity development, social-emotional functioning, parental relationships, independence, and moral thought. Mastery of all of these developmental milestones will be different among deaf teenagers and from hearing adolescents, as influenced by factors such as language acquisition, educational practices, and family relationships.

This transitional phase of adolescence holds particular importance for the individual's future mental health. The issues that arise during a deaf adolescent's passage into adulthood may without recognition and treatment become enduring issues throughout adulthood.

7 Deaf Children and Adolescents: Assessment

A mental health assessment is done for the purpose of establishing a diagnosis, if warranted, and more importantly, to formulate treatment interventions. A psychiatric or psychological mental assessment will examine how a child or adolescent feels, thinks, reasons, behaves, expresses him- or herself, and remembers (cognitive functioning). A mental health assessment for a child must be geared to the child's age and stage of development.

An assessment of a deaf or hard of hearing child is extraordinarily complex, and it is the burden of the clinician to acquire the specialized training and knowledge necessary for this type of work. Typically, mental health assessments are conducted by a clinical psychologist or a psychiatrist who is well trained in mental health assessments. Yet the complex nature of these assessments often supersedes what one learns in training or a residency program, and it is this gap in knowledge that this book attempts to address. The most dangerous of clinicians are those who feel adequately trained to do any type of assessment with any type of patient not recognizing the essential need for specialized understanding.

LANGUAGE OF THE ASSESSMENT

The first and foremost consideration in the assessment of a deaf child is that the language of the assessment match the child's preferred language. That is, if a child uses a signed language, then the assessment should be conducted in the same signed language. If a child uses spoken language, then the assessment should be conducted using the same spoken language. If the child utilizes an FM system, the FM system should be utilized in the assessment. It is the clinician's responsibility to match the child's language and not vice versa. Often a deaf or hard of hearing child will present with delayed or impoverished language, which again requires the clinician to be creative yet meaningful in his or her own language representation.

> One such client was Sadem, who was an 11-year-old congenitally deaf child who immigrated to Canada with his family one year earlier. In his home country, deaf children were not schooled, and although his nine hearing brothers and sisters had attended school, Sadem had not. Sadem and his family had developed a homemade rudimentary gestural system, which was the extent of his language acquisition. When Sadem came for a psychological assessment, it was a challenge to acquire a language register that would convey my questions as well as support his responses. The entire first interview took place through the drawing of pictures and shapes devoid of language. We then progressed to using action figures and puppets to display intent and emotion, but I was mindful throughout the entire process of the disparity in our language. All psychometric testing was nonverbal in nature, yet even that often has some cultural connotation that must be considered.

In situations where the clinician is not fluent in the patient's language, a sign language interpreter may be utilized. The addition of a sign language interpreter can change the dynamics as well as the accuracy of the dialogue unless both the clinician and the interpreter are knowledgeable about how to work collegially. In the event the language register of a child is very limited, a certified Deaf interpreter (CDI) may be required. A CDI is a deaf or hard of hearing individual who, in addition to general interpreter training, has undergone specialized training in the use of basic signs, gesture, mime, drawing, and other tools to enhance communication. The CDI usually has an extensive knowledge and understanding of deafness, the deaf community, and/or Deaf culture and can bring added expertise into uniquely difficult interpreting situations.

Use of an interpreter needs to be done with care. Interpreters should be regulated under local jurisdictions and work within a code of ethics to ensure confidentiality and professionalism. Unfortunately, few interpreter training programs have training in mental health interpreting, which requires a different set of skills and abilities. This means, again, that the burden is on both the interpreter and the clinician to establish a collegial working relationship mindful of the following issues:

- Confidentiality;
- Professionalism;
- Proper use of mental health terminology;
- Communication between clinician-patient and not patient-interpreter;
- Awareness of lag times;
- Knowledge of the meaning of nonverbal linguistic behaviors inherent in sign language such as deliberately averting eye gaze, wrinkling of nose, raising of eyebrows;
- Honesty when language is unintelligible or disjointed;
- Debriefing.

There are several issues that need to be considered when working with a deaf child/adolescent and a mental health interpreter. The interested reader is referred to Michael Harvey's (2003) book entitled *Psychotherapy with Deaf and Hard-of-hearing Individuals*, which has detailed chapters on communication and interpreting.

Children may be difficult for an interpreter to understand given their use of developmentally immature signs and/or use of homemade family signs, which tend to be seen in families where the parents are learning sign language at the same time/rate as the child. The interpreter may feel some pressure to supply words or fill in the gaps, or more simply may feel unsure how to voice what he or she sees signed. The mental health interpreter must be comfortable with and skilled at matching the developmental level of the child's signs while also maintaining the integrity of the clinician's questions and responses. The deaf child who uses sign language may choose to refrain from looking at the interpreter to avoid communication with the clinician or may conversely respond directly to the interpreter rather than the clinician. A skilled mental health interpreter will share these types of observations with the clinician rather than trying to manage or direct the flow of interactions.

An interpreter creates a therapeutic triad rather than a dyad. Despite their presence as the third person, the interpreter must be a broker of cultural and linguistic information and not a clinical support. There are times, especially if the child is known to the interpreter, when the interpreter may feel a connection and thus may attempt to subtly offer support or encouragement. The therapeutic alliance must remain between the clinician and the child, which requires both of the adults to be working toward the same goals with a clear understanding of their roles.

Family members should not be used as interpreters, especially in families where the parents or siblings may have less fluency in the child's language.

Eleven-year-old Shawna was brought for a psychological assessment by her mother. The mother had requested an urgent appointment and I scheduled her for the next day. I booked an interpreter as the mother was hearing and I was unsure of her ability to sign. At the start of the clinical interview the mother began sharing her concerns while Shawna and I watched the interpreter. The mother told a disturbing story of how Shawna had come home from school crying and terribly upset. When the mother asked her what was wrong, Shawna had responded that her friends had not invited her to a sleepover and that she hated her life and was going to hurt herself. While the mother was talking, Shawna was nodding her head while watching the interpreter (this is often a referential understanding of the dialogue rather than an affirmative agreement). At the same time, I noticed that Shawna's nonverbal behavior had changed and she sat forward alertly in her chair, intently watching the interpreter with a puzzled look on her face. As the mother concluded her story with the statement that Shawn wanted to hurt herself, the child quickly turned her attention to me signing urgently that what the mother said was not true. At that point, the child then turned to the mother and her signing changed from well-executed ASL to a gestural/sign-supported system that was difficult for the interpreter and I to follow. The child then switched back to ASL, at which point the mother became agitated and said, "I can't understand what she is saying." It became apparent that the sign system between the mother and the child was tenuous at best and that neither really understood the other. After much effort and a great deal of time, it was established that the mother had clearly misunderstood Shawna's signs the day before in terms of content and intent. Shawna shared that she had felt left out by her friend not inviting her to a birthday party (not a sleepover). She was upset by it and had decided she "hated the girl" (not herself) and that her feelings were hurt (not that she was going to hurt herself). The child's nodding while watching the interpreter was a common linguistic marker while processing sign and had little to do with agreement. This was a compelling example of miscommunication and misunderstanding.

TERMINOLOGY

Many mental health terms are not well-known to the general hearing lay community and this is a similar finding among the Deaf communities. This becomes an important issue for a clinician working with a mental health interpreter in terms of accurate translations of terms. Sign language is not universal; there are clear dialects and languages across regions and countries, and within languages there are differences in terms. For example, in the region where I practice, there are at least three different signs for the English word "autism." At times mental health signs are newly evolved out of necessity, yet there is not enough frequent use to ensure that the signs become well-known. More and more areas that provide services for the deaf are trying to mobilize forums with mental health interpreters as well as Deaf consumers to decide on accepted signs for infrequently used mental health terms.

The mental health clinician working with a sign language interpreter is advised to ensure that the interpreter has an adequate knowledge and vocabulary base of mental health terms and disorders to ensure accurate and meaningful dialogue. Ideally, interpreters interested in this type of work should obtain additional training to acquire this skill set. In reality, that does not happen in many areas and the burden then is on both the clinician and the interpreter to safeguard against language misunderstandings. The best way to do this is to schedule additional time both pre and post-appointment to review anticipated terms as well as to debrief. This is a critical part of the interpreter and clinician working within the circle of care with a deaf child/adolescent. Roles must stay clear in terms of scope of practice (i.e., clinicians don't interpret and interpreters don't diagnose and treat), yet both roles will be enhanced with clarification of all aspects of each session.

HISTORY

It is very important to get a clear and detailed history. The age of identification as well as etiology of deafness are both helpful data. For example, a child who was identified as deaf at the age of 4 years as compared to a child picked up in the newborn screening have potentially had very different life experiences. In terms of etiology, it is helpful to know if the deafness is congenital or acquired. For example, a child with a genetic deafness is more likely to *not* have an associated syndrome, although this needs to be considered. A child who is deaf from fetal alcohol syndrome will likely have associated cognitive delays. A child who is deaf from CHARGE syndrome (a genetic syndrome resulting in *c*oloboma of the eye, *h*eart defects, *a*tresia of the nostrils, *r*etardation of growth and/or development, *g*enital and/or urinary abnormalities, and *e*ar abnormalities and deafness) will have myriad issues to be considered. A child who is deaf from prematurity may have experienced other insults to his brain during the neonatal period, which may be expressed as learning disabilities or mobility issues. A child who is deaf from a high fever may have had early exposure to language prior to the fever that a child with congenital deafness did not. These examples serve as reminders of the importance of a thorough understanding of the etiology of deafness for the associated implications for the child.

A careful history with the parent is helpful. There is no call for judgment of parental language or educational decisions but the question needs to be asked if these decisions have been appropriately reviewed for efficacy. It is also evident from the preceding section that communication patterns between parent and child need to be assessed. This can be done most easily by observing the interactions between parent and child, although this can be a difficult task. For example, many parents feel that they alone can understand their child given the number of years and intimate moments they have spent together. Although this may be true for a child who is language delayed or impoverished, it also may *not* be true, as in the earlier example, when Shawna's mother truly believed that she understood the content and intent of her daughter's communications.

It is helpful to review developmental milestones with the parents. Assessment of a deaf or hard of hearing child should pay careful attention to the timelines of language acquisition as well as social behaviors. As explained in previous chapters, unlike an assessment of a typically developing hearing child, delays in language and social behaviors noted in a deaf child may be a result of delayed acquisition and exposure to language rather than a developmental delay.

And finally, a careful analysis of the presenting problem is crucial. It is my preference to get as many viewpoints as possible (i.e., mother, father, teacher, sibling) not with an expectation of congruent descriptions as children will behave differently in different contexts, but to establish a rich description of the presenting issue. The reason for this becomes evident in the following example.

Mr. and Mrs. Brown brought their 7-year-old deaf daughter Miranda for an assessment at the request of her teacher. Miranda was born full-term with a genetic non-syndromic bilateral sensorineural profound deafness and attended the local Deaf school from the age of 4 years. Miranda was immersed in a sign language environment from an early age; even though her parents were hearing, her maternal grandparents were Deaf. As such, Miranda's mother had grown up with ASL as her first language and used it with Miranda from birth. Despite this early immersion and exposure, Miranda's teacher reported that Miranda did not interact well with her peers, often complained of tummy aches, and frequently withdrew from class activities.

During the clinical interview, it was evident that Mr. and Mrs. Brown had excellent communication skills with their daughter, who signed animatedly and appropriately with them. Miranda appeared to be happy and engaged well with her parents. Intelligence testing placed Miranda solidly within the average range. Miranda's parents did not report any behavior problems, except for Miranda's occasional reluctance to go to school, and generally found Miranda to be a pleasant, easy child in the home environment. They were feeling that the teacher was judging their child unfairly and were genuinely puzzled why Miranda was not doing well in school, especially as she was somewhat advanced in her language skills relative to her peers.

Observations in the school environment, however, showed that Miranda was stressed about attending school, and a clinical interview with her revealed symptoms of a social anxiety related to the school environment. Cognitive behavioral techniques were implemented with good results, and over time Miranda became more involved with her peers and school activities. This example shows the importance of assessing *beyond* the deafness to diagnose a mental health disorder.

PSYCHOMETRICS OF TESTING

Great care must be taken throughout the assessment process that appropriate protocols are followed. Clinical observations are only as valuable as the skill of those observing. As such, the clinician is advised to learn about deaf children in as many ways as possible—observing how they communicate, how they play, how they interact, how they show defiance, how they show deference, how they show delight, how anger is expressed, and on and on. For example, it is common for deaf children to stamp the ground with their foot to get the attention of their peers through the vibration. This same action may be seen as aggressive or disruptive in a hearing child but is a common and accepted behavior in culturally deaf children. Knowing the normative psychology of your patient group allows for better identification of atypical presentations.

Unfortunately, there are still not a great number of psychological assessment tools appropriate for use with deaf and hard of hearing children. There are very few norm-referenced or criterion-referenced psychological tests for deaf children. Norm-referenced tests are standardized on a defined group and scaled so that the score reflects the student's performance when compared to the normative larger group, and criterion-referenced tests measure how well a student performs against an objective or criterion rather than another student. This means, then, that the psychologist wishing to modify standardized tests for use with deaf children must do so with caution both in the administration and the interpretation.

INTELLIGENCE TESTS

Intelligence tests are frequently used in psychological assessments to establish cognitive levels. Amidst great controversial debate, best practices formerly recommended only using nonverbal tests of intelligence and performance measures for deaf or hard of hearing children. Tests like the Universal Nonverbal Intelligence Test (UNIT) and the Complete Test of Nonverbal Intelligence (CTONI) were commonly used as nonverbal cognitive measures. This was because the verbal scales of an intelligence test were thought to measure more the language deficiency caused by hearing loss rather than measuring intelligence. Modifying the test into an alternate format such as sign language or cued speech posed threats to the validity of the test and also raised the question of whether verbal intelligence is actually the same construct in sign language as it is in spoken language. However, more recently the omission of the VIQ (verbal scale) has been questioned, as verbal intelligence has long been considered to be a better predictor for academic achievement in deaf children (Braden, 1992; Maller, 1997; Sullivan & Montoya, 1997). By not administering a verbal scale, what important tenet of "g" intelligence might we be missing?

It is a complicated question. Consider Tommy, an 8-year-old deaf child referred for a psychological assessment due to failure in school subjects. Tommy was identified as deaf at the age of 2 years and was placed in an auditory verbal class since preschool. When Tommy was tested, he scored as low average on the nonverbal scale but in the intellectually deficient range on the verbal scale. Recommendations included having Tommy repeat grades with part-time enrollment in a class for children with developmental delay. The concern is that Tommy may, in fact, have an average potential for verbal intelligence but due to limited language exposure scored very low on the verbal scale. To properly interpret this data, the psychologist must make it clear in his or her reports that the verbal intelligence score actually reflects Tommy's present verbal capability and the level of mastery of the language in which the test was administered. This therefore should not be a valid measure of his overall verbal intellectual functioning. There is still no clear evidence of validity of this scale for verbal intellectual functioning in deaf children (Maller & Braden, 2011). We are still in need of evidence-based answers to best direct clinicians in both the selection and administration of tests of intelligence for deaf children who use sign language.

A more recent and complicating issue are the observed trends in educational placements. In both the United States and Europe, the majority of deaf and hard of hearing children are being mainstreamed as auditory learners with hearing aids and cochlear implants and as such, verbal intelligence may be a more salient ability to assess. In fact, Sullivan and Montoya (1997) suggest that it is essential to understand the verbal intellectual abilities of deaf children when they are being educated in mainstreamed settings where academic subjects are language based. However, is verbal intelligence in oral deaf children the same construct as measured in their hearing peers, and if so, how is it fairly measured in a deaf or hard of hearing child? There is a compelling need for more research in this area, particularly between different subgroups within the deaf population. It is noted that more recent publications of test materials such as the Wechsler Intelligence Scale for Children—Fourth Version (WISC-IV) include a small sample of deaf participants as well as some suggestions for how to administer items. The small sample size, however, remains problematic in terms of making norm-referenced conclusions. The answers to these questions are beyond the scope of this chapter, and the interested reader is referred to Akamatsu, Mayer, and Hardy-Braz (2008) for a more comprehensive review. It should be evident, however, that the clinician who wishes to conduct intelligence testing with deaf and hard of hearing children must do so with careful thought as to the selection of tests as well as interpretation of results.

PERSONALITY TESTS

There are few personality tests that are appropriate for use with deaf children, as many of them tend to be language based. However, many clinicians find a simple projective drawing measure helpful to begin an interview with a child, although it again raises questions about validity.

Is there a "personality of the deaf"? Likely not, and furthermore, it may be a dangerous stereotypical assumption to make. The deaf population of children and adolescents is a very heterogeneous group. There may be similarities within subgroups, such as those with a cochlear implant, those using sign language, and those aided with amplification; however, those similarities have not been well studied nor analyzed. At this point in time, it is likely wise to recognize the subgroups within this diverse population of deaf children and to apply scientific reasoning in all clinical assumptions.

BEHAVIOR RATING SCALES

Rating scales can be very useful in terms of obtaining teachers' and parents' perspectives of children's behaviors. There are again, however, few standardized rating scales developed specifically for deaf children and adolescents. One notable exception is the Meadow/Kendall Social-Emotional Assessment Inventory (1980) an observational rating scale developed specifically for deaf children and adolescents, completed by teachers and school personnel to identify positive and negative classroom and school behaviors.

The Achenbach System of Empirically Based Assessment (ASEBA, 1991) scales, including the Child Behavior Checklist (CBCL), the Teacher

Report Form (TRF), and the Youth Self Report Form (YSR), have been frequently used with deaf students (Van Eldik, 2005; Musselman, MacKay, Trehub, & Eagle, 1996), modifying items to be more contextually relevant to the life of a deaf adolescent. For example, Wallis, Musselman, and Mackay (2004) changed the original items by asking them twice, first with reference to a deaf group and then with reference to a hearing group:

Original item: *I argue a lot.*
Revised items: *I argue a lot with deaf/hearing-impaired people.*
I argue a lot with hearing people.

Although the ASEBA website states that the forms have now been translated into 80 languages, none of the listed languages is a sign language. This is unfortunate, as it means that researchers are faced with establishing study-specific validity and reliability data, whereas clinicians would benefit from the development of standardized deaf norms.

For example, Susan was a 14-year-old Deaf child attending the Deaf residential school. Susan was referred for a psychoeducational assessment, which included both tests of intelligence and adaptive functioning. The adaptive testing used a standardized tool normed on hearing children and included items such as "Child is able to conduct a simple transaction with a cashier in a convenience store." An inexperienced clinician administering the test endorsed "0" for that item as Susan could clearly not communicate with the cashier in spoken language. However, the clinician's experience was an unfair developmental penalty, as contextually Susan had never been given that opportunity, and if in fact she had, she may not have achieved it due to the linguistic demands rather than the developmental demands.

The practice of using norm-referenced tools based on hearing children seems inappropriate when testing deaf children. However, critics might say that the child should be compared against the normative group within which he or she operates. In that sense, should a deaf child who is attending a school as the sole deaf student with an interpreter be compared against his hearing peers or his statistical deaf peers? These questions must be weighed carefully by the clinician and well documented in the psychological report.

INTERPRETATION OF RESULTS

It is essential that the interpretation of results be done within a contextual and developmental framework. That is, the clinician must assess the child within the context that the child exists, be that a signing deaf child, an oral deaf child, or a deaf child with limited language skills. In addition, a developmental psychopathology framework is useful for comparisons against typically developing deaf children. Developmental psychopathology, in its broadest sense, examines adaptive and maladaptive functioning from the perspective of developing systems over the life span (Kazdin, Kraemer, Kessler, Kupfer, & Offord, 1997). Multiple challenges arise in understanding adaptive and maladaptive functioning within childhood and adolescence. Quite simply, the range of biological, psychological, social, emotional, and sociocultural influences that shape the development of a child is staggering. Not only is there an enormous number of influential factors, the multiple interactions of these factors exponentially increase the complexity of development. The fields of child and adolescent psychology have devoted tremendous effort in studying these influential developmental factors, recognizing that the only way to understand dysfunctional and maladaptive patterns of behavior is within the context of typically developing and adaptive functioning.

The framework of developmental psychopathology is useful for the study of deaf children and adolescents. However, this framework is only useful if the contextual and influential factors are relevant to the paradigm under study. In this sense, clinicians serving deaf children and adolescents must have a solid understanding of their patients' worldviews and must apply clinical knowledge within these parameters.

For example, consider Robbie who was a 6-year-old profoundly deaf youngster in a mainstreamed Grade 1 class. Robbie became deaf from meningitis when he was 3 months old. Although Robbie was provided a sign language interpreter by the school board, neither Robbie nor his parents used sign language at home, as the parents felt that talking to Robbie was the most effective mode of communication. Although the board had the best of intentions, the only available sign language interpreter was a college student who had completed the first level of ASL studies. Prior to his entry to school in the previous kindergarten year, Robbie had attended a day care where communication had been through gestures and physical contact (i.e., carrying Robbie to the next activity). During his kindergarten year, Robbie was noted to have become more and more active and disruptive. When he wanted something, he took it. When he was tired of an activity, he got up and left. When he was mad, he had a temper tantrum. When he was excited, he clapped his hands and jumped up and down. The demands of Grade 1 required that Robbie sit in his seat for circle time, make a request of the teacher if he wanted something, and regulate his behavior with his peers. Despite the teacher and interpreter's best efforts to "talk" to Robbie, his behavior escalated and his activity level increased. The school psychologist assessed Robbie and diagnosed him with an Axis I attention-deficit hyperactivity disorder (ADHD-combined type), and the family doctor initiated a stimulant medication. Three months later, Robbie's behaviors had worsened; when he was not allowed to do what he wanted, he picked up the desk chair and flung it at the window, breaking it. Robbie was suspended and upon reentry to the school was reassessed by the school psychologist with an additional diagnosis of oppositional defiant disorder. But what if... .

- Robbie had been considered language delayed or language impoverished, thereby not understanding the world around him?
- Robbie had been assessed for the most effective and accessible language modality?
- Robbie and his parents had been given extensive sign language tutoring?
- Robbie had been assessed as reacting to the environment around him without the necessary social-emotional and linguistic tools?
- Robbie had been assessed for a possible learning disability?
- A qualified sign language interpreter had been made available to Robbie?
- The teacher had been given specialized training for working with a deaf child?
- Robbie's nonverbal disruptive behaviors had been interpreted as signs of his frustration?
- The psychologist had completed her assessment within a developmentally contextually appropriate framework?

Within the paradigm of a hearing child, the psychologist's assessment likely made a great deal of sense. Within the paradigm of a deaf child, there were additional influential factors, such as language exposure and acquisition, that needed to be considered. The important point is to encourage clinicians to adopt a contextually appropriate and comprehensive framework within which to complete an assessment. Robbie might well have had an Axis I ADHD-Combined type disorder and perhaps even an oppositional defiant disorder, yet the more heuristic approach would be to first examine the influential and salient factors of childhood development that intersect with childhood deafness.

DIAGNOSES

North American clinicians working with children and adolescents widely use the *Diagnostic and Statistical Manual of Mental Disorders,* 4th edition, text revision (DSM-IV TR) (APA, 2000) in terms of categorical classification of mental health disorders. The 4th edition of this handbook was published by the American Psychiatric Association (APA) in 1994 (with revisions in 2000); the 5th edition was published in 2013. The DSM-IV TR lists different categories of mental health disorders as well as the specific criteria necessary for diagnosis. In addition, clinicians in North America utilize the Achenbach System of Empirically Based Assessment (ASEBA) (1991) which offers a comprehensive dimensional approach, using questionnaires to assess adaptive and maladaptive functioning in children and adolescents. European clinicians working with children and adolescents tend to use the *International Classification of Diseases and Related Health Disorders* (ICD) published by the World Health Organization (WHO, 1992). The ICD is currently in its 10th edition, with the 11th edition expected in 2014. Although the APA and WHO are working toward publishing concordant editions of these diagnostic manuals, some differences remain, making international clinical collaboration and discussion somewhat difficult. Adding to this difficulty is the fact that none of these classification systems includes specific criteria for deaf children. Because of this lack of inclusion of deaf children, clinicians are often forced to fit symptoms into categories that may not necessarily be suitable. Although the DSM task force members are including more cultural information in future editions, there is still a need for a careful review of the differences (rather than the deficits) that deaf and hard of hearing children may experience in terms of mental health disorders.

FEEDBACK

Providing feedback to a child as well as his or her parents regarding a mental health diagnosis can be challenging in many situations. The transmission of psychological results to a deaf child is an important part of the process, yet again must be done with sensitivity and at the appropriate level. Inexperienced clinicians working with an interpreter may assume that there is a translation for every English word and may expect the interpreter to adjust the register accordingly. For example, there is no ASL sign for the term "psychotic episode," and the mental health interpreter will need to expand upon that concept using existing signs. This again highlights the advanced skill level required by a mental health interpreter in order to work effectively.

Providing psychological feedback to the parents of a deaf child must be done in a comprehensive yet sensitive way. The complex interplay of influential factors that deafness adds to the development of the child presents a real risk of clinicians either making a misdiagnosis or a "missed" diagnosis. Either might be life-changing for the child and her family, and certainly again places the burden on the clinician to become specialized and knowledgeable in this area.

A misdiagnosis in this context typically happens when the child's deafness is wrongly categorized as a mental health disorder. Examples abound in which a deaf child has been labeled as mentally retarded and placed in a class with hearing students with developmental disabilities.

In my own practice, a 16-year-old deaf girl moved into the region and the school board requested a psychological assessment. A review of her files indicated that at the age of 6 years she had been diagnosed with a moderate to severe mental retardation and had been placed in a residential institution. With the father's work transfer, the parents were now looking for a similar placement and thus approached the school board. During the interview with the parents, I was told that the girl had never learned any language, behaved much like an animal, and was unable to take care of herself in any way. Upon meeting her, I was in agreement that she had few, if any, linguistic skills. To my great surprise, however, she was observed to be copying signs as she watched the interpreter during the parent interview. Nonverbal testing placed her solidly within the borderline range of intellectual functioning, which was a significant leap from moderate to severe mental retardation. Although this child had clearly been misdiagnosed due to her deafness, her prognosis remained fairly bleak. At the age of 16 years, she did go on to learn some basic sign vocabulary with limited adaptive functioning skills but never to the potential she may have once realized.

A misdiagnosis in this context typically happens when the child's deafness wrongly becomes the predominant focus of clinical attention.

An example of this was 6-year-old Riley, who had a severe bilateral hearing sensorineural hearing loss. Riley was a very low birthweight premature infant and was failing to make academic progress in a self-contained mainstreamed classroom. The referral stated that past assessments had concluded that Riley's deafness was interfering with his ability to play appropriately with other children. In addition, the report went on to state that his deafness was causing him to engage in a number of maladaptive behaviors, such as perseveration with objects and eccentric mannerisms. A psychological assessment indicated that Riley had an autism spectrum disorder that had been entirely missed because of the over-attention to the deafness and the under-attention to the clinical symptoms he was manifesting.

SUMMARY

This chapter has described some of the constructs that need to be considered during the assessment process of deaf children and adolescents. These include the language modality used in the assessment to ensure that the best measure of mental health is obtained. In some situations, clinicians will require the use of an interpreter. It is criticially important to follow the guidelines for use of an interpreter to ensure that best practices in assessment protocols are maintained.

Issues that are specific and sensitive to deafness include the importance of obtaining an accurate history, especially including time of identification and etiology of deafness, language and educational decisions, mastery of developmental milestones, and the nature of the referral question. Following the initial history and clinical interview, the clinician must carefully consider the psychometrics of testing, including the selection of appropriate instruments for the testing of intelligence, personality, and behavior rating scales in deaf children and adolescents. Interpretation of results must be done cautiously and with care within the child's individual context. Comprehensive and sensitive feedback are essential to ensure that the efforts of the assessment process are realized.

8 Deaf Children and Adolescents: Mental Health Disorders

For more than 70% of adults living in Canada with mental health problems, symptoms developed in childhood or early adolescence (Mental Health Commission of Canada, 2012). There is ever-increasing evidence that many, if not most, psychiatric disorders first present in childhood and adolescence, and the past decade has seen considerable research devoted to this (Costello, Egger, & Angold, 2005). The need for research and clinical attention regarding childhood and adolescent mental health disorders was especially highlighted when the World Health Organization published the *International Classification of Functioning* (World Health Organization, 2001), which drew attention to the overall burden that mental health disorders placed on society. It is clear that efforts to reduce the overall burden of mental illness on society must focus attention on the early years of childhood and adolescence.

According to the World Health Organization (WHO), over one-third of the people in most countries report problems at some time in their life of enough severity to meet the criteria for diagnosis of one or more of the common types of mental disorder (2001). The Centre for Addiction and Mental Health (CAMH) report that one in five Canadians will experience a mental illness in their lifetime and furthermore that the remaining four will have a friend, family member, or colleague who will (2002). Etiologies or causes of mental disorders are diverse and in some cases unclear or unknown. Evidence-based theories may incorporate findings from a range of fields, and mental illness is rarely as straightforward to diagnose as many physical conditions. The clinician must be knowledgeable about the context within which the person exists (i.e., culture, disability, gender, race, etc.) in order to understand differences that may represent maladaptive behaviors, perceptions, or emotions. There are not simple blood tests to confirm and/or identify the presence of mental distress; instead, the clinician relies on his or her knowledge of the human condition within research-driven theoretical paradigms.

DEAF CHILDREN AND MENTAL HEALTH

A change in hearing structure or function does not in itself cause mental health disorders, and as such there is no causal relationship between deafness and childhood mental health disorders. However, there are various implications of what may be *associated* with deafness that may indirectly or directly heighten the risk of mental health issues. For example, a profound bilateral deafness may be just that—a profound bilateral deafness. In this sense, the Deaf child does not hear, yet is quite capable of achieving developmental milestones, language, and a sophisticated theory of mind. However, that same profound bilateral deafness is more likely to heighten the probability of developing emotional and behavioral problems and neurodevelopmental disorders for a variety of reasons (Hindley, 2005; Gentili & Holwell, 2011).

In the United Kingdom, Hindley (2005) estimated that the prevalence of mental health problems in community samples of deaf children was approximately 40% and that Deaf children were estimated to be 1.5–2 times more vulnerable to mental health problems than hearing children. This data suggested that 15–20% of all deaf children in the United

Kingdom have clinically significant mental health problems. American data suggest that Deaf children and adolescents exhibit higher levels of behavioral and attention-deficit hyperactivity disorders than the general population (Haskins, 2000; Chritchfield, 2002) and that while Axis I mental health disorders do not differ between hearing and deaf populations, Axis II (personality disorders and intellectual disability) and childhood behavior problems are three to six times more prevalent for deaf persons (National Association of the Deaf, 2008). Canadian data have been hard to obtain, likely because of the vastness of the country and its relatively lower population. It is the opinion of the Canadian Association of the Deaf (CAD, 2007) that no fully credible census of Deaf, deafened, and hard of hearing people has ever been conducted in Canada. The CAD suggests with some caution using the traditional "one in ten" formula for estimating statistics, concluding that there are 310,000 culturally Deaf Canadians and 2.8 million hard of hearing Canadians. It is generally estimated that one in five or 20% of Canadian children (Children's Mental Health Ontario, 2012) will experience a mental health disorder. More specifically, Waddell, McEwan, Shepherd, Offord, and Hua (2005) published a meta-analysis indicating that 14% of children aged 4 to 17 years (which represents over 800,000 children and youth in Canada) experience mental disorders that cause significant distress and impairment at home, at school, and in the community. These authors also speculated that unfortunately fewer than 25% of Canadian children with mental health disorders receive specialized treatment services. If the existing Canadian system is meeting the needs of less than a quarter of the children in mental health distress, it is not hard to speculate that special and extraordinary groups such as deaf and hard of hearing children and youth are receiving even less service and less support.

DEAFNESS AS A RISK FACTOR

Deafness as a risk factor appears to be of more significance in deaf children from hearing families than Deaf children from Deaf families (Moores, 1996). This is likely because many of the hearing parent-deaf child dyads present with less than adequate levels of intra-family communication, family acceptance (Du Feu & Fergusson, 2003), and overall acquisition of language development (Gentili & Holwell, 2011) as compared to Deaf parent-Deaf child dyads. Deaf children of Deaf parents tend to follow similar developmental trajectories as hearing children of hearing parents. Deaf children of Deaf parents then should be considered as prone to developing significant mental health disorders as their hearing peers.

This parallel in development includes language acquisition and appears to offer protection against risks associated with mental health disorders. Clearly, the "sameness" between parent and child offers protective advantages. This implies that those dyads experiencing "differences" must perhaps more directly ensure that relevant protective factors are in place. Absence of these protective factors, which may result in more severe language and cognitive problems, appears to place the deaf child more at risk of developing emotional and behavioral problems later in life (Willis & Vernon, 2002).

As has been outlined elsewhere in this book, deaf children who are language impoverished or language delayed will show differences in their overall development, their ability to regulate their emotions and behavior, and their development of executive functions. These developmental deficits all have the potential to potentiate psychiatric conditions. For example, language is fundamentally linked with the regulation of emotional states (Lieberman et al., 2007) in addition to executive functions.

> Consider Sarah, a 12-year-old child with bilateral moderately severe hearing loss of unknown etiology. Sarah's hearing parents divorced following considerable turmoil and fighting, which was witnessed by Sarah and her two hearing siblings (one older brother and one younger sister). The family sought counseling for the three children to minimize their distress as related to the parents' divorce. The focus of the counseling encouraged the children to clearly understand and differentiate their feelings apart from those expressed between the parents. This was effective for Sarah's siblings, yet Sarah had extreme difficulty understanding the concept of describing and labeling emotions and instead responded with extreme and destructive temper tantrums.

Executive functioning refers to the psychological processes responsible for planning, abstract thinking, rule acquisition, initiating appropriate actions and inhibiting inappropriate actions, and selecting relevant sensory information. Children with weak executive functioning often have difficulties with planning, organization, memory, study skills, time management, receptive and expressive language acquisition (Alloway, 2006). Poor executive functioning is a risk factor for the development of psychiatric disorders, and poor language acquisition has a negative impact on executive functions (Gentili & Holwell, 2011). It can be seen, then, that deaf children with less than optimal language development as an indirect result of their deafness are at higher risk for the development of various mental health disorders.

In addition to specific risk factors, deaf children may present with a different prevalence of psychiatric disorders, as well as clinical symptoms, from hearing children. The literature greatly varies in terms of prevalence rates; in response, van Gent, Goedhart, Hindley, and Treffers (2007) specifically examined prevalence and correlates of psychopathology in deaf adolescents using a multi-method multi-informant approach. Overall, their findings suggested a higher prevalence in psychopathology in deaf adolescents than hearing adolescents, and they argued for the importance of early detection of emotional and behavioral problems by using a multi-informant assessment protocol. In addition, their results supported the idea that it is not the deafness itself that contributes to the psychiatric problems, but more the implications of issues associated with hearing loss.

A US residential psychiatric treatment center of emotionally disturbed deaf youth showed differences between deaf and hearing adolescents in the rank order of their diagnostic syndromes at the time of admission (Willis & Vernon, 2002). Hearing children tend to show a rank order pattern of mood disorders, behavioral disorders, followed by psychotic disorders, whereas the Deaf children admitted to the national Deaf Academy more frequently presented with mood disorders, psychotic disorders, followed by behavioral disorders (Willis & Vernon, 2002).

DEVELOPMENTAL DISORDERS

Autism Spectrum Disorders

Autism spectrum disorder (ASD) refers to a collection of complex neurodevelopmental disorders that affect the way the child's brain functions. This effect on brain functioning results in a triad of core ASD behaviors involving social impairments, communication difficulties, and restricted, repetitive, and stereotyped behavioral patterns. The cause of ASD is not entirely known, although there is considerable evidence that it is under genetic influence (Rutter, 2000; Newschaffer et al., 2007).

It can be very difficult and somewhat confusing to tease out the accurate diagnostic indicators of ASD in deaf children. Children with autism typically show delays and disturbances in their language development. Deaf children also may show delays in their language development, especially if there is a mismatch between the child and an accessible first language. The important and fairly consistent difference, however, is that a deaf child typically shows communicative attempts, whereas the child with autism does not.

It is essential that parents and clinicians be able to differentiate between disturbances in language development due to autism and/or due to language choices related to deafness. For example, a clinician who is not knowledgeable about typical language development in deaf children may wrongly identify delays and lack of communicative initiatives to be indicative of a symptom of ASD, when in fact the child may be showing significant signs of language delay due to an inaccessible language and/or lack of linguistic exposure. Conversely, an inexperienced clinician may attribute a delay and/or disturbance in the development of language in a deaf child as typical of all deaf children, when in fact this may be a marker of an autism spectrum disorder (Chovaz, Anderson, & Goldstein, 2011). Szymanski and Brice (2008) suggested that clinicians assessing deaf children for an ASD heed the following red flags:

- Poor eye contact;
- Difficulty initiating facial expression;
- Difficulty engaging in shared attention (looking in same direction as caregiver);

- Inflexibility to clearly communicated changes in routine;
- Obsessional interests.

Edwards and Crocker (2008) compiled the following as diagnostic indicators of an ASD in a deaf child:

- The absence of communicative intent;
- The absence of joint attention skills;
- The presence of behavioral disturbance suggestive of disorder rather than simple delay.

A consultation with Nicholas, an 11-year-old boy attending a local mainstreamed school, illustrated the difficulties in differentiating the effects of autism from the effects of deafness. Nicholas had been identified as having a moderate bilateral hearing loss when he was 5 years old after his parents became concerned that he was not yet talking. Nicholas was aided at the age of 6 years, yet 5 years later the school, audiologists, and parents remained perplexed and frustrated that Nicholas had not yet developed any kind of language skills. The audiologists had tried a series of different aids that in their words "should be having some effect," yet there was negligible, if any, language gain. Instead of participating in class activities, Nicholas quietly and persistently counted and recounted a sack of small pebbles that he insisted on carrying with him at all times, appeared to have little interest in the other children, insisted on only wearing jeans that were several sizes too small for him and periodically engaged in violent temper tantrums for reasons unknown to his teacher or parents. A clinical assessment, including a detailed history of Nicholas's early years, concluded that the child clearly had an autism spectrum disorder. Sadly, 5 years had been wasted trying to better his hearing aid prescription, when careful clinical observation would have revealed the essential markers of autism including an absence of any communicative attempts, behavioral disturbances, and minimal joint attention skills.

Intellectual Disabilities

Diagnosis of an intellectual disability (also called a developmental delay) requires that a child has an IQ below 70, demonstrates significant limitations in two or more areas of adaptive behavior, and that these limitations were apparent in childhood. Examples of adaptive behaviors include communication (knowing the rules of conversation and expressing wants and needs effectively), personal care skills including health and safety, functional reading and writing, and social skills.

Identifying deaf children who have intellectual disabilities can be difficult and hence these disabilities are sometimes missed. Deaf children who are language delayed may have associated deficits related to their lack of language rather than deficits in intellectual functioning. Mainstream testing of IQ typically utilizes tests of intelligence that are language loaded which are both inappropriate and unfair for use with deaf children. Use of these tests of intelligence by uninformed clinicians may yield both false negatives (concluding that a deaf child is intellectually intact when he or she is not) and more commonly false positives (concluding that a deaf child has an intellectual disability when in fact he or she does not).

Some of the etiologies of childhood deafness, such as meningitis, maternal rubella, prematurity, and cytomegalovirus, are often associated with neurological involvement (Moores, 1996). This neurological involvement may result in changes or damage to the brain, resulting in lowered intellectual functioning. In this sense, then, the child may present with deafness *and* a true intellectual disability, and a comprehensive psychological assessment is essential to accurately identify both. This highlights the importance of inquiring about the etiology of the deafness, if known, for the further diagnostic information this may yield. It is critical to differentiate a true developmental delay from the far-reaching, critical effects that a hearing loss may have on childhood development of cognitive (thinking) and linguistic (language) skills (Pollack, 1997).

It is essential to *accurately* identify intellectual disabilities in deaf children to ensure that appropriate resources and supports are in place. Unfortunately, the misidentification of an intellectual disability in deaf children (i.e., a false positive) can have powerful and at times long-lasting effects on the individual's life. The wrong identification of an intellectual disability when in fact the child is showing the effects of a hearing loss on his or her developmental progress could potentially result in a deaf child being placed in an institution or class for children with developmental delays. And unfortunately, the child might remain there for the rest of her childhood, only then to be placed in an institution or group home for the mentally delayed as an adult. It is also a concern when a child's deafness may be overlooked or minimized, particularly in those with more severe intellectual deficits and very limited communication skills. Parents, teachers, and clinicians may interpret behavioral symptoms as only a function of the child's intellectual disability rather than recognizing the potential implications of a hearing loss (diagnostic overshadowing). It is unacceptable to rely on inappropriate psychometric tests or inadequate clinical knowledge when these may result in enduring and negative changes in the life of the deaf child.

An intellectual disability in hearing children has been found to be significantly associated with a higher risk of psychiatric disorders (Sinkkonen, 1994). Mental health disorders appear to be even more prevalent in deaf children with an intellectual disability (Schlesinger & Meadow, 1972), given that each in its own right can result from CNS damage (Hindley, 2000). In addition, a deaf child (who is already more vulnerable to abuse than a hearing child) is even more likely to experience emotional, physical, and sexual abuse when he or she also has an intellectual disability (Knutson, Johnson, & Sullivan, 2004).

The clinical assessment of a deaf child with an intellectual disability is extremely complex and challenging. Often, deaf children with an intellectual disability have even more compromised language abilities, which can make the evaluation of thought processes difficult if not impossible. In these situations, the clinician, after exhausting every possible mode of communication, will likely need to engage in careful observation of behavioral manifestations of mental health disorders, as well as relying on extensive reports from teachers, parents, and background history (Carvill, 2008).

AFFECTIVE DISORDERS

A review of the literature shows many methodological problems in the assessment of psychiatric disorders in deaf children. Many of these methodological problems are related to uninformed or inexperienced clinicians using inappropriate tests (i.e., language loaded), failure to establish a therapeutic rapport, and comparison to inaccurate normative groups. This means, then, that the research must be reviewed with some caution.

Affective disorders, including anxiety, mood disorders, and disruptive disorders, are the most common mental disorders among children (US Department of Health and Human Services, 1999), and there appears to be an even greater prevalence of these emotional and behavioral disorders among deaf children (van Eldik, Treffers, Veerman, & Verhulst, 2004; Mathos & Broussard, 2005; Hindley, 2000). Although the biology of deafness does not cause these disorders, it is again likely that risk factors such as language deprivation, family issues, and barriers created by society associated with neurological vulnerability all contribute to a deaf child's developmental deficits. The outcome of this has a significant impact on how deaf children experience and react to the world around them. Difficulties with constructs such as theory of mind and the understanding of "self" and "other" likely contribute to the development of affective states such as worry, mistrust, and negative thoughts.

Depression

Some studies report that deaf children present with higher rates of depression than hearing children (Theunissen, Rieffe, Kouwenberg, Soede, Briare & Frijns, 2011). A German study (Fellinger, Holzinger, Sattel, Laucht, & Goldberg, 2009) confirmed this higher rate of depression, as well as the lack of a relationship between depression and the degree of hearing impairment. These authors suggested that both deaf and hearing children may share the same risk factors of being teased, maltreated, or neglected, but that deaf children may also have significant problems making themselves understood, which contributes to the overall higher prevalence rate of depression. This again highlights the association between language and the manifestation of psychiatric disorders such as depression. The following are signs that may be associated with depression in hearing children and adolescents (Ianelli, 2009):

- Frequent vague, non-specific physical complaints such as headaches, muscle aches, stomachaches or tiredness;
- Frequent absences from school or poor performance in school;
- Talk of or efforts to run away from home;
- Outbursts of shouting, complaining, unexplained irritability, or crying;
- Being bored;
- Lack of interest in playing with friends;
- Alcohol or substance abuse;
- Social isolation, poor communication;
- Fear of death;
- Extreme sensitivity to rejection or failure;
- Increased irritability, anger, or hostility;
- Reckless behavior;
- Difficulty with relationships.

Reflect upon the child within the context of deafness exhibiting these clinical symptoms. Clearly, the deaf child with limited language skills may have difficulty communicating thoughts of running away from home, fearing death, or engaging in non-specific physical complaints. The deaf child who is already somewhat isolated, especially if he or she attends a hearing mainstreamed program with hearing peers, may already have distant relationships, may feel somewhat bored, and may not have any regular playmates. This means that parents and clinicians may need to be very attuned to the more vegetative signs of depression, which is also problematic as these symptoms are not always easily identified in children and adolescents.

Annalise was a 14-year-old deaf child of hearing parents attending a main-streamed program with an interpreter. Annalise was referred for a psycho-educational assessment, yet it became apparent throughout the assessment that Annalise showed signs of a clinical depression. At the conclusion of the assessment, Annalise became confused when the counselor (fluent in sign) attempted to explain how her particular symptoms indicated depressed feelings. Finally, the girl signed, "but I thought everybody always felt this way," illustrating her profound lack of understanding of normative states of well-being, as well as her inability to label her own affective states.

Consider also Michelle, the 11-year-old Deaf child of hearing parents. Michelle's mother telephoned the crisis line asking for an immediate appointment for her "suicidal daughter." At the appointment, the Deaf psychologist, through a sign language interpreter, asked the mother to summarize her concerns. As the interpreter signed what the hearing mother was recounting regarding her daughter's intention to kill herself, the Deaf daughter became visibly agitated and finally jumped up, signing "no no she does not understand me and I never said that." Sadly, the mother had misunderstood her daughter's tearful description of not receiving a birthday invitation from a popular girl in school as suggestive of suicidal intent. With the interpreter present, the mother and daughter had one of their first meaningful conversations about feelings.

Anxiety

Clearly, one of the difficulties that clinicians face is the diagnosis of affective disorders in deaf children who may be language compromised or delayed. Many of the typical psychometric tests or interviews to explore affective feelings involve language and as such are likely not appropriate for use with many deaf children. A Dutch study (van Eldik et al., 2004) explored the prevalence of anxiety from the perspective of the parent, with their results showing that Deaf children aged 12–18 showed more anxiety than their same-aged hearing peers. It is likely important, especially when a deaf child presents with limited communication skills, for clinicians to seek information from parents and teachers. This practice, however, must also be undertaken cautiously with hearing parents and deaf children, given the typically poor communication pathways between the hearing parent and the deaf child.

Deaf children may be more vulnerable to developing anxiety disorders, given their limited understanding of the world around them, difficulties communicating with those around them (especially in a mainstreamed setting), and their almost inevitable feelings of isolation. The results of a study by Bat-Chava and Martin (2003) showed how deaf students, rather than being actively disliked, were more neglected by their hearing peers in term of socialization. This neglect over time may have a cumulative effect and, combined with other risk factors, may make a deaf child vulnerable to the development of an anxiety disorder.

The manifestations of anxiety in a deaf child may present somewhat differently. In a world that does not make sense (i.e., language, theory of mind, emotions etc.) deaf children may seek to impose order upon their chaos through engaging in perseverative and obsessive behaviors.

One deaf child, Jake, was referred for his annoying habit in the classroom of lining up his colored pencils on his desk. Jake would line them up, shuffle them, and do it again repeatedly throughout the day. An assessment indicated that this was but one of many symptoms of anxiety that Jake was displaying. Lining up pencils was a reassuring and comforting task for Jake in an intimidating classroom environment.

Bat-Chava (1993) suggested that there are generally three factors for deaf children that are directly linked to anxiety and self-esteem:

1. Parental attitudes: Parents who attempt to understand issues associated with their child's deafness in a positive way will then impact their children's self-esteems positively.
2. Clear communication: The enormous advantages of open and meaningful communication at home generalizes to a child's social world.
3. Deaf role models: Deaf children who are able to able to identify with people within the deaf community tend to develop stronger language skills, a critical sense of belonging, and a better understanding of their place in the world around them.

BEHAVIOR REGULATION DISORDERS

Attention-Deficit Hyperactivity Disorder (ADHD)

It has been suggested in the literature that deaf children show greater degrees of impulsivity than hearing children. Teachers and parents often report that the deaf child is fidgety, distractible, and not able to maintain attention on task. However, observations and reports of greater impulsivity in deaf children (even though these observations are clearly accurate) does not necessarily lead to higher rates of attention-deficit hyperactivity disorder (ADHD) among deaf children, especially when these children are assessed using accessible and appropriate measures. Hindley and Kroll (1998) concluded that deaf children with hereditary deafness are not at greater risk of developing ADHD, but that children with acquired deafness are at significant risk. The reasoning for this difference is likely related to the medical conditions (i.e., etiologies), the family dynamics, and the language delays that distinguish these two groups. This differential between the two groups (i.e., hereditary vs. acquired) has been observed repeatedly in clinical practice, as illustrated by the following patient.

Tim was a 6-year-old child identified at the age of 4 years with a bilateral moderate-to-severe deafness of unknown etiology. At the age of 2 years, Tim had sustained a very high fever from a viral infection. Tim was aided and mainstreamed in a classroom, with the teacher using an FM system. At the time of the assessment, Tim was reported by both the parent and the teacher as being inattentive, distractible, unfocused, and fidgety. He had difficulty making transitions, was disorganized, was socially immature, did not interact well with his classmates, and was not making academic gains. At the start of Grade 1, Tim had not made any expressive or receptive language gains. Nonverbal testing of intelligence was within the average range of functioning, while language-related measures were significantly lower, and a severe deficit was noted in Tim's working memory. Standardized measures completed by parent and teacher used to specifically assess for ADHD approached significant clinical levels or were only mildly elevated. These results were somewhat surprising, given that the parents and teachers provided a convincing description of a young boy with an attention-deficit hyperactivity disorder.

Further and careful testing showed that Tim had a very significant language delay, weak working memory, and presented as a much younger child in terms of his development of theory of mind, peer relationships, and socialization. Although Tim looked and acted like a child with ADHD-combined type, objective testing did not confirm this and instead highlighted significant areas of deficit and delays more likely related to his deafness and lack of language acquisition.

Conduct and Oppositional Disorders

Oppositional defiant disorder (ODD) and conduct disorder (CD) are a group of behavioral and emotional problems in youngsters. ODD is characterized primarily by aggressiveness and a tendency to purposefully bother and irritate others, while children and adolescents with CD have great difficulty following rules, accepting authority, and behaving in a socially acceptable way. Children with ODD or CD are often labeled by other children, parents, and teachers as "bad" or delinquent, when in fact they are suffering from a psychiatric disorder. Many factors may contribute to a child developing ODD or CD, including brain damage, genetic vulnerability, overly harsh parenting practices, child abuse/neglect, school failure, and traumatic life experiences.

Clearly, the list of risk factors that contribute to the development of behavioral disorders are also evident for many deaf children and adolescents. Children with sensorineural hearing loss, in particular, show significantly higher rates of externalizing behavior problems (van Eldik, Treffers, Veerman, & Verhulst, 2004; Vostanis, Hayes, du Feu, & Warren, 1997) than children with normal hearing (Hinshaw & Lee, 2003). Why is this? The etiologies of some deafness (i.e., meningitis) may contribute to adverse behavioral outcomes, even though the deafness per se is not the causal factor. Many deaf children experience academic failures and are also vulnerable to abuse. Hearing parents experiencing frustration communicating with their deaf child may resort to overly harsh, controlling, and intrusive parenting practices, which in turn may contribute to defiance and rebellion in their child. And finally, there appear to be strong links between language and behavior problems, as hearing children with language disorders show a higher incidence of behavior problems and, conversely, hearing children diagnosed with behavior problems show a higher incidence of language disorders (Barker et al., 2009). It remains unclear whether deficits in language lead to behavior problems, if language deficits are the result of behavior problems, or whether both language and behavior problems are independent factors of a more general developmental process (Beitchman et al., 2001) What is clear, however, is that deaf children of hearing parents may be considered to be at even a greater risk of behavior problems as either a direct or indirect function of their language delay or impoverishment, in addition to other known risk factors. This is not to imply, however, that Deaf children of Deaf parents are excluded from the development of mental health disorders, although likely the genesis of the disorder is rooted in different processes.

For example, Jeff was a 16-year-old Deaf son of Deaf parents. Jeff attended a school for the Deaf and had one Deaf sister. Jeff's first language was American Sign Language, and he was both fluent and eloquent in it. Jeff had a large and supportive extended family, including Deaf paternal and maternal grandparents. Jeff had been a defiant youngster and the parents had sought a referral by the age of 10 related to Jeff's aggressiveness within the home and school settings. Jeff was given a diagnosis of Oppositional Defiant Disorder (ODD) and was referred to a local children's mental health agency. Unfortunately, the recommended wrap-around treatment approach was not successful, largely because of the agency's unwillingness to provide interpreters for the various social services that became involved with the family. By the age of 15 years, Jeff had been apprehended twice by the police and was facing charges as he had set an empty shed on fire. Jeff was using marijuana on a regular basis, stole alcohol from his parents' home, and refused to attend school on a regular basis. Jeff's parents understood the diagnosis following an assessment with a Deaf psychologist, yet services were still very difficult to put in place due to linguistic and cultural barriers. By the age of 17 years, Jeff had left his family home, was living on the streets, and had little contact with his parents.

SUMMARY

Children with hearing loss can and do develop psychiatric disorders at higher rates than hearing children. It appears that deaf children of hearing parents are at an even greater risk of mental health disorders related to the myriad risk factors associated with language development, neurological involvement, and open family dialogue. It is essential that clinicians working with deaf and hard of hearing children not consider all maladaptive behavior solely as a function of the deafness, thereby missing true clinical disorders and therapeutic opportunities for recovery. Similarly, it is a challenge for the clinician to consider maladaptive behavior in exclusion to the risk factors associated with the deafness (i.e., language delay, intra-family communication dynamics etc.), which in themselves should be targeted for intervention strategies. Clearly, the deaf and hard of hearing child and adolescent pose challenges to themselves, their parents, their teachers, and their clinicians. Yet they remain children, and the onus must be on the adults to become duly educated as to clinical presentations, diagnostic challenges, and appropriate therapeutic interventions within the context of deafness and mental health.

9 Deaf Children and Adolescents: Treatment

THE NEED

The treatment of deaf children and adolescents with mental health disorders is complex and multifaceted. The need for treatment is often unfortunately met by a service delivery system that is inadequate and poorly prepared for a variety of reasons. Steinberg (1991) estimated that 90% of the deaf population's mental health needs remain unserved. Why is this? First, due to the low incidence of childhood deafness, it has been difficult to secure funding and to establish specialized clinical services tailored for this unique population. Instead, mainstream services have attempted to provide care without having the necessary expertise, knowledge, and language to do so.

Second, it has proven difficult to recruit deaf people to both define and provide competent culturally and linguistically accessible care. This is likely related to the lower literacy levels of many Deaf adults, which precludes admission to mainstreamed university programs. This is unrelated to cognition and is directly related to the difficulties associated with teaching a deaf individual how to read a phonics-based language. This is unfortunate and calls for change in how universities determine entry criteria, as well as how courses are taught. Clearly, Deaf professionals and paraprofessionals are much more likely to be fluent or native users of sign language, thus providing more effective communication.

Third, there is a need for more rigorous research regarding deafness and mental health to drive clinical practices. It is neither valid nor sufficient to modify research based on hearing individuals, as this ignores the uniqueness of this population. This is especially true for children who are also facing monumental tasks of language acquisition, development of theory of mind, and a sense of identity.

And finally, not only is there a paucity of treatment providers for deaf children and adolescents, there is a woeful lack of community supports and resources to promote and maintain mental health stability. Effective treatment for deaf children and adolescents with mental health disorders requires a continuum of care.

> A true continuum of culturally affirmative care for deaf children means that services are available in a variety of settings and are customizable to meet the specific clinical needs of the child. Ideally, there should be a range of services from in-patient to outpatient services, available in the home and in the school. It also means that such a program would have strong ties with schools serving deaf students. (Hamerdinger & Hill, 2005, p. 11)

This means that not only do deaf children and adolescents with mental health disorders require culturally and linguistically affirmative care well grounded in theory, they also require ongoing and available supports throughout their childhood, adolescence and into adulthood to ensure stability. It is evident that planning strategies and funding devoted to the mental wellness of deaf children and youth would repay many times over in terms of an overall healthier Deaf adult community.

TREATMENTS

Understanding the mental health disorder from the perspective of the deaf child/adolescent is necessary for effective treatment. In some situations, the child's deafness may be directly related to the etiology of the psychiatric disorder, whereas in other situations the deafness will be incidental (Roberts & Hindley, 1999). For example, central nervous system (CNS) disorders are highly significant risk factors for any child, increasing the risk of developing a mental health problem by six times (Hindley, 2005). Given that we know that disorders involving the CNS are often associated with deafness such as syndromes (e.g., CHARGE), the complications of severe prematurity, intrauterine viral infections such as cytomegalovirus (CMV), or bacterial meningitis in infancy, deaf children with these etiologies who are at higher risk for the development of mental health disorders should be identified for early interventions.

Treatment strategies will be most effective if all of the information in the preceding chapters is duly and thoughtfully considered by clinicians. The following factors must be considered:

Language

Interventions must first and foremost be in a language that is accessible to the child, be that sign language, spoken language, or a combination thereof. The best treatment strategy in the world will be ineffective if the child is not able to understand and participate in it.

Once the clinician establishes the child's best mode of communication, efficacy of treatment will further depend on a number of factors, such as if the family shares the same language as the child.

> Russ was a 15-year-old attending a residential school for the Deaf who considered ASL to be his first language. Russ had hearing parents who had very limited sign language skills. At bedtime one evening, Russ told his residential counselor he was very unhappy and wanted to hurt himself. The counselor called his parents, who immediately drove one hour to the school. The

counselor met with the parents and their son to review the boy's comments. It quickly became apparent that the level of communication between Russ and his parents was so superficial and limited that the meeting was postponed until the next day when an interpreter could be booked. Russ responded sadly by saying that if his parents loved him they would not need an interpreter to talk to him. Although the parents were very loving and supportive of Russ, their differences in language created an emotional distance that may also have been a contributing factor to Russ's depression.

A different scenario was seen with Melissa, who was a 16-year-old Deaf adolescent also attending a residential school for the Deaf. Melissa's parents signed regularly with their daughter, although they saw her only on weekends and holidays. The mother considered herself fluent in ASL and usually interpreted for Melissa on outings. Recently the parents had noticed that Melissa seemed to be eating much less than previously and appeared very thin. The mother made an appointment with their family doctor who scheduled the family to see a nutritionist. Not far into the interview, the nutitionist began to ask more in-depth questions about Melissa's nutritional intake, calories, and planning of meals. Unfortunately, the mother only knew very basic signs for "food," and the interview quickly deteriorated as Melissa was not able to follow the questions. In this scenario, two things are evident. First, family members should not be utilized as interpreters; second, the parent's competence (realistic, rather than perceived) can be vital to the success of intervention.

Developmental Level

The mental health of all children and youth is best conceptualized on a continuum ranging from developmentally typical behaviors that can be addressed in everyday home and school life to problems that require expert assessment and clinical interventions. Due to the complexity of language acquisition in deaf children (late identification of deafness, language exposure, accessibility, goodness of fit, parental attitudes, language choice), typical developmental milestones may be delayed or present somewhat differently. This has implications for mental health interventions in that strategies must be individually tailored to the child or adolescent's developmental level.

For example, the public health unit was holding a "blitz" campaign, visiting all area high schools with a barrage of materials, lectures, and videos on illegal substance use and abuse. When the public health nurses arrived at the Deaf school, they were bewildered by the students' lack of response to their presentation. What the nurses did not realize was that the Deaf teenagers' lexical knowledge of health risks, street awareness, and use of slang drug terms was much different from that of the hearing youth. In order for the presentation to be effective, the nurses needed to present the material in a way that made sense to the Deaf youth.

In addition to the importance of assessing developmental level to ensure the delivery of appropriate interventions, clinicians may need to provide more psychoeducation during the initial phase of treatment. Psychoeducation of the relevant concepts needs to be presented in the child's preferred language and at the appropriate developmental level. Providing psychoeducation buffers against deficits in incidental learning, which the children or youth may not have had access to in their world. This may be particularly true regarding the naming of emotions, understanding of theory of mind, and other psychological constructs.

Robert was a 16-year-old deaf student in a self-contained signing class in his home school. Robert had a cochlear implant when he was 7 years old and communicated orally until high school. At that time, Robert decided he would rather use ASL and began learning the language. In Grade 10, Robert was diagnosed with bipolar disorder and was referred for counseling. During the first session, it became apparent that Robert did not have any linguistic understanding in either spoken or sign language of the terms "depression," "mania," or "cycles." Therefore, the first five sessions of counseling were devoted to explanation of these terms in language and level of thought that Robert understood.

Visual Strategies

Although it seems evident that visual strategies would be helpful with some deaf children and youth, many clinicians are unsure how to implement these in their interventions. Therapists need to consider how visual approaches such as play therapy, drawing, sculpting, role playing, observing, and mime can all be very useful, especially with deaf children with any degree of language lag.

For example, Nina was an 8-year-old Deaf child attending a residential Deaf school. Nina was diagnosed with generalized anxiety disorder, and it was difficult for Nina to articulate in sign what her worries were about. The therapist helped Nina cope with these worries by meeting together each morning and having her "blow her worries into a brightly colored balloon." Then the therapist and Nina would release the balloon into the air watching the worries float away.

MENTAL HEALTH INTERVENTIONS

Although expertise in a specific mental health intervention model is important, the clinician's attitudes toward the deaf child or youth will directly influence the efficacy of therapy (Sussman & Brauer, 1999). This means that understanding and appreciating the influential variables, such as age of etiology of deafness, identification, language choice, language sophistication, school background, and cultural affiliation, will more positively affect the outcome of any mental health intervention. In addition, regardless of theoretical orientation, clinicians who focus on the strengths and resilience of the deaf children and youth, rather than pathologizing their deafness will better empower their young clients.

Mary was a 14-year-old deaf child attending a mainstreamed program where all other students were hearing. Mary communicated using an interpreter. Mary's two older hearing siblings attended the same high school. Mary's mother was diagnosed with depression and was often unavailable to her children. Despite being the only deaf child and having a mother who had her own mental health needs, Mary excelled in school, was happy, and had numerous friends.

It is this resilience that deaf children and youth often show which is sometimes not well captured in the literature and which certainly serves them well in terms of mental health outcomes.

Type of Interventions

Regulated mental health clinicians working with deaf children and youth utilize evidence-based therapeutic treatment interventions. There is, unfortunately, far less in the research regarding what treatments are evidence-based for deaf children and youth than there is for hearing children and youth. However, a fundamental premise of evidence-based practices for this population is delivering treatment in an accessible language. In terms of signing Deaf children and youth, efforts must continue to increase the number of trained clinicians who are fluent in the relevant sign language and are culturally affirmative (Hamerdinger & Hill, 2005; Willis & Vernon, 2002; Mason & Braxton, 2004; Glickman, 2013). In terms of oral deaf children and youth, the burden must be on the clinician to determine the accessibility of the language of the therapeutic model.

Consider Diane, who was a 12-year-old oral deaf child with bilateral digital hearing aids. Diane had a phobia of birds that was so frightening that she refused to leave her house to attend school in case she saw a bird outside. The school psychologist began a series of desensitization training sessions as part of the therapy regime but was puzzled as the child would not participate in the relaxation strategies critical to the therapy. After several unsuccessful attempts, the psychologist met with the parents, who inadvertently mentioned how much their daughter relied on speech-reading for communication. It was then that the psychologist realized that asking the child to close her eyes to participate in the visualization/relaxation exercise effectively cut her off from communication, and therefore the child resisted.

Given the shortage of sign language–fluent clinicians, there is a critical need to ensure that interpreters are well trained to work within a mental health setting. Mental health interpreters working with Deaf children and youth may face issues such as the child bonding with interpreter rather than the clinician due to the shared language, children who are extremely language impoverished or delayed, in which case a certified Deaf interpreter should be recruited, or finally, tensions with the clinician if the interpreter feels that the clinician is not knowledgeable on critical aspects of deafness. It is very important that the mental health interpreter and the clinician work well together, sharing their expertise yet respecting mutual boundaries.

SCHOOL-BASED SERVICES

As mental health is directly related to both the learning and development of the child, it makes good sense to offer support within the school systems. In terms of deaf children, however, mainstream educational programs often lack clinical staff trained to assess the mental health needs of deaf children as well as provide treatment. In the past, the residential schools for the Deaf often employed culturally and linguistically sensitive clinicians; however, the decline in enrollment with the move toward mainstream programs has often meant a reduction in available clinical services. Regardless of whether the child uses sign language, is an oral deaf child, or is a child who uses a cochlear implant, there is a need for qualified staff to be recruited, trained, and retained to provide support across the educational placement continuum.

FAMILY EDUCATION

Given the many potential issues facing hearing parents of deaf children and their families, resources to address these needs should be readily available. Again, these services should be easily attainable without financial hardship and should reflect the linguistic and cultural needs of the child and family. It is known that many deaf children may face multiple risk factors for mental health disorders, so clearly society needs to plan accordingly and respond with routine levels of intervention to screen, identify, and treat disorders.

INPATIENT SETTINGS

Deaf children and adolescents admitted to inpatient settings face formidable challenges with accessing the therapeutic milieu and in forming meaningful relationships with their peers. These challenges are above and beyond the presenting mental health concerns and are often directly related to communication issues with staff. For example, treatment protocols on adolescent inpatient units involving other patients, such as group therapy, or social skills modeling programs immediately pose difficulties for a child who signs or who speech reads.

Issues such as these, in addition to the unique nature of the population, suggest that likely the most effective inpatient setting is a specialized one for deaf children and youth where all staff are well trained on the relevant issues of deafness. An example of this is Corner House in London, England, which is a six-bed specialist inpatient service for deaf children and young people with severe mental health, emotional, and behavioral problems. A multidisciplinary team staffs the unit, and both deaf and hearing staff are proficient in British Sign Language (BSL) and SSE (Sign Supported English). The program provides detailed assessment and inpatient treatment through a variety of goal-focused interventions.

OUTPATIENT RESOURCES

Access to specialized services is critical for deaf children and youth with mental health needs. Similar to all other service providers, outpatient resources must ensure that deaf children receive appropriate therapy from clinicians who are linguistically fluent and culturally affirmative. Usually, outpatient resources differ from community social service resources in that the child and the family have access to a multidisciplinary team, including a psychiatrist and/or clinical psychologist to diagnose and assess disorders.

The Deaf Kids Mental Health Clinic was opened in 2008 in London, Ontario, Canada, under the directorship of one of the authors to specifically serve deaf children and adolescents and their families. The multidisciplinary team provided services to deaf children of any type of communication philosophy and their families. The clinic recognized that children with any degree of deafness may present with unique mental health needs that are often extraordinary, significant, and enduring, which without treatment have the potential for long-term emotional effects on the child, family, and society in general. Despite an overwhelming request for services, the clinic was forced to close within three years given that families were already facing undue financial hardship and were unable to pay on a fee for service model. Recognizing that families already have higher financial responsibilities (the cost of hearing aids, sign language classes, auditory-verbal training, etc.), these services must be available to families without financial cost.

More recently, the National Deaf Child and Adolescent Mental Health Service (NDCAMHS) was established in the north of England with the mandate of addressing the mental health needs of deaf children and their families. This service uses specialist intervention and is available to all deaf children experiencing emotional and behavioral disorders and their families (Sessa & Sutherland, 2013). The NDCAMHS is government funded, and the multidisciplinary team works on the premise that deaf children are more likely to experience mental health issues, that families often experience communication issues, and that, for a variety of reasons, the developmental pathways for deaf children differ from those of their hearing counterparts. The service recognizes that these factors need to be properly considered for intervention to be effective.

Community Social Service Agencies

Community agencies offering mental health interventions are another integral treatment strategy. Community social service agencies are a system of care in which the child's community is the primary provider of primary level care. An example of this is the PAH! program in Ontario, Canada. "PAH!" is an American Sign Language (ASL) sign equivalent to the English phrase "finally, at last!" PAH! provides mental health services to Deaf and hard of hearing children and youth, and their families. PAH! is a partnership between two associations that provide funding. Services are client centered and strength based. The services include individual and family counseling, group programs, art and expressive therapy, and consultation to agencies and professionals. All services are provided in the child's preferred language and are linguistically sensitive and culturally responsive. This type of community agency is exemplary for the services it provides to deaf children and adolescents.

THERAPEUTIC FOSTER HOMES AND FOSTER PLACEMENT

Deaf children can be extremely vulnerable to abuse and/or neglect. In situations where authorities have removed deaf children from their homes for their protection and well-being, it is absolutely essential that the foster placement options are accessible and appropriate (Hamerdinger & Hill, 2005). Recognizing how traumatic removal from a home is for the child, it is imperative that linguistic and cultural needs be addressed in order to ensure that mental health needs are well served.

> Nadine was a 7-year-old Deaf child of hearing parents who attended a day program at the Deaf school. Nadine came to school one day with a badly swollen and cut face, and the school notified Children's Services. Nadine disclosed to the social worker in play therapy that her father had become angry with her that she did not speak and hit her across the mouth repeatedly with a wooden spoon "to make her mouth work." Nadine was placed with loving foster parents who unfortunately did not know any sign language. Although it was a protective environment, it was not an enriched one, and Nadine became very withdrawn and refused to engage in any interactions with the foster family.

TECHNOLOGY

Technology has provided deaf children and youth with more options for interacting with each other over distance. For example, a videophone is a telephone with a video display, capable of simultaneous video signed communication between people in real-time. Although videophones are excellent for casual signed conversations, they are limited in their efficacy in a counseling situation. Some agencies now utilize videoconferencing (groupware) that also operates on simultaneous two-way video transmissions but differs from videophone calls in that it is designed to serve a conference or multiple locations rather than individuals. This allows agencies to develop programs for long-distance counseling with ASL-fluent counselors, to involve family members from various locations, and to facilitate group interactions/therapy. It is essential that clinicians become educated in the use of these types of technological advances, especially to facilitate services for deaf children and youth living in more rural areas.

SUMMARY

This chapter has described treatment interventions with deaf children and youth. It is helpful for counselors to conceptualize their work as a form of cross-cultural counseling where language, values, beliefs, customs, ethnicity, gender sexuality, religion, and socioeconomic status may be different from those of the larger majority society (Munro, Philip, Lowe, & Biggs, 2005). Within that context, sensitivity must be given to language preference and sophistication, family dynamics, and other important variables such as etiology. Evidence-based treatment strategies may be very effectively modified to reflect a culturally and mentally affirmative treatment strategy. Research must continue to develop and test theoretical paradigms that are appropriate and accessible for deaf children and youth.

10 Mental Health of Deaf Adults: Introduction

As described in Chapter 2, Deaf people are born into Deaf or hearing families from all walks of life; as adults, they are found throughout society and have roles in work, family, and social life, in the same way as all people of large or small communities. As they are usually in a minority group situation, their experiences of life are affected by the attitudes toward minorities within their families, in their peer group, and in society generally.

Deaf people are a diverse population, not only with regard to the nature or degree of their deafness, but in their cultural identity in the wider community, which may already be bicultural, for example, British Asian or Hispanic American. Deaf people may have other Deaf family members or, more commonly, be the only Deaf person in their family. They may or may not actively identify themselves as part of the Deaf community. The cause of deafness may have had additional effects on their physical health, on their vision, or occasionally on their appearance. All these factors affect Deaf people in different ways. Some causes of deafness may also cause different degrees of intellectual disability.

As for everyone, childhood experiences have a strong and lasting influence on adult mental well-being. As described in Chapters 3 through 9, for Deaf people this can be particularly important, especially with regard to language development and its implication on adult life.

EARLY STUDIES

In a historical overview of Deaf psychiatric patients, Vernon and Daigle-King (1999, p. 52) paint a disturbing picture of Deaf people in mainstream hospitals before the development of Deaf mental health services, describing their predicament as "in many respects, the essence of a snake pit environment for a deaf person needing mental health care." Similarly, Rainer et al. (1963) found many Deaf inpatients who were needlessly diagnosed with schizophrenia. In fact, Vernon and Daigle- King (1999, p. 52) described this as being "used as a waste basket category for deaf patients whose poor oral and English communication skills made their diagnosis more difficult." Other early researchers, such as Denmark and Warren (1972), noted the extremely negative impact of strict oral educational policies on the mental health of their patients. Remvig (1969) noted a high proportion of patients with organic brain damage due to non-genetic causes of deafness, such as meningitis, prenatal rubella, or birth trauma.

EPIDEMIOLOGY

It is known that Deaf people have a higher rate of mental health problems than the general population (Fellinger et al., 2012), but epidemiological studies have been difficult. Community studies are limited by the fact that there is usually no definitive background information about Deaf people in any catchment area population (WICHE, 2006). There is usually no database of Deaf or hard of hearing people, and the definition of deafness used is varied or imprecise. There are some voluntary registers as, for example, in Norway (Kvam et al., 2006), but these are not inclusive. Even studies of college students (Van Eldik, 2005) or deaf club members (Fellinger et al., 2005) may be looking at a population that does not include the entire range of deaf people.

Many studies have focused on caseloads of Deaf people who have been referred to specialist deaf mental health services. These studies can also have serious limitations. There may be an artificial peak in apparent incidence of, for example, schizophrenia, as new services receive a backlog of referrals. Deaf people who are more seriously ill or who have more disturbed behavior are referred from long distances in an undefined catchment area, in comparison with a hearing series of patients. This may result in comparing two unlike caseloads with different referral patterns (Appleford, 2003). Deaf people with additional difficulties in residential services have a high proportion of mental health problems compared with similar facilities for hearing people (McClelland et al., 2001). Øhre et al. (2011) give a full account of these epidemiological studies.

Despite the difficulties in epidemiological research, several trends emerge. Overall, it is estimated that mental health problems in deaf children are up to one a half times those of hearing children (Hindley, 2005; Fellinger et al., 2012). In community samples in deaf young people and adults, there is an excess of psychological and emotional distress, anxiety, and depression. This excess can be more than double the rates in the general population (Kvam et al., 2006).

In outpatient series, the proportion of Deaf patients with schizophrenia vary between 8% (De bruin and de Graff, 2005), 17% (du Feu, 2009), and 27% (Appleford, 2003).

In the inpatient series, the most common diagnoses vary between adjustment disorders (Denmark & Eldridge, 1969), schizophrenia (Haskins, 2004), and post-traumatic stress disorder (Black & Glickman, 2006).

Studies have shown that Deaf inpatients have longer stays than hearing patients, often to an extreme degree, with Deaf patients spending many years in hospital (Timmermans, 1989). More recent research (Appleford, 2003; Baines et al., 2010) shows inpatient stays twice as long as for hearing patients, mainly because of difficulties with complex problems and delays in making suitable discharge arrangements.

A further distorting factor in the epidemiology of mental health problems in Deaf adults is the longer duration of illness that results from difficulties in accessing even general health care (RNID, 2004). There are then further barriers to appropriate mental health services. These will be discussed further in later chapters.

DEAF PEOPLE WITH LANGUAGE DELAY

Many caseload studies of the Deaf people presenting to mental health and Deafness services have described a significant proportion of them as experiencing delayed language development and functioning below their potential. The terms used seems to follow literature where Deaf adults have been described to have "primitive personalities" (Rainer & Altshuler, 1971) or "primitive personality disorder" (Vernon & Miller, 2005), or even have been diagnosed with "surdophrenia," a term coined by Basilier (1964) that has since been dismissed. It is now accepted that, when present, lower functioning in Deaf adults is attributed to early language deprivation and acquisition delay and not to deafness itself. In other words, lower functioning is the result, not the cause.

Glickman (2009, p. xxi) describes Deaf adults who function at a lower level as "language and learning challenged." They have levels of intelligence at least in the borderline range of average IQ or, if intellectually disabled, are in the mild range. They are not fluent in any language modality but usually have a little sign rather than speech. They have minimal literacy and have adjustment and behavior problems that may include challenging behavior. Their problems are associated with inadequate language development, and they are traditionally an under-served group. Many of these Deaf people can be difficult to treat, as their problems are entrenched and they may not have the knowledge or motivation to use mental health services. They may present to services because of behavioral problems or offending.

RISK FACTORS

Deaf adults are subject to the same risk factors for developing mental health problems as the general population, but many of these factors fall more heavily upon them.

Neurological Risk Factors

Deaf adults, particularly those with non-genetic causes of deafness, have a raised neurological risk, and it is known that people with central nervous system disorders have higher risk for mental health problems (Hindley, 2005). Most identified neurological risk factors have been researched in relation to schizophrenia, and this is reflected below. In the general population, low birthweight, premature birth, perinatal hypoxia, and intrauterine infections are all implicated in the aetiology of schizophrenia (Picchioni & Murray, 2007). Childhood nervous system infections also raise the risk for adult schizophrenia (Rantakallio et al., 1997). Congenital anomalies in functional neural impairment are also associated with an increase in schizophrenia spectrum disorder (Waddington et al., 2008). Epilepsy increases the risk of psychosis (Qin et al., 2005), and cognitive impairments are an independent risk factor for schizophrenia (Owen, 2012).

Mason et al. (2008) studied the connection between middle ear disease and the development of schizophrenia. Interestingly, auditory hallucinations were associated with middle ear disease but not with hearing loss. The odds ratio of recorded middle ear disease predating schizophrenia was 3.68, and this excess was particularly associated with disease in the left ear. The proposed link is through damage to the overlying temporal lobe. There are some prospective cohort studies of prodromal symptoms of schizophrenia in young people, and it is suggested that hearing loss increases the risk of schizophrenic illness. However, the levels and duration of these hearing losses are retrospectively self-reported, and profoundly deaf people were excluded from the cohort (David et al., 1995).

Maternal rubella may be a specific risk factor for non-affective psychosis. Brown et al. (2000) followed up a mixed cohort of Deaf and hearing people with average intelligence who had been affected by maternal rubella in the 1964 epidemic in New York. Compared with an unexposed cohort, the relative risk of developing non-affective psychosis was 5.2.

Psychological Risk Factors

Like all adults, Deaf people are significantly affected by their experiences in earlier life. In fact, the language and communication environment of the family is a crucial variable affecting the psychosocial well-being of Deaf children and young people. The small proportion of Deaf children who are born into Deaf families do not show an excess of mental health difficulties (Schlesinger 1969). Sinkkonen (1994) shows the positive effect of early family communication in hearing families who had signed with their Deaf children from infancy (Gentili & Holwell, 2011).

Where Deaf children have attended residential school, this can result in disruption of secure relationships within the family. For many years, most Deaf children went to residential schools, many from the age of 2 or 3. Some went home for the weekend, others were separated from their parents for the duration of every school term, and some went home only for the summer. They often lacked a parental figure while at school. This was recognized by Ewing (1957, p. 327) who stated, "The need to provide parent substitutes during school term, in the case of young Deaf children, has not received formal recognition." Adverse attitudes from family members, at school, or in society contribute to neglect, rejection, and scapegoating (Rutter, 2005).

Social Factors

As part of a minority group, Deaf adults are subject to the risk of social exclusion in the domains of employment, housing, health, education, and access to community services (RNID, 1999). It is well established in the general population that social exclusion is known to increase the risk of mental health disorders (Huxley & Thornicroft, 2003); and that this effect is more marked when a minority forms a small proportion of their local community (Picchioni & Murray, 2007).

Abuse

Abuse in childhood continues to affect Deaf adults. In fact, Deaf children are at increased risk of abuse (Sullivan et al., 2000) and it is well recognized that abuse increases the risk for many psychiatric disorders (Keyes et al., 2012). Deaf children are at risk both within the family and in institutional care. Deaf children who attend residential schools may be alone with many different adults and in effect are more vulnerable to abuse. Their vulnerability from being away from home, coupled with their diminished language skills, significantly reduces their ability to report abuse. Physical and sexual abuse, as well as emotional neglect, are frequently reported by Deaf adults who reach mental health services.

PROFESSIONAL ATTITUDES TOWARD DEAF PEOPLE

Mental health professionals, when seeing a Deaf adult with mental health problems for the first time, may feel unskilled and have a "shock, withdrawal, paralysis" reaction (Schlesinger & Meadow, 1972). They may be unwilling or unable to obtain a sign language interpreter, and there can be a partial or complete breakdown in communication. Deaf people often have some spoken language or literacy skills, and the clinician can be misled and think that a sign language interpreter is not needed. The clinician can underestimate the Deaf person's ability and negative attitudes can complicate this further.

"Every village has one." Comment of community psychiatric nurse about a disturbed Deaf man with untreated schizophrenia.

"Environmentally acquired intellectual disability due to being deaf and dumb." Clinical psychologist's observation about the same Deaf man.

After observing an interview with a severely intellectually disabled Deaf man with autism, a clinical psychologist asked, "Has he got intellectual disability or is he just hearing impaired"?

"Perhaps we should get an interpreter once a year." Comment by consulting psychiatrist for schizophrenic Deaf woman.

A depressed Deaf man who lived on his own attended a local day center for several years. They could not communicate with him. A sign language interpreter came to the center to see him, with a mental health nurse, and offered to enable the center manager to converse with his client. The Deaf man was delighted and told the manager about a recent family wedding. The manager was so disconcerted to discover that the Deaf man was capable of fluent conversation that he cut the interview short and left the room.

More positive attitudes are fortunately held by the many hearing clinicians who work hard to do their best for Deaf patients and co-work with Deaf mental health services whenever possible.

MENTAL HEALTH INTERPRETING

Interpreting is a highly skilled role, and it must not be assumed that because someone is bilingual that they can automatically fill it. Qualified and registered interpreters should be used for mental health work. Interpreters have a strict code of ethics, including confidentiality, they undertake a wide range of work, and not all sign language interpreters are experienced in mental health.

There are too many occasions where Deaf people who have some spoken language and lip-reading skills have been seen without interpreters, and this creates a bottleneck of communication. The same phenomenon is seen in bilingual people with two spoken languages. More psychopathology is explored when someone is interviewed in their first language (Farooq & Fear, 2003). Nelson Mandela said, "If you talk to a man in a language he knows, that goes to his head, if you talk to him in his own language that goes to his heart" (Mandela, 2011, p. 144). Vernon and Miller (2001) point out that translation of standard psychiatric instruments such as the Minnesota Multiphasic Personality Inventory into American Sign Language took years to carry out. The sign language interpreter in a mental health assessment interview is performing a similar task in real time.

There have been situations in which Deaf people have been seen for assessments using relatives as interpreters. The Report of the Independent Inquiry into the Care and Treatment of Sarwat Al-Assaf (2004) describes a situation in which a Deaf man was assessed for the risk of violence to his family using his wife as interpreter. The use of family members should be avoided except in dire emergency. The risk to confidentiality, the chance of missed interpretation, and the distortions due to the relationship all adversely affect a proper assessment, which can become more problematic when hearing bilingual children are called to interpret their Deaf relatives.

A 25-year-old Deaf woman went home from the maternity hospital with her new baby. She had an older hearing child; her husband was also Deaf. After a few days the new baby became unwell. The parents, uncertain what to do, went back to the maternity ward. The mother gave the sick baby to a nurse and then fainted as she was unwell herself. When she recovered, there was no sign of the baby. No one could communicate with her and she thought the baby had died. She became extremely upset and tried to jump out of a window. Using only the child as an interpreter, she was admitted to the locked psychiatric ward. Two days later, she was discovered to have a bad chest infection; when this was treated, the mother eventually discovered that her baby was alive and well.

When a sign language interpreter is used in a mental health setting, it is important that the service user has the choice of an interpreter, either in a general way, in preferring a male or female interpreter, or for a named individual if this is possible. This is particularly important for regular appointments and even more so for psychotherapy (de Bruin & Brugmans, 2006). The interpreter will probably be already known by the patient, and could be the hearing son or daughter of a Deaf friend. This could increase the patient's trust in the interpreter or could lead to difficulties, for example, in the disclosure or discussion of childhood sexual abuse.

GUIDELINES FOR USING AN INTERPRETER

Although a sign language interpreter can sign while a hearing person is still speaking, there will always be a slight delay, especially as sign has a different word order; often the whole sentence must be completed before it can be translated into sign.

- People should speak one at a time and the interpreter should not be left to, in effect, chair a meeting.
- The interpreter should sit next to the hearing person and opposite the Deaf person so the Deaf person can face the interviewer and watch the sign simultaneously, while the hearing person talks to and sees the Deaf person and not the interpreter.

- There should be a neutral backdrop and the light should be on the speaker's face and on the interpreter, not behind them, otherwise they will be in shadow.
- Reflecting badges, clattering bracelets, clicking pens, and rustling keys are all distracting for the Deaf person or the interpreter.
- Background noise makes it very hard for the interpreter to follow what is being said.
- If written information is used, the Deaf person will break eye contact with the interpreter, who needs to wait until he looks up again.
- The interpreter will interpret everything that is said or signed, so no side conversations must be undertaken.
- It is important to check that proper two-way communication is taking place. A Deaf person may just nod to be polite, or in order not to seem afraid or confused.
- The speaker should speak in a normal tone and at a normal pace. The interpreter will indicate if she or he cannot hear or cannot keep up.
- Speech should not include long complicated sentences, compound questions, double negatives, or English idioms. Topic changes should be well indicated.

Interpreting is much more than translating. It is a complex process and a bridge between two cultures. As Leigh and Pollard (2011, p. 217) note, "too many clinicians assume that the presence of an Interpreter automatically resolves communication barriers between themselves and deaf patients." In an interpreted interview there can be errors and misunderstandings. Sometimes there may be an omission in a chaotic situation.

> A Deaf man was rushed to the hospital after stabbing himself. It transpired that during the resuscitation process he had indicated that he had also taken an overdose, but this information did not emerge until he was re-interviewed a day later. Fortunately, he had received almost an exchange transfusion of blood, so the potentially lethal amount of medication that he had swallowed was substantially reduced.

Information may be misunderstood and this misunderstanding can be perpetuated through the interpretation process.

> The child of a Deaf couple was rushed to hospital after a collapse at home. The parents described hitting the child. They meant they were trying to resuscitate him.

The interpreter may need to expand on a question, working with the clinician. For example, in British Sign Language there is no general term for "medication." Therefore if a doctor asks about medication, the interpreter has to explain that he or she must ask about tablets, liquids, inhalers, patches, and injections at different sites. The generic term for an operation (a thumb stroke across the palm) is not always recognized and may therefore be taken literally as an operation on the hands, so if the doctor wants to ask about operations, the interpreter must indicate different parts of the body and/or ask the doctor to be more specific.

The interpreter may also need to ask the clinician to expand on terms such as agoraphobia, which may be unfamiliar to the Deaf person and do not translate word for word into sign language.

The interpreter has to be careful that the Deaf person knows that the questions are coming from the clinician.

> A doctor asked the Deaf person his name and address. The question was relayed by the interpreter to the patient, who replied in astonishment, "But you know me, you know where I live."
>
> A 75-year-old Deaf woman thought that the interpreter was asking the questions himself in order to spread gossip about her.

Deaf patients will sometimes ask advice directly from the interpreter, or, if they have previously known the interpreter in a professional or personal capacity, may ask him or her to explain their problems on their behalf. The interpreter sometimes has to make clear to both the doctor and the patient that he or she cannot participate in the dialogue between them.

Both closed and open questions can be quite difficult. Open questions can be hard for some Deaf people to answer, for example, "How are you feeling?" The Deaf person might just respond, "fine," but on further inquiry will have feelings such as anxiety or depression. However, closed questions, such as "Are you happy?" or "Are you sad?" can lead an acquiescent patient, who may agree just to be polite, because he doesn't understand, or to stop the questioning. There is a particular difficulty in listing options, as the Deaf person may respond to the last on the list as the simplest answer. The interpreter should not turn a question into a list without asking the clinician.

> A Deaf 25-year-old man was thought to have autism. He just copied back the interpreter's signs. In an effort to get a spontaneous answer, the doctor asked, "Do you have a pet at home?" The inexperienced interpreter asked the patient "What do you have at home, a cat or a dog?" He answered, "a dog." The doctor then thought this was a spontaneous response.

A major difficulty for sign language interpreters in mental health interviews is the normalization of disordered sign. In other situations interpreters will do their best to maximize meaningful communication, but this can disguise symptoms in a mental health assessment. However, word for word interpretation into speech in sign word order will sound thought disordered even when it is not.

The clinician working through an interpreter has the difficult task of establishing rapport with a patient with whom they are not talking directly in the same language. It is important that rapport is established, as empathy is needed for the patient to trust the doctor with what may be distressing or embarrassing symptoms. There are different models of mental health interpreting: the impartial model, the community model, and the advocacy model (Cambridge et al., 2012). In the impartial model, the interpreter aims as far as possible for strict translation, remains impartial, and displays empathy while maintaining a professional distance from both parties. The community model is often viewed as an advocate or cultural broker who goes beyond the traditional neutral role of the interpreter and will intervene for expansion or clarification. The advocacy model interpreter goes even further to mediate between the patient and the clinician and guides the former through the encounter.

All models of interpreters will clarify relevant linguistic and cultural issues as requested, and all will indicate where there is abnormal signing or when effective communication is not taking place.

> A 40-year-old Deaf old man who had been isolated from other Deaf people since he left school had limited old fashioned sign language from his school days. When interviewed with an interpreter, he seemed just to be copying what the interpreter was signing. However, as the interview progressed, it was clear that he was practicing signing again, and by the end of an hour he was producing spontaneous signs. The interpreter was able to comment on this.

Interpreters can have ethical dilemmas with mental health patients who are particularly vulnerable. Although it is advised that an interpreter should talk with a Deaf client before any assignment in order to get used to the person's level of sign, this means that the client can confide information to the interpreter before the interview starts. When the doctor is seeing, for example, a relative who is hearing, the client and the interpreter may be together outside the room. The client may also leave with the Interpreter. At all these times, the client may ask questions or disclose information that has not been included in the interview. The interpreter needs to encourage the Deaf person to tell or ask the doctor whatever is necessary and can only disclose information of a nature that would lead to disclosure in other circumstances, such as abuse of a child or a risk to life.

Many mental health services with Deaf people see patients over extremely wide areas. The use of video telecommunications for interpreting could save a great deal of time and travelling. Many Deaf people are more familiar with the use of these technologies than clinicians (Austen & McGrath, 2006). However, particularly for first assessment interviews or for complex interventions, the limitations on communication and rapport can be considerable.

Relay interpreting by a trained Deaf person whose first language is sign can facilitate communication with Deaf people with limited or idiosyncratic language. The relay interpreter signs with the patient and translates into standard sign for an interpreter or signing clinician. This is a skilled and important role.

MULTILINGUAL MULTICULTURAL INTERPRETING

This is a particularly complex field but it is not an unusual one. In large conurbations there are many spoken languages and also sign languages from different countries. Some cultures, such as the Aboriginal and Torres Strait Islanders in Australia, have their own sign languages that are used by hearing people. A Deaf person may code switch between their own Deaf sign language, "contact signing" that is used with their hearing community, and also use some limited spoken or written language. Extreme multicultural sensitivity and several interpreters, including Deaf relay interpreters, may be needed to make an appropriate assessment of a Deaf patient in these circumstances (Faye'herbe & Teuma, 2010).

SUMMARY

Deaf people have the same range of mental health disorders as the general population, but the risk factors for these problems can press particularly heavily upon them. Adverse neurological, childhood, psychological, and social factors result in an excess of mental health problems. Deaf people can then experience significant delays in presenting to appropriate services. Mainstream services need to use sign language interpreters, but also need knowledge of Deaf people's cultural issues and life experiences.

11 Deaf Adults: Assessment

INTRODUCTION

A Deaf adult presenting to mental health services may have complex problems. There may be a cause of deafness associated with health, sight, or neurological problems including intellectual disability. The Deaf person may have had a path through life that has exposed him or her to many risk factors for emotional and psychological problems. Even a Deaf person with a successful and fulfilling life may have gaps in information and general knowledge from an inadequate education. There can be incomplete information about the patient's baseline level of functioning before the mental health problem developed.

The assessment therefore needs to examine the Deaf person's path through life very carefully in order to consider all these complex and interacting factors in the light of the person's present mental state.

REFERRAL INFORMATION

When a patient is referred from primary care to a mental health service, the referral letter will usually contain a comprehensive summary of the patient's background and family circumstances, with a description of the presenting problem. In general adult mental health practice it is assumed, usually correctly, that the patient's level of functioning, both within the family and in society is, or was until the onset of the present difficulties, within the normal range for his age and culture. It is also assumed that the patient's family will be able to give a corroborative account of his history and describe recent changes in his mental state.

For a Deaf person, none of this may be true. The primary care referrer has recognized the Deaf person's need for further assessment and in making the referral has potentially given him access to interventions that may be long overdue. However, the referrer is highly likely to be inexperienced in relating to and assessing Deaf people with mental health problems and, despite good intentions, incomplete or inaccurate information may be given. What happens next determines whether a vital opportunity is taken or is missed, perhaps with prolonged and serious consequences for the Deaf person with the mental health problem.

Good communication with a patient is the bedrock of mental health practice. History taking, mental state examination, the clinician/patient relationship, informed consent to and compliance with treatment, psychological assessments, therapy programs from formal psychotherapy to supportive counseling, community and recovery programs—all these obviously depend on sharing a common language. Deaf people whose first language is sign language can be excluded from all these basic aspects of mental health assessment, treatment, and care, even when they have managed to surmount the first barriers to services by accessing primary care and being referred to a mental health team.

Referral letters sometimes do not even make clear that the Deaf patient is a sign language user.

A referral was made by a mainstream mental health service to the Deaf mental health service. The referring clinician stated that the young woman disliked being Deaf and did not sign. He added, "she is physically agitated and restless, constantly moving her hands." She was in fact using some signs while speaking and was a fluent sign language user.

The referring clinician may have communicated with the Deaf person using a mixture of speech, lip reading, and writing, aware of the limitations of these but not realizing that the Deaf person signs. The Deaf person may not have known his right to an interpreter or may have expected from past experience that because of the expense or shortage of interpreters, his request would be refused. So the referring doctor may be under the impression that the Deaf person does not sign and may never have thought of finding out.

A referring letter to the Deaf mental health service of a patient who was later diagnosed with schizophrenia stated that "he has hearing and speech difficulties and his preferred communication is by simplified writing." The patient when seen had fluent sign language.

THE INTERVIEW

When the mental health clinician first meets a Deaf patient, the priority is, therefore, to establish the Deaf person's preferred means of communication. This may be sign language, speech/lip reading, or a mixture of the two, as in Sign Supported English, perhaps with finger-spelling and/or writing for some words with proper names. Some Deaf people with additional sight problems use hands-on sign or finger-spelling with the Deaf Blind alphabet. Others who have had limited access to sign language may have idiosyncratic "home" signs developed within their families. Others may have older signs from their school days or have a strong regional sign accent.

At the beginning of the interview, it is important that the seating and environment are appropriate for the Deaf person. Introductions are important, as the Deaf patient may not realize why he is being seen. The patient may not have been able to read the appointment letter and may not know the roles of the doctor, nurse, or other professional. The patient may be inexperienced in using an interpreter. The clinician needs to establish effective communication, explaining his or her role and the reason for the interview. Seating must be arranged with regard to lighting, acoustics, and distractions, so that the patient, the interpreter, and the clinicians are all comfortable. Privacy needs to be assured. A glass panel in the door may cut off spoken communication, but there will be no privacy for a signer, who will also be distracted by people passing the door. If it is a home visit, the Deaf person may be unaware of intrusive background noise such as a barking dog. Visual distractions such as a television, even if silent, should be turned off. Eye contact is vital for effective communication.

> A junior doctor in a Deaf mental health service felt that the patients did not trust him. On discussion, it was noted that in his culture it was rude to look directly at people. The Deaf patients felt his lack of eye contact was dismissive of them.

If the Deaf person wants a relative or, for example, a social worker to be present, the clinician needs to be aware that an interpreter must interpret everything and should not conduct spoken side conversations. Further information about mental health interpreting can be found in Chapter 10.

There is a need to create rapport with the patient, as a lot of intrusive questions will be asked in a mental health interview. Deaf patients may well also ask personal questions of the interviewer, and these can be answered briefly and appropriately. They may include questions about the clinician's hearing or deaf status.

TAKING THE HISTORY

When the history taking starts, it is of fundamental importance to realize that, unlike other users of cultural minority languages, Deaf people
cannot be presumed to have fluency in their own language, even in the
absence of any mental health problems (see Chapter 2). A relevant example that captures the dilemma of parents' choices appears below.

> A 5-year-old Deaf child was referred to child mental health services because
> of behavioral problems. Although his hearing parents acknowledged that
> there was a severe communication difficulty between them and their child,
> they were very angry with suggestions that sign language would improve his
> communication and language development. It transpired that they had an
> older Deaf son who had been brought up by the strictly oral method. Although
> this had been of extremely limited success, they could not bring themselves
> to recognize that their hard work had been in vain, and they were not pre-
> pared to change in response to the needs of the younger child.

Therefore, even with a sign language interpreter, it cannot be
taken for granted that clinician/patient expressive and receptive
communication will be comprehensive. This raises many important issues, regarding both interpreting and the entire assessment
and treatment process. Deaf people from Deaf parents are of course
more likely to have fluent sign language, but even then exceptions
can occur as the parents themselves may have had limited early signing opportunities.

PERSONAL AND FAMILY HISTORY

History taking should cover all standard information gathering, but
every aspect is colored by the Deaf person's perspective and life experience. Even basic information about his family may not be readily available to the Deaf person.

A 60-year-old woman who had been profoundly Deaf from birth was visited at home. She had lived with her parents until they had died and had become increasingly isolated. She described her older siblings accurately but was vague about her younger siblings. She had been sent to residential school at a very early age and had stayed there until she was 20. She only come home only for school holidays, and her family could not communicate with her. She therefore never had clear information about the birth order and ages of her younger siblings.

A Deaf teenage boy was struggling at school and was falling further behind. He had partial hearing from birth and had functioned well with two hearing aids. He had good speech and extensive vocabulary. However, his hearing had gone down further and this had not been recognized. He was falling behind at school and had been moved to a intellectual disability class without a formal cognitive assessment. His family was extremely reluctant to consider any total communication, sign support, or bilingual approach. It transpired that the young man had a paternal uncle who was also Deaf. This man had been sent away to a signing boarding school and had been abused and had not received a good education. The young man's parents therefore were afraid of their son following the same path, and the boy had not even been told that he had a Deaf uncle.

Inquiries about a Deaf person's family must be tactful, as he may have been told about family events but has missed details. For example, if a cousin has had a baby, the Deaf person may not necessarily know whether the baby is a boy or a girl, and it is important to wait for people to volunteer information of this sort rather than embarrass them by asking directly.

A young Deaf man was describing his school career. He said that he had been taken to see a child psychiatrist when he was about 8. He had gone as a day pupil to a bilingual school, which he liked very much, but then he had refused to go and had become increasingly distressed. He explained that eventually it was realized that his parents had asked the teachers to tell him about his grandmother's death in sign language, as they themselves did not sign. He had become terrified to go to school in case other family members died.

As for every patient, information about birth, milestones, and early life should be sought from patients themselves and from records or family informants, but for Deaf people this can be of particular significance. Both the facts, as far as they can be obtained, and the patient's and family's perception of the facts are important. Deaf children do not all easily discover that others are hearing.

> A Deaf 75-year-old woman described how her Deaf older brother had explained to her that they were different from hearing children when she was 5 and about to go to school.
> A Deaf 40-year-old man said that when he was a child he would go to the front door, open it, and look out. When asked why he did this, he said to his parents, "When you open the door, Grandma's there."

Some Deaf children who have never met Deaf adults have believed that they will die, or will become hearing, when they grow up.

It will be evident that the authors of this book do not regard deafness as a medical construct but as a cultural/linguistic issue in a social context. However, the fact remains that many causes of deafness, whether genetic or non-genetic, can have additional effects, and these must be considered both for any meaning they hold for the Deaf person and for any physical, cognitive, or neurological consequences. These will be further discussed in the following chapters.

Many Deaf people do not know the cause of their deafness. Sometimes their families do not know or have not told them. Relatives may believe they have told the Deaf person, but he or she has not been able to understand the information because of the communication barrier.

Some patients and their families have erroneous beliefs about the cause of deafness. There have been cases where hearing parents have thought that their child's deafness was a curse or a punishment. One child was told his deafness was due to the violence perpetrated by his father on his pregnant mother. The deafness may have been attributed to incidents in babyhood, such as a fall from a crib, when subsequently another cause such as rubella is found. Guilt, anger, and blame may persist and affect family relationships.

> A young Deaf man, the only Deaf member of his immediate family, did not know the cause of his deafness. He had many problems with anger and with accepting his Deaf identity. He had a hearing sister. When he was 14 he had a new cousin, a boy, who was born Deaf on his mother's side of the family. He concluded that his deafness was his mother's fault and that if he had been born a girl he would have been hearing. This added to his bitterness and his conflict with his family.

Ascertaining the cause of deafness can alert the clinician to the likelihood of coexisting physical, neurological, sight, or cognitive problems. Further relevant history taking with regard to family members and indicated physical investigations can be pursued. Sometimes the cause is only recognized when the Deaf person is seen by specialist mental health services.

The history continues by considering the circumstances surrounding recognition of the deafness and the family's reaction to this. Even the elderly parents of middle-aged Deaf people may still recount the experience of learning that their child was Deaf and the consequences of this in vivid detail and are obviously still grieving.

> The 80-year-old hearing mother of a 50-year-old Deaf man described how she had to send her son at the age of 3 years away to a boarding school. She described how she was unable to explain to him what was happening and that when she picked him up at the end of his first term there, he was frightened and bewildered. Particularly poignant was the fact that she had knitted and made clothes especially for him, but then she found that all the clothes were put into a communal wash and the children just wore what they were given.
>
> A 65-year-old Deaf man described arriving at the boarding school with his parents when he was 3. He was given a sandwich. He looked down at his plate, and when he looked up his parents had gone. His parents told him many years later of their distress when they were prevented from seeing him the following day to say good-bye.

Many families at the time of the diagnosis, although distressed, experience some relief that their concerns were at last recognized after having been dismissed as the worries of over-anxious parents.

Before universal hearing screening programs (which are still not implemented in many countries), a child's deafness may only have been realized when, for example, a saucepan was dropped or a tractor started. Even marked delays in speech may have been missed as causes for concern, or the child would have been described as shy, badly behaved, or, more seriously, as intellectually disabled.

The Deaf person's obstacle course through life begins at birth; the recognition of deafness, the implications both psychological and medical of its cause, and the effect on the family are all vital parts of the history. Deaf children in Deaf families are naturally accepted and welcomed, though some Deaf parents may be apprehensive that their children will have the same life difficulties that their own generation experienced. Some are so afraid of this that they do not have children.

A 70-year-old Deaf woman who had been at boarding school during her childhood described her feelings when she became pregnant at the age of 40. She was delighted to be having a child but was terrified that the child would be Deaf and would be subjected to the same experiences and abuse that she had suffered at school. When the child was tested and found to be hearing, she wept with relief.

Other developmental milestones may be normal or delayed. If the Deaf person is the oldest child, new parents may not have realized any delays at the time but retrospectively recognize them when subsequent children reach milestones significantly earlier. If the Deaf child was a second twin and the deafness was due to birth difficulties, these other delays, if present, will have been obvious at the time. Some parents have believed that the other delays were due to the deafness alone.

EDUCATIONAL HISTORY

The next important part of the history concerns the language and educational choices and decisions made for the Deaf child in early life. The important word here is "for" and not "by." Obviously, the child is too young to take part in these decisions, which were made by parents in good faith; however, it is clear that many Deaf adults would have made different choices for themselves as children (Gregory et al., 1996) (*In the Land of the Deaf*, 1992).

> The psychiatrist was signing to a 30-year-old Deaf man with a depressive illness on a home visit. He had asked for his mother to be present. He was doing well, but as the conversation in sign proceeded, the doctor became aware that the young man's mother was crying. When asked what was troubling her, the mother explained that she was crying because a stranger could come to her son's house and communicate with him better than she could. She said that she had always been told never to learn sign and now she felt it was too late. She also said that her son became angry with her and did not believe that she was only following advice in not learning to sign when he was young.
>
> A young Deaf woman with a schizophrenic illness, an inpatient in a Deaf mental health service, was in the psychiatrist's office with her hearing parents who were visiting. The parents asked the psychiatrist to sign to their 30-year-old daughter that they loved her. The Deaf woman signed back, bitterly, "That's all very well but I spent my whole childhood trying to learn to speak and they spent not one hour trying to learn to sign." The mother started crying and said that they had done what they had been told to do.

It is only recently that Deaf adults have been included in the consultation process for newly diagnosed Deaf children so that their experiences, positive and negative, can be considered when these important decisions are made. Also, more rigorous review of these decisions means that Deaf children are not set on one particular course, which is then pursued to the point of failure.

Many of the Deaf adults who present to mental health services have not benefited optimally from the language and education decisions that were made for them decades ago. Even signing Deaf children from Deaf families may have been prevented from using sign language at school. The linguistic, psychological, emotional, cognitive, educational, and social consequences for them form the core of a comprehensive mental health assessment of a Deaf person.

Inquiring about school yields information about what can be the most formative time of a Deaf person's life. Where and when Deaf people are born have been the most powerful predictors of their educational pathway. National and local policies about speech, sign, mainstream schools, partial hearing units, and boarding schools dictated what happened, far more than the assessed needs and preferences of individual children and their families. The historical background of this has been described in Chapter 2. The decisions made for Deaf children could suit them very well. Attendance at boarding school with a Deaf peer group and an effective bilingual program can give a Deaf person a secure identity, a good education, and lifelong friends, and can provide access to a successful personal and social life as well as employment. Others have been less fortunate. Poor language development in either speech or sign, minimal literacy, estrangement from their families, and physical and/or sexual abuse have been the experiences of many Deaf people at residential schools. Recently, more Deaf children have been mainstreamed. Many have benefited from this educationally, but sometimes at a cost to their identity (i.e., feeling between Deaf and hearing identities in adult life). Others have been isolated or bullied as the only Deaf child in a hearing school, in addition to missing a lot of education because of communication barriers.

A intelligent young Deaf woman became quite agitated when describing her experiences at school. She repeatedly said that she could not understand what was happening and used the sign for information just going straight past her. She thought she was stupid and her brain did not work properly. She was asked her about her confidence in various areas of her life. She explained that she could not read subtitles while watching television, could not read forms or bills or understand newspapers. She signed that her husband's literacy was better than hers and he would help her, or other relatives would help.

SOCIAL AND EMPLOYMENT HISTORY

After leaving school, some Deaf people have had access to further education or training. Others have returned to their family homes after years of boarding school and found that they have poor communication with their families and difficulties in obtaining employment. Their educational level may be below their potential and it becomes increasingly hard to remedy this. Links with boarding school friends can be broken, especially in the past for people with poor literacy and before access to video communications, texting, and e-mail. Their sign may fall into disuse as they become more isolated. Receptive sign may last longer than expressive sign, as isolated Deaf people may follow sign when given the opportunity, but may take some time to recall and use sign to express themselves.

MEDICAL AND PSYCHIATRIC HISTORY

With regard to the medical history, many mental health patients are poorly informed about this and about their past or present medication. This is especially true for Deaf people. Deaf adults sometimes describe going to the doctor with a hearing family member as being like a cat or dog being taken to the vet. People speak over them, they cannot follow the conversation, and they have no idea what their illness or treatment is. Deaf people who have had operations have signed consent forms with no real understanding of what is going to happen. Deaf people can be understandably reluctant to see a doctor, as even if they can manage to make an appointment and then be called into the consultation room in an appropriate manner, they may then be unable to understand the doctor, read the prescription, or comprehend the pharmacist's instructions. They may not realize they need to continue the treatment or may collect repeat prescriptions for a long time without a review. Sometimes medical conditions cause the apparent mental health problems (see Chapter 12).

FAMILY PSYCHIATRIC HISTORY

Deaf people may not know important information about their family mental health history. Information about family mental illness may have been kept from the Deaf person, or the family has not thought to ensure that he had been informed, even with regard to family deaths. If a relative had died by suicide, the Deaf person may have been "protected" from this information.

> A Deaf young man presented with depressive symptoms. His father informed the doctor that the young man's cousin had committed suicide but the young man himself didn't know the cause of his cousin's death. However, in the interview the Deaf man was preoccupied by thoughts of hanging, which had been his cousin's method of death.

THE PRESENTING PROBLEM

When considering the presenting problem, one of the important questions, as for all patients, is "Why is this person presenting now?" The problem may, of course, be recent and present appropriately. The patient and her family may be fully aware of the time of onset of the symptoms and have come for help at an appropriate time. For Deaf people, however, as for all patients, the symptoms and distress may in fact have been long-standing and an external event has precipitated the referral. For Deaf people, the time before presenting may last for years, or even decades. The Deaf person may be functioning poorly due to a mental health problem but this dysfunction has been attributed to her deafness. The reverse can be true, and a Deaf person is thought to have schizophrenia or an intellectual disability when he in fact has been language deprived and over-protected or institutionalized. A Deaf person in any of these long-standing situations may only present to mental health services when a relative dies, a ward closes, or a Deaf person commits an offense.

> A Deaf young man presented to Deaf mental health services after being arrested after starting a fight at a family wedding. When interviewed in sign, he explained that he was angry because his twin had not been invited to the wedding. He did not have a twin. When his parents (who couldn't sign) were asked how long he'd had the delusional idea of a twin they were astonished, but then said, "Oh that's why he's been buying two of everything for a year."

PREMORBID FUNCTIONING

The family informants, who would in most circumstances be able to compare the patient's past functioning with recent changes and report significant conversations, may be unable to do any of these tasks. Their Deaf relative may have been away at school from an early age and the family may have had little contact with teachers and care staff. Family communication may be limited to the point that although relatives can report observed mood and behavior, even florid psychotic symptoms have been missed for long periods.

The history will give an account of the patient's life in the context of early experiences in the family, Deaf or hearing, in education, language, peer group experience, and age-appropriate development. The history should also make clear, as for hearing patients, what the patient's baseline optimal level of functioning has been. The presenting problem can then be evaluated in this context. Once more, the situation with regard to Deaf people may be deceptive. Deaf people with normal or high intelligence may not have achieved their potential due to educational and language delays and deprivation.

A Deaf woman in her forties who had obtained a copy of her educational records as part of a court case was seen for a psychiatric report. She was very distressed to see how negatively they had commented on her and also by the phrase "She has a mental problem with language." She had been brought up by the strict oral method but had started to sign since leaving school. She had married, worked, had children, and made a success of her life. However, she still had very poor confidence and self-esteem and ongoing problems with literacy. When the assessment in sign was over, the woman asked the psychiatrist what she thought. The psychiatrist replied, "I think you are a brave and intelligent woman who has been able to overcome all the things that went wrong in your childhood and at your school." The Deaf woman was surprised and she signed, "Do you mean I have become intelligent since I've grown up?" When the Doctor replied, "No, you have been intelligent all along," the woman burst into tears and signed, "So it was them, it wasn't me, it wasn't me."

Deaf people may have a poor employment history due to inadequate literacy or discrimination. They may have reduced daily living skills due to parental over-protection. Sometimes, the level of functioning can be deceptive. For example, Deaf people may be able to drive but not be able to read signs or maps or ask for directions. They can only drive a familiar route or with another person to direct them. The key obstacle for many Deaf people driving is now the written theory test. Therefore, it can be hard to find a meaningful baseline for any presenting difficulty in these areas of life. Because there have been low expectations of Deaf people by teachers, family, and society, depressive or negative symptoms or cognitive decline for any reason can be missed as the previous level of functioning was artificially low.

In hearing families, if a hearing son aged 35 with normal intelligence could not read, use money, travel, or live independently, this would be seen as anomalous; but a Deaf man in a hearing family could be in this situation even before any mental health problem developed.

> The hearing mother of a Deaf man who had been seen by mental health services for anxiety asked the doctor if she felt it was all right to leave him in the house on his own for the weekend while she and her husband went away. The mother was not worried about her son's mental health problems but whether he would be able to manage on his own. He was 32.

The key point in history taking is not to assume anything in advance of seeing an individual Deaf patient, whatever the original referral information. The referral may be exactly right in all respects but the clinician must start with a completely open mind.

When a history has, as far as possible, been obtained, the question to be answered is "Does the course through life experienced by this Deaf person explain his or her distress and problems and situation now, or is there an additional mental health problem?" Whether the answer is yes or no, further exploration, discussion and therapeutic interventions are needed; but this question needs an answer and the mental state examination goes further to answer it.

THE MENTAL STATE EXAMINATION

"The mental state examination is dependent on facility with language because that is the tool with which psychiatric practice is conducted" (Oyebode, 2008, p. 33). The whole interview will have yielded key information. The clinician will have been observing the patient during the history taking. The Deaf person may have little idea of why she is seeing the psychiatrist or other mental health professional. She may be uncomfortable because she is in unfamiliar surroundings or because she is afraid of hospitals or clinics. There may be a stigma attached to the premises where the interview is being held. Conversely, the venue may be a familiar one such as the Deaf Center office, but the patient is anxious about confidentiality. If it is a home visit, the patient may be unused to visitors and may be anxious, suspicious, angry, or embarrassed because of this. The clinician must not assume that these are due to mental health problems. The patient's appearance can tell the clinician a good deal. Physical characteristics associated with different causes of deafness may be apparent. There may be sight problems or neurological difficulties such as cerebral palsy, or syndromes such as Waardenburg's with different colored eyes and a white forelock, or Klippel-Feil with stiffness of the neck and a bent posture. The level of self-care can be observed, but this may be deceptive. A relative may have helped the patient to present himself well, or he may have made a special effort for the appointment.

The patient may be unused to using an interpreter and may be anxious about confidentiality. His experience of communicating with hearing people may have always been limited and difficult. He may believe that he is in trouble and does not know why.

The detailed examination of speech for disorders of form or content is obviously fundamentally affected by conducting the interview in sign language, whether or not through an interpreter. First, the serious considerations with regard to the Deaf person's own sign fluency must be noted, as described above. Second, sign is affected in the same ways as speech in disorders such as autism, Tourette's syndrome, intellectual disability, specific language disorders, schizophrenia, mood disorders, dementias, and stroke. This means that any abnormalities of the Deaf person's sign could be due to early language deprivation, limited or idiosyncratic sign-ing, and/or to subsequent changes due to mental health or neurological problems.

The patient's mood may be obvious from observation, but further exploration may be limited by the patient's vocabulary. Although sign language can express the whole range of emotions with a subtlety at least equal to spoken languages, a particular Deaf individual's sign vocabulary may be restricted to basics such as happy, sad, fed up, stressed, angry, or afraid.

> A Deaf young man who had been brought up by the strict oral method and, though of normal intelligence, had limited speech or sign, found it almost impossible to explain how he felt. He said he was "a mad dog." The psychiatrist tried to ask if he thought he was feeling differently from everybody else and he looked at her with astonishment and scorn. He said, in his limited spoken English, "How would I know how other people feel?"

Linguistic facial expressions in sign language must be separated from expressions of mood. The clinician must also be alert to whether the patient is describing his own mood or other people's and whether this is in the past or the present. For example, in a description of a signed conversation, a Deaf person will need to switch between interlocutors and will role-play the participants by expressing their signing accordingly. This means that when he is recalling an angry conversation, he will look angry, and this can be misleading. Animated sign can look agitated or even hypomanic or can mask depression. Small or hesitant sign may be due to poor confidence, limited sign language, depression, anxiety, or poverty of thought.

Exploring thought content may be difficult, and in imposing closed questions such as "Do you feel sad?" the clinician may inadvertently lead a suggestible patient who may not really understand, or answer "yes" or "no" in an attempt to please the interviewer or to stop the questioning.

With regard to thought content, Deaf people may have mistaken ideas or insufficient knowledge about topics due to limited access to education and overheard information. For example, a Deaf person may believe that only Deaf people are abused, or that Deaf people cannot go to prison, or that everybody who has a mental health problem is hospitalized. Even more extreme ideas can still be due to misunderstandings and must not be taken as delusional.

> A Deaf young man stated that electricity came out of the wall. What he actually meant was that the switch was on the wall and that made the electricity work. He had no idea how this actually happened.

Deaf people with psychotic illnesses can experience hallucinations in all modalities, including auditory, and careful examination is vitally important. This is further discussed in Chapter 13.

With regard to general knowledge and orientation, a Deaf person's response can be very misleading. Deaf people may not have had access to written information such as a daily newspaper or TV subtitles, so they may seem disoriented in time. The person may have been brought by others to an unfamiliar place. He may not be aware of recent events in the news, or he may have thought they were part of a television drama. Conversely, a television program about past events may have seemed to be the current news. It is important to inquire tactfully about a Deaf person's access to literacy, for example, about whether she finds the subtitles helpful or whether she uses texting.

Standard memory tests with words, letters, and numbers can be confusing and inappropriate (see Chapter 12). A Deaf person's intelligence can be totally misrepresented by low educational achievement.

> A Deaf woman was asked her age and wrote "old, 2572 yeas." She was asked when her birthday was and she wrote "biradaner Happy." This was her way of writing happy birthday and what she gave as her age was actually her date of birth.

A Deaf person may have no basic information about mental health or even physical health concepts. Mental health problems may have an even greater stigma than is usual. Assessment of insight should be done with extreme caution, as the patient may have limited knowledge or unrealistic ideas about mental health and may be afraid or in denial.

SUMMARY

The mental health assessment of a Deaf patient presents complexities over and above the standard history taking, evidence gathering, and interviewing of hearing patients who share the language and culture of the clinician. These issues will be further explored in the following chapters.

12 Physical and Organic Disorders and Intellectual Disability

PHYSICAL ILLNESS

Deaf people can find it hard to see a doctor, and when they do attend a medical appointment, there may be poor communication.

> A 40-year-old signing Deaf man with depression asked for further appointments with the signing psychiatrist after his depression had resolved. He wished her to correspond with his family doctor about his back symptoms and then explain to him about his diagnosis and treatment. His family doctor had always refused to provide an interpreter for his appointments.

Deaf people are likely to have reduced access to information and awareness about physical health, medical procedures, and treatment. Communication breakdowns can then have serious consequences.

A 40-year-old Deaf woman was having frequent blood tests by her doctor, who was investigating her diabetes and heart disease. The doctor became concerned when she refused all further tests. When seen to discuss this, she signed, "Is it dangerous, will I die?" She had believed that she was being drained of all her blood.

A 60-year-old Deaf man was given a mouth spray to use when he had angina. He thought the spray was for his sore throat and used it regularly, causing severe headaches.

Deaf people attending a mental health appointment either with signing staff or with an interpreter may disclose information about untreated medical conditions. Medical problems can in fact themselves cause the symptoms that have led the Deaf person to present to mental health services.

A Deaf woman with diabetes was interviewed without an interpreter by the practice nurse with regard to healthy eating. She did not understand the connection between diet and her illness and became angry, as she felt the nurse was making personal comments about her weight. She left the consultation prematurely and defaulted from further checkups. She was thought to have mental health problems and was referred to Deaf mental health services.

A 60-year-old Deaf man was seen after a hospital admission for chest pain. He had no concept of the cause of his diagnosis, and as his angina had occurred while out walking, he had subsequently refused to leave the house and was thought to be agoraphobic.

Many causes of deafness can be associated with physical health problems, and these may not be recognized. Pendred's syndrome, for instance, is a recessive genetic cause of deafness that also causes thyroid deficiency. With modern screening this can be picked up in early life so thyroxin levels can be monitored and any deficiency can be treated. However, both early and late onset cases have been missed.

> In a long-stay intellectual disability hospital, a 60-year-old Deaf woman was found to have severe thyroid deficiency and was retrospectively diagnosed with Pendred's syndrome. Thyroxin supplements were too late to correct her short stature and intellectual disability.
>
> A socially isolated Deaf woman failed to attend social work appointments to arrange her benefits. The social worker became concerned and visited the house with a member of the Deaf mental health team. She was in bed in an almost comatose state with hypothyroidism.

There are causes of deafness that are associated with kidney disease (Cassady et al., 1965). It is important that the Deaf patients understand their illness and its treatment. The combination of the kidney problems and the deafness can make families over-protective and the patient excessively anxious.

> A young Deaf woman with kidney problems needed repeated hospital appointments. She did not understand much of what was happening and became anxious and depressed. When she was referred to the Deaf mental health service for counseling, it became clear that she was much more intelligent than her parents had realized. Cognitive testing showed that she was within the normal range, and this led to her taking more responsibility for her treatment, and her parents encouraged her to have much more independence.

Physical problems such as asthma can be undiagnosed or poorly treated.

> A 25-year-old Deaf man who lived with his parents was referred for what appeared to be anxiety and panic attacks. He was visited at home. He had been diagnosed with asthma and had been given an inhaler, but he had not understood the instructions on how to use it and was having worsening asthma attacks.

A Deaf-aware general practice demonstrated a higher incidence of diabetes in Deaf people (Schatzlmayr, 2001). Diabetes can present as a psychiatric problem.

A 35-year-old Deaf man living with his parents refused to move into an apartment that he had applied for. He had recently been diagnosed with diabetes and had become very anxious. He believed that he could not be left alone at any time as he could go into a coma.

A Deaf man with mild learning disability attended a day center. He became increasingly irritable and disturbed and had been excluded. He had been diagnosed with diabetes. He did not understand how to manage his illness and had been having hypoglycemic episodes.

Sometimes people who have already been identified by Deaf mental health services present with new physical illnesses.

A young Deaf man living with his male partner was being treated for schizophrenia. His mental state improved, but then he stopped his medication and did not attend further appointments. He was followed up and he explained that he did not like the medication because it had given him an unpleasant rash. He turned out to be HIV positive, and his rash was Kaposi's sarcoma.

When a person is Deaf and is known to have psychiatric problems, he or she is at a special risk for physical illness being missed.

A 55-year-old Deaf woman with mild intellectual disability and recurrent depression was not eating and had lost a significant amount of weight. This was attributed to her depression, but when she was seen by the Deaf mental health service it was clear that she was physically ill. She died from cancer of the esophagus.

Medication may lead to mental health problems.

A young Deaf woman was prescribed steroids for rheumatoid arthritis and became progressively psychotic.

A Deaf woman with epilepsy had hallucinations caused by her prescribed medication.

A Deaf elderly man became delirious due to his medication for cancer and attacked his wife in the night.

EPILEPSY

Deaf people have an increased incidence of epilepsy (Hindley, 2005) due to the neurological risk associated with many non-genetic causes of deafness, such as birth anoxia and meningitis. It is well recognized that epilepsy has wide-ranging neuropsychiatric manifestations (Agrawal & Govender, 2011). The risk factors for psychopathology in epilepsy can apply to excess in Deaf people. They include low socioeconomic status, low educational level, social stigma, difficulties adjusting to the consequences of the illness, external locus of control, fear of seizures, and over-protection by families. In addition to this, some Deaf people may have limited understanding of the nature of epilepsy or the treatment for it. They are at risk of having their medication unreviewed for long periods of time.

A 30-year-old Deaf woman presented to Deaf mental health services with poor self-care, apathy, and over-dependence on her parents. She had been on high doses of phenobarbitone since she had some fits at the age of 13. This had remained unreviewed. She had a new EEG and after slow reduction of her medication she became much more alert. She had no further fits and entered a rehabilitation program.

A 42-year-old Deaf man presented to mental health services with anxiety and depression after having a recurrence of seizures following his decision to stop his medication. He had been on anticonvulsant medication after a mild head injury in a road traffic accident at the age of 18. At the time he had been advised that he would probably remain on the medication for some years. He had asked for a specific estimate and had been told "until you are about forty." He had therefore finished the pills on his fortieth birthday.

Deaf people can have depression, anxiety, and transient psychosis associated with their epilepsy in the same way as the general population, but these may not be identified. Deaf people can also have difficulties in getting appropriate help until the situation escalates.

> A 65-year-old Deaf woman with long-standing grand mal epilepsy had always relied on her mother, who lived with herself and her husband. When her mother died, her husband became impatient with her and she became progressively more afraid of having a fit. This led to repeated hospital admissions with both grand mal seizures and pseudo seizures. Eventually, the marriage broke up and the woman went into residential care.

RARE ORGANIC SYNDROMES

Many neurological syndromes may also affect hearing, but there are some in which the deafness precedes neurological symptoms by many years. Psychiatric symptoms may present before any neurological deterioration. This is one of the reasons that it is important, if possible, to establish a cause of deafness. For example, if a Deaf teenager seems to be losing cognitive function, it could be due to one of these rare syndromes. However, if another cause of the deafness is well established, such as rubella, the apparent cognitive decline is much more likely to be due to depression or to the negative symptoms of schizophrenia.

> A 16-year-old severely Deaf boy presented with poor self-care, ritual behaviors, disturbed sleep, and abnormal posturing. The cause of his deafness was not definitely known but was thought to be due to a head injury sustained in a traffic accident when he was about 3 years old. He also had a mild learning disability attributed to the same cause. However, there had been no clear history of his hearing level or cognitive functioning before the accident. He was partially hearing and used hearing aids, lip reading, and speech. A family history showed some undiagnosed mental health problems in distant relatives and some possible cases of deafness that had been attributed to non-genetic causes. After investigations for abnormalities of metabolism with equivocal results and an MRI scan that did not show any new changes, early onset schizophrenia was diagnosed, and he eventually responded well to Clozapine.

This contrasts with a similar presentation.

A 22-year-old Deaf man presented with social withdrawal and self-neglect. He had previously worked in a shop but had lost his job due to poor time-keeping. He was in a relationship that his parents disapproved of and he was estranged from his family. It was thought that he was depressed due to losing his job. He had a family history of deafness, with two Deaf siblings, one of whom had died as a child after a seizure during what seemed to be a febrile illness. Neurological investigation showed that he had metachromatic leucodystrophy, an autosomal recessive condition that causes abnormal neural lipid metabolism. The rarer later onset cases can present with psychotic symptoms. The patient died within a year of diagnosis. His Deaf sister also developed the psychiatric and neurological symptoms and died the following year.

Schilder's disease (diffuse cerebral sclerosis) is another rare sporadic and genetic syndrome. It is associated with widespread demyelination and glycolysis in the white matter of the hemispheres. It can present psychiatrically and then rapidly progresses. Denmark (1994) describes a Deaf woman who presented with a puerperal psychosis and was diagnosed with Schilder's disease after she died.

Mitochondrial encephalomyopathy (MELAS syndrome) can affect many organs, including the central nervous system via a dysfunction in mitochondrial metabolism. Petty et al. (1986) described a series of 66 cases, 27% of whom showed prominent involvement of the central nervous system, which included deafness. Dementia was common in this group.

A 35-year-old man who had been profoundly Deaf from early life presented with delusions of persecutions and auditory hallucinations that his neighbors were banging on the wall and disturbing him. These noises were not witnessed by his hearing relatives and did not alert his hearing assistance dog. He also had some loss of memory. A neurological referral for further investigation resulted in a diagnosis of mitochondrial encephalomyopathy. The psychiatric symptoms responded to anti-psychotic medication, but his physical health deteriorated and he developed progressive dementia.

INTELLECTUAL DISABILITY

Deafness and intellectual disability frequently coexist, as many genetic and non-genetic causes of early deafness can also cause neurological problems, including intellectual disability. It has been estimated that the prevalence of hearing impairment is at least 40 times higher in people with intellectual disability compared with the general population (Carvill, 2001). Some causes of intellectual disability, such as Down syndrome, are also associated with a higher rate of hearing loss, usually in later life. In addition to developing conductive/sensorineural hearing loss, people with this cause of intellectual disability may also have central auditory processing problems (Kiani & Miller, 2010). Many genetic and non-genetic causes of early deafness also cause intellectual disability. Rubella is a common cause of early deafness, and depending on the trimester during which the mother was infected, other consequences such as cardiac abnormalities, sight problems, and intellectual disability may coexist with the deafness. Other genetic causes of deafness and intellectual disability include CHARGE syndrome, Didmoad syndrome, Noonan's syndrome, and Goldenhar syndrome; these also have multiple physical effects (Kiani & Miller, 2010).

People with intellectual disability should be screened carefully for both hearing and sight problems. Appropriate communication will help them to achieve their potential.

Deaf adults who have grown up at a time or in a place that did not have early screening for deafness or facilities for comprehensive assessment may have reached adult life with an undiagnosed intellectual disability. Conversely, Deaf adults may have been regarded as intellectually disabled when this was not the case. If there has been diagnostic overshadowing from the deafness, combined with language delay and deprivation, someone of normal intelligence may be functioning at a lower level. In addition, there are Deaf people of low normal intelligence or borderline intellectual disability who have been functioning at even more reduced level with regard to language, social, and psychological development in personal relationships and independent living. Deaf people functioning like this may present to services after a change in their circumstances, or with behavioral difficulties.

A 49-year-old Deaf man, the only Deaf person in his family, had been admitted to psychiatric hospital at the age of 18, when he left boarding school to return home. He had been brought up by the strict oral method but had learned sign language from other boys at school. His alcoholic widowed father could not communicate with him, and they became violent with each other. The Deaf man was admitted to the hospital, where he remained 30 years later. During these years he acquired the diagnosis of schizophrenia and intellectual disability, though there was no evidence for either. He was described by staff as someone who "made a funny noise and tried to escape." He had not been able to use sign language throughout his stay in hospital. His ability to sign was only discovered when he was visited by a Deaf social worker as part of the hospital closure program.

Sometimes Deaf people with additional problems have had inappropriate school placements in which Deafness has not been accounted for.

A 50-year-old Deaf man with sight problems and a mild intellectual disability due to maternal rubella was sent to a school for blind children, and his deafness was not considered. He has little language of any sort.

A young Deaf woman with cerebellar ataxia spent her childhood at a school for physically disabled children where there was minimal communication.

Sometimes Deaf people are in intellectual disability services for long periods with little communication.

A 55-year-old Deaf man lived with his elderly widowed mother. He was profoundly Deaf due to maternal rubella and went regularly to a workshop and day center for people with significant intellectual disabilities. He was very solitary there. He had learned a bit of sign language at school but had no one to use it with. When he was reassessed, his nonverbal IQ was well within the normal range. This meant that he lost his placement without any other suitable placement being available for him.

Sometimes people fall between services.

A 50-year-old Deaf man was taken to a psychiatric hospital after being found on a railway station, apparently trying to jump under a train. He was profoundly Deaf but knew no sign language. He had limited speech and literacy. He was isolated and depressed. He was admitted to the Deaf mental health service but on discharge neither the intellectual disability service nor the general adult mental health service would take responsibility for his care, as testing showed that his IQ was exactly 70, the usual cut-off mark between these services.

COGNITIVE TESTING ON DEAF PEOPLE

As standard cognitive tests are standardized on the general hearing population, testing can be misleading in profoundly Deaf adults. Clearly, the verbal part of a test such as the Wechsler Adult Intelligence Scale (WAIS), is unsuitable, but even the nonverbal tests are difficult to administer in a standard way. A Deaf person cannot look at sign language instructions while also looking at the task to be performed. Some of the signed instructions will also prompt the subject in unintended ways. Timed tests will be affected as the subject has to look up to take any further instruction.

In addition, Deaf people may be unfamiliar with the concept of testing and need some rehearsal time. For example, on the pictorial tests in Raven's matrices (Raven, 1976), the pattern matching may be unfamiliar as an idea and therefore the subject would seem to perform badly. However, if provided with sufficient explanation of the task's demands and, if possible, a practice example, they can often go on to perform very well. Practice items, however, should be kept to the minimum to avoid confounding the result of the test with a learning effect.

A Deaf man with some sight problems was being tested with the Raven's progressive matrices. It took him some time to understand what was required of him and he was quite slow performing the test. However, he was doing very well until he got tired. He then made a deliberate mistake as he realized this would end the testing.

There have been translations of tests into sign language, and also the new WAIS IV test contains specific instructions and advice on testing Deaf people (Wechsler, 2010). The assessment of intellectual disability with Deaf adults has been reviewed by Baker and Baker in *The International Journal of Mental Health and Deafness* (Baker and Baker, 2011).

MENTAL HEALTH PROBLEMS IN DEAF PEOPLE WITH INTELLECTUAL DISABILITY

Mental health problems are more common in intellectually disabled people whether Deaf or hearing (Cooper et al., 2007). A population study of over a thousand adults did not associate a further excess due to hearing impairment, but the case ascertainment was through intellectual disability services, which Deaf people do not always reach. In the studied population, point prevalence of mental ill health was 40% and the most prevalent type of problem was with behavior. However, this group contained mostly people with severe or profound learning disability, and Deaf people with intellectual disabilities who present to Deaf mental health services are usually in the moderate to mild group. A study of affective problems in hearing adults with mild learning disability (Collishaw et al., 2004) showed a sixfold risk of chronic depressed mood. This was largely mediated by variations in socioeconomic disadvantage and ill health, suggesting that positive interventions could reduce this morbidity.

Deaf people with intellectual disabilities can be affected by the entire range of mental health problems. Diagnosis may be difficult due to the complexity of the person's history and presentation.

Deaf adults may present when they are already in mainstream intellectual disability services, in residential care, or with their families. Sometimes intellectual disability has not been previously recognized and the limitations in independent functioning have been attributed to the deafness alone. A full history and mental state examination will reveal any mental health problem as part of a complex and multifactorial situation.

Deaf adults with intellectual disability may also develop a mental illness. Some case histories illustrate this with reference to psychotic disorders, schizoaffective disorder, and depression.

PSYCHOTIC DISORDERS

A moderately Deaf woman with Turner's syndrome lived with her elderly parents until they died. She then became increasingly unable to manage; eventually, after a fire at her house, she presented to mental health services. She had some speech and lip reading and literacy and no sign language. It became clear that, in addition to the deafness and the mild intellectual disability, she had a long-standing psychotic illness, and it was this that had caused her deterioration in function. When her illness was treated with antipsychotic medication, she was able to live semi-independently in sheltered accommodation.

A Deaf young woman with mild intellectual disability due to rubella became increasingly disturbed in her family home. She was admitted to a psychiatric hospital and schizophrenia was diagnosed. She defaulted from follow-up as she had persecutory delusions about her psychiatrist. She believed he was following her in various disguises. She was subsequently transferred to intellectual disability services and accepted further treatment.

A deafened man of 35 refused to sleep in his bed. He had severe deafness and moderate learning disability due to anoxia from epilepsy in childhood. He had limited speech and no literacy. He did not sign. His mother was reluctant to accept his deafness. His family had changed his bed and tried different mattresses to make him go to bed to sleep. On mental state examination it was found that he had somatic hallucinations of being gnawed by rats when he was in the bed. This was his sole psychotic symptom and proved difficult to treat.

SCHIZOAFFECTIVE DISORDER

A Deaf man with mild intellectual disability, in long-term sheltered accommodation, became increasingly disturbed and overactive. He was elevated in mood and had auditory and visual hallucinations of people visiting him from where he used to work in a sheltered placement. His sign was quite limited and further distorted by his illness. A Deaf relay interpreter was needed in the examination of his mental state. He responded to treatment with mood stabilizers and antipsychotic medication.

DEPRESSION

A 45-year-old Deaf man with moderate intellectual disability was a resident in a psychiatric facility that had been opened after the old long-stay hospital closed. He had been admitted to the old hospital at the age of 13 after behavior problems at school. The cause of this deafness was not known. He still had a little contact with his family, but they could not sign with him. He was becoming increasingly withdrawn and was losing weight and was seen to be tearful. He had been on long-standing sedative medication but had not shown behavior problems for many years. The medication was reduced, a Deaf support worker visited him, and he started to use his sign language more. He then became able to travel independently on the bus to the Deaf Center and he gained some computer skills. He improved without antidepressant medication.

BEREAVEMENT

The loss of a parent is a major life event for any person, but for a Deaf person who is particularly close to one parent and may have few or no other people to confide in, this is a particularly difficult time. Deaf people with learning disability may have incomplete information to understand what has happened.

A 33-year-old Deaf woman at an intellectual disability training center lost her mother to cancer after a long illness. She had been at her mother's funeral and signed about her mother in heaven watching over her. However, she was anxious and perplexed. When asked directly what she was worrying about, she asked, "How did my mother get into that jar?" She had not gone to the crematorium with her family after the funeral. She had seen the urn with her mother's ashes but had no idea what had happened.

BEHAVIOR PROBLEMS

Deaf people with intellectual disability often present to mental health services with disturbed behavior, while there are also cases in which these people have been over sedated in residential care or at home.

A 40-year-old Deaf woman who had meningitis as a baby lived with her parents. She was on so much medication that she was asleep for most of the day. She had a history of challenging behavior, and due to poor communication with mental health services, only medication had been offered. She had side effects that were thought to be due to a lowered seizure threshold, but were in fact oculogyric crises. Sign language was encouraged with the young woman, both at her day center and with an assistant who would take her out. She responded to a behavioral program. Her medication was reduced and the side effects ended.

A 58-year-old Deaf man was in long-term residential care. He had been unable to cope alone after the death of his parents. He had very little sign and his behavior was often disturbed. Because of this, he was eventually placed in a highly staffed unit for people with intellectual and physical problems. Some of them had abnormal mouth movements, and as he did not know whether they were speaking, he assumed they were making rude comments about him, which worsened his behavior. When he was brought to the attention of Deaf mental health services, it was apparent that he had only mild intellectual disability. A Deaf support worker visited and showed him family photographs of his own father at school with the Deaf man. He recognized him immediately but only knew him by his number, as when he was at school, the pupils were known by the numbers of their pegs in the cloakroom. The Deaf man's sign language returned with practice, and he was resettled in a residential home with other Deaf people.

Deaf people who come with their families from other countries may have not had access to language or education and the cause of the deafness is usually not known. It then can be very difficult to tell if there is a baseline learning disability, particularly if language development remains extremely delayed. However, with intensive support, particularly with regard to sign language development, these young people can slowly improve in their psychological, emotional, and social functioning.

SUMMARY

In all mental health assessments, it is essential to consider physical illness and organic disorders as factors in the presentation of mental health problems. Premorbid and current cognitive abilities also form a vital part of the clinical picture. For Deaf people, these aspects of assessment are especially important in order to provide appropriate treatment and care.

13 Schizophrenia

INTRODUCTION

The diagnosis of schizophrenia leading to the treatment and care of those who are afflicted with this common and serious psychiatric illness is one of the core tasks for mental health services.

Schizophrenia is a multifactorial disorder; therefore, with the neurological and psychosocial risks that Deaf people are liable to, it could be expected that the incidence and prevalence of schizophrenia would be raised in this group. However, as described in Chapter 10, the evidence is not clear or decisive.

DURATION OF UNTREATED PSYCHOSIS (DUP)

Deaf people face many delays and difficulties in accessing treatment, as recognition of the illness by the patient's family, primary, and even secondary mental health services can be delayed by many years or even decades. There may be limited communication between a Deaf person and the hearing family, and absence of family involvement in seeking help is a major contributor to delay in presentation to services (Morgan et al., 2006). In Norway, public information campaigns were shown to reduce the duration of untreated first psychosis (Joa et al., 2008), but the Deaf community has limited access to these, so even Deaf people in communicating Deaf families can have delayed presentation.

Therefore, for Deaf people there can be a greatly increased risk of a longer duration of untreated first episode psychosis (DUP). In general population studies, the delay in presentation can be correlated with an insidious onset of illness, which in itself leads to a poor prognosis (Morgan et al., 2006). For a Deaf person, illness may be of florid onset and may still remain untreated for a prolonged period.

A 45-year-old Deaf man was arrested for an assault after drinking. He had a long history of arrests for such assaults and was finally referred for a mental health assessment. He was floridly deluded and hallucinating. His family had previously tried to get help for him, but his late mother would not allow them to do so, as she was very protective of him and attributed his difficulties to his deafness. He had been ill for nearly 20 years.

In DUP research, evidence suggests that the end-point is contact with mental health services (Morgan et al., 2006). This is not necessarily true for Deaf people, as even then the illness may not be diagnosed.

A 16-year-old young woman, Deaf from maternal rubella, was suspended from school for unruly behaviour. She was usually a good student and took this badly. When she returned to school she became increasingly withdrawn and was diagnosed as depressed by mainstream mental health services. She left school and returned home to her parents. She became difficult to manage, with ritualistic behavior and reduced communication, and she was then thought to be autistic. She was eventually admitted to a Deaf older adult residential service, as there was no other available placement with sign language. By the time she was referred to a Deaf mental health service, she had untreated schizophrenia for 15 years.

Deaf people may be socially isolated or may live with people, including close family members, who cannot communicate with them. There may also be a low expectation of a Deaf person's functioning, so that any shortcomings in independent living, or strangeness of behavior, may be attributed to the deafness itself. The illness may continue unnoticed until an event precipitates a referral.

A profoundly Deaf 22-year-old woman presented at the Emergency Department of a general hospital. She wanted surgery on her face as she had delusions that it was distorted. She had already made cuts in her face herself.

A 35-year-old Deaf single mother was referred for a psychological assessment, as she was repeatedly preventing her 8-year-old daughter from going to school. On assessment she was deluded and hallucinated, believing that the sun was following her, the tap water was poisoned, and she had leaves in her veins. She was therefore afraid to let her daughter leave the house.

A 30-year-old profoundly Deaf man was becoming increasingly withdrawn at the sheltered workshop he attended. He worked in the kitchen and had previously been happy at the day center, though there was only minimal communication with him. He had visual hallucinations of dead relatives, and he believed that staff at the day center were planning to kidnap and kill his young nephew, so he refused to attend.

All of these patients had, in retrospect, been ill with schizophrenia for several years.

ASSESSMENT

Taking the History

When the Deaf person with schizophrenia finally presents to mental health services, there are still formidable obstacles to accurate diagnosis. Chapter 11 outlines some of the pitfalls in general mental health history taking and assessment. These are all of enhanced significance with the patient with schizophrenia. Deaf people's ability to give a full history and description of their symptoms may be seriously compromised by language delay and impoverishment, even when the clinician can sign or an interpreter is present. Family informants may be unable to communicate with their relative or have distorted views of what is "normal" for a Deaf person.

> A 35-year-old Deaf man with schizophrenia was seen for a mental health tribunal assessment. He asked to be seen with his parents present. The signing psychiatrist explained that she could not be the interpreter for his parents, who did not sign, but he still wanted them to be present. He started to sign to her that they were not his real parents and that he had been born on another planet. The psychiatrist felt uncomfortable having this conversation in front of his parents and asked the young man if she could share with them what he had just signed. He readily agreed. When they heard what their son believed, his parents laughed and said, "Deaf people are so stupid, aren't they?"
>
> A 50-year-old Deaf woman who had frequently been in the hospital with schizo-manic relapses was seen at her home, where she lived with her elderly mother. The psychiatrist asked her how long her daughter had been ill. Her mother replied, with some exasperation, "She isn't ill Doctor, she's deaf and dumb."

At a crucial time in late adolescence for the development of schizophrenia, the Deaf person may have been at a residential school and any change may have been attributed to the return home to a different environment.

Family history of mental health problems may be unknown to the patient or may have frightening significance.

> A Deaf woman was taken into care as a child when her hearing mother developed schizophrenia and was hospitalized long term. When the young woman herself became ill, she and her Deaf husband hid her illness, as they were afraid that they too would lose their children.

MENTAL STATE EXAMINATION

The main areas of significant difficulty in the diagnosis of schizophrenia in Deaf people are thought disorder, delusions, and hallucinations.

THOUGHT DISORDER

Categories of thought and language disorder are fully described in psychiatric texts such as *Symptoms in the Mind* (Oyebode, 2008). It is important that the writing of Deaf signers is not used for diagnosis of thought disorder, as Deaf people's literacy may be poor, or the writing is in sign language word order.

> A Deaf woman in her thirties, without thought disorder, wrote about her anxiety "poor commication—still Disgust—much poor I really got danger fright that makes afraid because keep alway trouble. Hard thinks—much force—no relax."

Disordered sign language in Deaf people with schizophrenia has been described in detail (Thacker, 1994; Trumbetta et al., 2001). Signers show errors specifically related to the production of handshape, particularly with regard to classifiers (pronoun handshapes for objects, people, and vehicles) (Chatzidamianos, 2013), which are unrelated to any movement disorders associated with schizophrenia, and which can cause significant impediments in the overall language production (Chatzidamianos, 2006). Thought disordered signs may be produced backward, with changed use of right and left hands, or may be meaningless newly created signs. Signing may perseverate or be derailed, use "rhyming" handshapes or loosened associations; just like disordered speech. There can be poverty of sign, sometimes to an extreme extent. This may only become clear as the illness is treated.

> A young Deaf woman was sent by her family in the Caribbean to live with her grandparents in England. They could not communicate with her, and her behavior deteriorated. Eventually, she was admitted to a psychiatric hospital and started on antipsychotic medication, which calmed her. However, when she was transferred to a rehabilitation facility, she was so sedated that it was difficult to work with her. She was referred to the mental health and deafness service and the medication was gradually reduced. She became extremely disturbed, did not communicate in any way, and stood posturing for long periods in the hospital corridor. A presumed diagnosis of schizophrenia with catatonic symptoms was made and a new antipsychotic started. Within two weeks the woman's sign language started to return and within three months she was back at her residential placement and subsequently started a college course.

If the Deaf person's language is impoverished or disordered for whatever reason, the rest of the history taking and mental state examination is made especially difficult. Elucidating symptoms such as thought insertion, thought blocking, and thought broadcasting requires time, care, and patience.

A 40-year-old Deaf man with suspected schizophrenia was asked if people could hear his thoughts. After a pause, he responded with a mixture of suspicion and relief, "How did you know?"

A 30-year-old Deaf man believed that the police were following him in order to broadcast his thoughts on their radio.

A 50-year-old Deaf man with long-standing schizophrenia said that thoughts were put into his head by the devil writing a postcard and posting it into his brain.

DELUSIONS

Delusions can be florid or subtle. They must be put into the context of the patient's background and beliefs. The patient may have mistaken ideas and appear delusional.

A Deaf woman described going to a hospital appointment and having "wires put into my head." She had an EEG (electroencephalogram).

Conversely, delusions may be missed because they seem plausible or are attributed to a Deaf person's limited experience. The way the person's belief is held is as important as the content of the belief. This can be especially important for persecutory beliefs. A Deaf person may truly have been treated badly and be sensitive, suspicious, or hostile for understandable reasons. However, these ideas may also be delusional in form and intensity.

A 40-year-old Deaf man with a strong family history of schizophrenia explained that he was being persecuted by his neighbors. He had indeed been the target of their hostility following a sexual offense. However, when he presented to mental health services several years later, he believed they were entering his house and putting water and electricity into his clothing. He described them as sending signals with the street lights where he lived.

There can be delusional memory.

> A 30-year-old Deaf woman demanded dental treatment, as she believed that at the age of 11, teachers at her school had extracted some of her teeth and put in dog's teeth. These new teeth were receiving messages from angels and she wanted them removed. She described in detail the episode at school where the teachers had performed this operation on her. She had some speech and was first seen by general adult services without an interpreter. They arranged a dental appointment for her. She then assaulted the dentist, who refused to extract her teeth.

Closely related to delusional memory is the phenomenon of delusional confabulation.

> A 65-year-old Deaf woman believed that her late mother, who had died 15 years previously, was still alive. She had not been to the funeral but had seen the grave and was assured by all her relatives that her mother had indeed died. If alive she would have been over a hundred. She described ever more elaborate circumstances that explained her mother's disappearance and brought her late mother into any topic of conversation, describing road accidents and floods and historical events where her mother had been present.

HALLUCINATIONS

Many clinicians with Deaf mental health services have described Deaf people with schizophrenia experiencing hallucinations in all modalities, including auditory (Remvig, 1969; Altshuler, 1971; Critchley et al., 1981; Evans & Elliott, 1981; Schonauer et al., 1998; du Feu & McKenna, 1999). The concept of someone who is profoundly Deaf experiencing verbal or nonverbal auditory hallucinations in a schizophrenic illness is a counterintuitive one. It has unsurprisingly been the subject of controversy. Mainstream psychiatrists may fail to ask Deaf patients about these experiences, as they believe they cannot exist. The description of auditory hallucinations in Deaf people by hearing clinicians has been viewed as a cultural misconception (Paijmans et al., 2006). The phenomenology has been investigated in detail, both for the better assessment and treatment of Deaf patients and in the search for the basis for the hallucinatory phenomenon in all schizophrenic patients (Atkinson et al., 2007).

One point of discussion has been whether Deaf people who have auditory hallucinations are only those who had some hearing in early life. Some series have described this (Evans & Elliott, 1981). Others have described auditory hallucinations in those who have always been profoundly Deaf (du Feu & McKenna, 1999). However, it can be extremely difficult to establish whether a Deaf person has ever had any residual hearing, even with some genetic causes of deafness (Bitner-Glindzicz, 2002). Many of the causes of deafness for Deaf adults are unknown and the actual age of onset imprecise.

In clinical practice, there are accounts suggesting that the priority should be to explore the patient's symptoms and to accept her account of what she is experiencing (Briffa, 1999b). No one, Deaf or hearing, who has not actually experienced auditory hallucinations can truly know what they are like; in the same way that psychiatrists accept a patient's accounts of such symptoms as being penetrated by x-rays, they should accept a patient's description of what is troubling him, however counterintuitive. As Jaspers (1912), the father of psychiatric phenomenology, wrote, "the only real observers in the study of hallucinations are the patients, not ourselves" (cited by Remvig, 1969, p. 111).

It is very important to take the history carefully and to enable the patient to describe his experiences as clearly as possible, despite any limitations in his signing. Interpreters and, if necessary, Deaf relay interpreters need to work together if the clinician is not a full signer. When interviewing a Deaf patient, it is not sufficient to ask "Do you hear voices?" because the answer may well be "No, I'm Deaf," or "On one side when I have my hearing aid in," or some other such factual answer. By the time this point in the interview is reached, the clinician should have gained the patient's trust, have maximized communication, and feel able, for example, to ask "I know you are Deaf, but have you ever had the experience that you are sitting quietly, and then you feel alerted to something, but no one is there and you look round and there is nobody and it's like perhaps you are hearing something, and I know you are Deaf but...." " and so on, using some role-play, and the patient will either respond, "No, I have never experienced that," or he will try to explain whatever experience he has had, and then more discussion can take place. Often, patients describe voices or other noises spontaneously. When a Deaf person does disclose auditory phenomena, he will often exhibit relief at being able to describe a disturbing and inexplicable experience to someone who is willing to discuss it and try to understand what is being explained. Despite the fact that Deaf people understand that hearing people communicate with each other by speech, the concepts of loudness, recognizing voices, and local-izing them are less familiar. However, when Deaf people with schizophre-nia experience auditory hallucinations, they often describe them in these ways. A Deaf person experiencing hallucination may go out of the room to locate the voices, or attribute them to parts of his anatomy, to light fixtures or other parts of the room, or to other people, whether present or not. They may identify voices that they could never have heard, including people who are themselves Deaf signers. They may write down what the voices are saying, or obey their instructions to stand or sit. There may be command hallucinations, which can be distressing, and which require further clinical investigation in relation to risk. Deaf people may respond in sign to their hallucinations, but it is important to note that Deaf people may sign to themselves, just as hearing people may talk to themselves.

A young Deaf man described hearing a constant voice talking to him. He said he could not understand what was being said as the voice was speaking in French. He had never been to France and knew no French Sign Language and did not speak or read French. However, he was insistent that he was hearing a voice talking in the French language.

A 65-year-old Deaf man with schizophrenia had moved many times, as he felt he was being persecuted by boys he could hear talking in his apart-ment. He signed eloquently how every time he moved, the voices would fol-low him to his next apartment. He contacted the police, but they suspected him of asking boys to his apartment and investigated accordingly. It was not realized that he was ill. With treatment, the voices of the boys disappeared and he was able to stay in his home.

A 30-year-old Deaf man was tormented by hearing his ex-girlfriend and her new partner arguing in his head. At other times, he believed he saw them following him in a car, although they lived in another country.

A 40-year-old Deaf man with a long history of treated schizophrenia continued to hear his late mother's voice, which he had never heard in life. She gave a continuous running commentary on all actions. He found this very distressing. He felt he had no privacy and that other people could hear his mother's comments.

A 50-year-old Deaf woman with a long history of treated schizophrenia reduced her medication and her symptoms returned. She became disturbed, deluded, and hallucinated. When she was once more treated, her remaining symptom was that when she went into the shower and switched the water on, she heard the voice of a Deaf girl she had known at school many years ago. She had never heard this girl's voice, as they were both Deaf and used sign and not speech. However, she was convinced that the voice she heard was of this girl. This experience was not accompanied by any visual hallucinations.

Other people describe hearing nonverbal sounds, including music.

A Deaf man in his fifties on long-standing treatment for schizophrenia described how he heard "music in the sky." He had never heard music and was perplexed by this experience.

A 40-year-old Deaf woman with schizophrenia constantly heard music. She said it followed her in the street. She described it as Chinese music. She could not explain how she heard the music or how she knew it was Chinese.

Doctors and patients have all struggled to explain these auditory hallucinations in Deaf people. Patients are usually prepared to discuss the voices they hear, and are either perplexed by them or offer various explanations, such as "Sometimes I'm Deaf, sometimes I'm hearing," or "I can hear through Jesus Christ, who allows me to hear," or "I can hear on one side," but may also state, "I am completely Deaf." One woman believed that her voices came to her along the motorway on motorbikes. Most Deaf people who experience hallucinations found their voices distressing, and some would argue with them and ask them to be quiet.

Clinicians' explanations for the auditory hallucinations that Deaf people describe have included the perception of air currents and delusional thinking (Remvig, 1969) and the perception of vibration rather than sound and an element of wish fulfillment (Altshuler, 1971). Some patients who indicate "talking" have been describing visual hallucinations of signing, lip reading, or finger-spelling (Critchley et al., 1981). Recent research has also explored the sub-vocalization hypothesis (Atkinson, 2006; Atkinson et al., 2007).

Deaf people have hallucinations in other modalities, including visual, somatic, and olfactory. Visual hallucinations may be quite complex. Sometimes Deaf people see people signing, and these may be thought of as "auditory hallucinations" in another modality. Other visual experiences are not accompanied by any communication.

> A 40-year-old Deaf woman with schizophrenia was tormented by faces from television programs appearing on the wall in her apartment. They did not communicate with her.

There can be somatic and olfactory hallucinations.

> A 35-year-old Deaf man with schizophrenia living with his mother was becoming increasingly disturbed and his mother was frightened. He had developed a strong recurrent somatic hallucination that his clothes were being made wet, and he blamed his mother for this.
>
> A 40-year-old Deaf man with schizophrenia used to work on a farm. When he relapsed, he had the sensation of the photographs of cows in his farming magazine breathing onto his face. He could feel and smell their breath.
>
> A 40-year-old Deaf woman who lived alone only presented when a friend persuaded her to see the signing psychiatrist, after becoming increasingly isolated and withdrawn. On mental state examination it was apparent she was tormented by sensation of wires pulling on her spine inside her abdomen.

NEGATIVE SYMPTOMS

As for hearing people, negative symptoms of schizophrenia, especially if insidious, can predominate in the presentation.

A 28-year-old Deaf man who had little communication, despite normal intelligence, became increasingly withdrawn. He slept during the day and went for long walks every night. When eventually he presented to services and was treated, he became an active member of the Deaf community and an accomplished artist.

A 65-year-old Deaf man lived alone in the house he had been brought up in. After his parents died, he became increasingly reclusive. It was thought that he was unused to caring for himself, and it was only several years later, when his house had fallen into an extremely neglected state, that psychiatric opinion was sought. He was found to be floridly deluded and hallucinated. He responded well to antipsychotic medication and chose to move to a sheltered apartment.

DELUSIONAL SYNDROMES

Deaf people may present with persistent delusions in an otherwise stable mental state. The delusion may be plausible and cause considerable distress to the Deaf person and his or her family before presenting for help.

A Deaf woman had been bullied at school. This had included being put into an extremely hot shower. Although there were no ongoing physical effects, she remained preoccupied with this. By the time she was seen, several years later, she had a fixed delusion that her skin was boiling.

A 30-year-old Deaf woman living with her family was very self-conscious about her appearance. This developed into an obsession with her hair being cut in a certain way so her fringe was absolutely straight. She became convinced that people were looking at her to check this. She would take hours to get ready to go out and in the end refused to go out at all.

A 40-year-old Deaf man was convinced that he was being stalked by a man he believed his wife was having an affair with. He believed this man followed them on holiday. He complained about his wife's unfaithfulness to all his family, who berated her for her behavior. She was at risk of losing her job because of his repeated visits to her work to check on her. Eventually, delusional jealousy was diagnosed and he responded well to treatment.

Treatment and rehabilitation for Deaf people with schizophrenia will be described in Chapter 20.

SUMMARY

Deaf people with schizophrenia have the same positive and negative symptoms as hearing people. Because of barriers to presentation and diagnosis, the duration of untreated psychosis may be prolonged for Deaf people. Evaluation of thought disorder in sign language, the nature of delusional beliefs, and the exploration of hallucinations all need particular care when a Deaf person is assessed for the presence of a schizophrenic illness.

14 Mood Disorders

INTRODUCTION

The assessment and treatment of mood disorders in deaf people can be one of the most complex tasks clinicians face. People may take years to present, and if their problems are not appropriately assessed in a way that is acceptable and gains their trust, they may not present again and face further years of suffering.

The debate about biological versus reactive depression has continued for decades. Maj (2011) asks, "When does depression become a mental disorder?" and summarizes the different ways to answer this question, all of them highly relevant to deaf people. The contextual approach sees depression illness as a discontinuity, in that the low mood in depression is different from normal sadness in intensity, duration, degree, and expression, even if there is an apparently precipitating event. The qualitative approach describes depressive illness as including symptoms that are clearly abnormal, with psychotic depression as the severest example of all. Maj then describes the pragmatic approach where the boundary between sadness and depression is drawn, as in standard classificatory systems, by criteria that include the number and duration of symptoms to reach a threshold for a diagnosis.

For deaf people, the recognition of depression has a checkered history. Leigh and Pollard (2011) pointed out that mainstream clinicians may dismiss depression as a normal consequence of being deaf. Because deaf people did not initially present to early mental health and deafness services, clinicians like Rainer et al. (1963) concluded that depression was rarer in deaf people. They formulated theories such as deaf people having insufficient ego-development to become depressed, quoting Freud's comment that "the ego wears an auditory lobe." In fact, deaf people with depression may not present to services until intensive liaison strategies are put in place. Identification and assessment of depression in deaf people in the community demonstrate difficulties in ascertainment and standardization of assessment (Connolly et al., 2006).

PREDISPOSING FACTORS FOR DEPRESSION

Deaf people with fluent sign language and satisfying lives can become depressed, just as anyone else in the general population. They then need assessment and treatment by clinicians who understand their culture and can communicate with them in their own language in the same way as any patient deserves.

For many deaf people, the situation is not so straightforward. Their past history and baseline functioning not only make them more at risk for depression, but can also mask depression as part of a continuing situation. A deaf person's life history can predispose him to the development of the negative cognitive triad—negative views about one's self, one's future, and one's surroundings—which renders him vulnerable to depressive illness (Goldberg et al., 1994, p. 200). For example, deaf people may know that their parents had genetic counselling to avoid having another child like themselves.

An only deaf child in the family can feel left out, particularly at mealtimes and occasions like Christmas with the wider family. At mainstream school, the deaf child may feel isolated, excluded, and uncertain about his identity as a deaf person, sometimes feeling like a second-class hearing person. If he or she does badly in literacy and academic achievements, this can lead to low self-esteem.

In adult life, deaf people have described being outsiders in a hearing world. They can be the last to know about family or work information, and may be overlooked for promotions and left out in meetings if no interpreters are booked. Many spend their break times watching hearing people talking, like silent goldfish in a bowl.

Deaf people can be socially excluded, unemployed, or employed at work that does not realize their true potential. This creates situations in which deaf people perceive themselves as powerless; if they have poor coping skills, they can become overwhelmed.

Protective factors include confiding relationships and belonging to a social group. The Deaf community has often been described as a village where people know and care about each other. This may have many benefits, but it can be difficult for people who wish to keep their problems private or who feel stigmatized by them.

Deaf people can therefore have a baseline that includes negative feelings about themselves, and psychological and emotional issues from their childhood. If childhood experiences include emotional, physical, or sexual abuse, their baseline mental state may include features of post-traumatic stress disorder. Relatedly, Brampton (2008) said that "there is no direct line to depression, although a history of abuse is a more direct line than almost any other" (p. 76).

PRECIPITATING EVENTS

Deaf people may take some time to present for help with depression, partly because of difficulties in access to any sort of medical care and partly because of lack of mental health awareness in the Deaf community. When an event does lead to presentation, this may be part of a complex situation with the depression not being immediately apparent.

Family problems or breakdowns in relationships may either precipitate or result from depression.

A 45-year-old deaf married woman with three children was discharged from hospital after a hysterectomy. She became depressed, but this was attributed to the after-effects of the operation. Her husband became impatient with her and did little to help. When the depression was treated, she realized that her husband had always had a negative and unsupportive attitude toward her, and despite relationship counseling, the marriage ended.

A 32-year-old deaf woman became depressed after having her third child. Her own and her husband's family believed that she wasn't coping because of her deafness, as she had not coped well after her previous two children were born. It was eventually realized that she had recurrent post-natal depression, and when she was treated the whole family dynamic, including her marriage, improved.

Transitions can precipitate or expose depression.

A 30-year-old deaf woman who had been educated orally found it difficult to manage at work due to poor literacy. Eventually she went to a bilingual training college, where she was overwhelmed by what she had missed in her life. At the same time, she found it hard to function in a signing environment, as she had no experience of this. She presented after taking a serious overdose.

A 25-year-old woman who had apparently done well with an oral education gained a place in an art and design university program. She had been admitted on the basis of her art portfolio. When she started the program, she found it very difficult to manage, particularly with written material. She gave up the course, returned home, and became increasingly depressed. With further examination, it was found that she was dyslexic and her problems in literacy were not due to educational difficulties arising from her deafness. When her depression was treated, she was given educational support to return to college.

Depression can present after bereavement.

A 40-year-old man became depressed after his wife died suddenly from heart disease. Not only did he have to cope with his grief, he also started looking back over his life and had increasingly intrusive thoughts of abuse in childhood. He had also depended on his wife for help with literacy and felt ashamed that he could not help their children with their homework as she used to do.

> A 59-year-old deaf woman became increasingly hypochondriacal after her husband died from cancer. Information about the severity of his illness had been kept from her by the doctors and by her family. She went for multiple tests and was confused about various medications she had been given. She had developed an agitated depression.

Disclosure of abuse can be associated with a depressive illness. Either the thoughts of the abuse become more intrusive as the depression develops, or disclosure of abuse leads to negative thoughts and painful emotions.

> A 50-year-old deaf man enrolled in a Deaf history course at a university Deaf studies department. When he started to read material related to his time at school, he found that people who had abused him were included in the textbooks. He found it impossible to come to terms with this, dropped out of the course, and became increasingly depressed.

HISTORY AND MENTAL STATE EXAMINATION

As the history is taken, predisposing and precipitating factors will be revealed and the account will be coloured by the patient's mood.

> A young man was describing his family history. He and his brother were the only deaf members of his family. He signed, "I feel very sorry for my mother, poor her, having two deaf children."
>
> A young depressed woman signed, "I wanted a happy life, but that's impossible, I'm deaf."
>
> A depressed deaf man signed, "My children are deaf, God is punishing me."

Other people describe themselves as having always been slow, dim, or stupid. When asked about school experiences, many deaf people at a first interview are unwilling to describe this, and deeper exploration should usually be left until an appropriate time.

The patient's signing may be slow, hesitant, or in a small space. Their linguistic and emotional facial expression may both be subdued and reduced. As for all patients, deaf people know the obvious symptoms of depression, such as low mood and tearfulness, but may not be aware that sleeplessness, poor appetite, irritability, and reduced concentration are also significant. When this is explained, the deaf patients will often feel relieved at the recognition of their thoughts, feelings, and experiences.

Anxiety may be a major feature of depression. It may resolve as the depression improves or may need treatment as the primary disorder.

> A 50-year-old deaf man presented with chronic anxiety and more recent depressive illness. He had been sexually abused at school. He had a supportive wife and only presented for treatment when she became physically unwell herself. His extreme anxiety had prevented him from receiving counseling for the abuse or treatment for his depression.

Psychotic depression can present with delusional thoughts or actions based on them.

> A 35-year-old deaf woman was seen after the death of her mother. She had lost a lot of weight. She believed that her stomach no longer existed and her ribs were moving toward her pelvis.
>
> A 45-year-old deaf man with depression was discharged from a psychiatric hospital without being interviewed with an interpreter. When he arrived home, he became extremely distressed and had to be readmitted immediately. He was deluded that the house was full of dead bodies of his relatives.
>
> A 60-year-old deaf man was an inpatient in Deaf mental health services with severe depression. When he was told there was fish for lunch he thought that there were fish swimming in the unit and that the water level was rising and that everyone would drown. This was despite the fact that the sign for fish to be eaten is in a different signing space from fish swimming freely.
>
> A depressed 50-year-old deaf man became preoccupied with the belief that people thought he was cruel as he recalled looking after his little sister when he was a child and she fell over and hurt her leg.

SUICIDE

There are no definitive studies of suicide in deaf people. Risk factors such as unemployment, poor physical health, alcohol consumption, drug misuse, poor identification and treatment of depression in primary care services, and social isolation are all factors that affect deaf people. Abuse, both sexual and physical, are strong risk factors for suicidal behavior, especially in young people (Bruffaerts et al., 2010). Effective detection and treatment of depression and continuity of care with family and social support all reduce the risk (Appleby, 2012).

BIPOLAR DISORDER AND SCHIZOAFFECTIVE DISORDERS

Many patient series (see Chapter 10) show a low incidence of bipolar disorder in deaf people to the point that Markowitz and Nininger (1984, p. 895) stated, "one might wonder why bipolar disease should spare the deaf." Altshuler (1971) described few patients with hypomania, but Shapira et al. (1999), in a retrospective study, concluded that under-diagnosis may be a significant reason for this. They identified deaf patients with bipolar over a 15-year period, as representing about 40% of the admissions. However, no catchment area figures were given, so the incidence and prevalence in the Deaf population remains unspecified.

In a review of complete cumulative caseloads in mental health and deafness services in Northern Ireland (2003–2010) and the Republic of Ireland (2005–2011), a total of 505 patients (du Feu, 2011) showed a strikingly low incidence of bipolar disorder (three patients). In addition, there were 11 patients diagnosed with schizoaffective disorder. The question arises of whether people with bipolar experiences have been missed because they have presented when their mood was low and were potentially misdiagnosed with depression. Past episodes of restlessness and irritability may have been misunderstood. It is known that in the general population this occurs (Smith et al., 2011). It is also possible that the schizoaffective presentations may at times be manifested either as bipolar disorder or schizophrenia. However, a detailed review of the caseloads in

Ireland of those deaf people with schizoaffective experiences showed that mood incongruent psychotic symptoms coexist with the depressive or hypomanic mood change, often in multiple episodes.

> A 63-year-old deaf woman had recurrent hypomanic and depressive episodes for 30 years. On each occasion the mood change was accompanied by complex religious delusions. She responded to lithium and antipsychotic medication.

When a deaf patient presents with hypomania, it can be quite traumatic, with florid symptoms and irritable behavior, which may even lead to arrest.

> A deaf 35-year-old man was arrested for criminal damage. When he was in prison he set fire to a mattress in his cell and complained that he was being targeted by aliens. His history revealed several episodes of both depression and hypomania. He had committed the offense while he was ill.

In other situations, people have caused chaos within their family before it was realized that they were hypomanic. A person with depression can later become elevated in mood.

> A 50-year-old deaf man was referred for counseling. He had become low in mood and isolated after moving away from his previous proximity to the Deaf center. However, as his depression progressed, it was clear that he was ill. When antidepressants were started he became very elevated in mood and hostile toward his family until his mood could be restabilized.

TREATMENT OF MOOD DISORDER

The treatment of depression in deaf people is described in Chapter 20. It is particularly important that treatment addresses not only the current illness, but the background issues in a person's life that not only predisposes him to illness but could perpetuate it. There are poor outcomes with chronically adverse and interpersonal circumstances (Goldberg et al., 1994).

SUMMARY

As for hearing people, deaf people with depression can present in many ways. Clinicians need to be culturally sensitive and to understand the underlying difficulties that may have been present in the lives of many deaf people, in order to offer assessment and treatment, which may have been long delayed.

15 Other Disorders

EMOTIONAL AND PSYCHOLOGICAL DISORDERS

Emotional and psychological disorders such as anxiety and adjustment disorders are common and affect approximately 15% of the general population at any time (Sharpe et al., 2010). The different diagnoses of generalized or situational anxiety, panic disorder, obsessive-compulsive disorder, behavioral and adjustment disorders all manifest themselves with a combination of emotional cognitive and behavioral disturbance. They are often accompanied by physical symptoms such as sweating, tremor and increased heart rate. People often try to manage their symptoms in ways that in fact make them persist, such as avoidance behaviors or self-medication with alcohol or drugs. They may give their fears intermittent reinforcement by trying to overcome them, for example by going into an anxiety-provoking situation, but then withdrawing in response to the renewed stress.

Belonging to a minority population, Deaf people can be particularly vulnerable to this range of mental health disorders, as they are at risk of stress and uncertainty in their everyday lives. Even going to a shop or using public transportation can give rise to difficulties and misunderstandings due to communication problems, and a sensitive or vulnerable Deaf person can become anxious or avoidant if problems recur. In more serious situations, especially in early life, the foundations can be laid for patterns of sensitivity to stress leading to these disorders. At times of change, uncertainty and a lack of information, confidence, or support can precipitate and prolong adjustment disorders.

The severity of emotional and psychological problems for deaf people may be increased by delays in presentation to services.

POST-TRAUMATIC STRESS DISORDER (PTSD)

According to established classificatory systems, post-traumatic stress disorder is diagnosed when symptoms occur after a significantly traumatic event and subside with time. However, many Deaf people have features of these disorders that have endured for many years. There may have been a single or cluster of traumatic single or repeated events, such as a sexual assault(s) within a short period of time, or there may have been long-term serious stressors, such as physical and sexual abuse for many years at school (Sullivan et al., 2000). There may be isolated symptoms of occasional flashbacks or sensitivity to particular topics. There may also be enduring changes in a person's life, including living a long way away from the place, such as the school, where the events occurred. People may avoid school reunions or even cut themselves off from the Deaf community entirely. There may be lifetime patterns of psychological and behavior difficulties, such as poor self-esteem, anger, or substance abuse. Many Deaf people who present with other mental health problems often have these underlying difficulties (Kessler et al., 2010).

A 30-year-old Deaf man presented with depression and anxiety due to marital problems. He was unable to compromise with his wife, over even minor decisions, as he described being ordered about all his life by his parents and being abused at school. He became very angry with his wife over any disagreement, however trivial. He realized his anger was due to past events, but could not control it. He then disclosed other symptoms of PTSD.

In Ireland, the publicity surrounding the revelation of abuse in residential schools and by the clergy has resulted in these topics becoming openly discussed. This has led to more disclosures, but also to an increased sensitivity about this issue. The Deaf community is small, and people are concerned about their privacy. Many people find relief from disclosure and have been able to attend specialized counseling services with interpreters. This has in turn been a difficult situation for many clients and interpreters, especially if interpreters have Deaf parents and are known to the Deaf patient. Many Deaf people choose not to have these interpreters for abuse counseling, as it is understandably difficult to discuss childhood sexual abuse in the presence of a son or daughter of personal friends, however much they may trust the interpreter in other circumstances.

SUBSTANCE ABUSE

There is no definitive information about the level and nature of alcohol and drug abuse in the Deaf population. Available research suggests that the prevalence is similar to the general population (Austen & Checinski, 2000). There are communication barriers to assessment and treatment programs and few specific treatment services for Deaf people (Guthman et al., 2010). The Deaf community, as in so many areas of knowledge, has reduced access to information about the facts about alcohol and drugs. Social meetings, as for any population group, often revolve about alcohol, either in the Deaf clubs or at other venues. This means that if a Deaf person seeks to give up drinking, it is hard for him or her to avoid social occasions where alcohol is available and may be pressed upon them. While socializing in hearing situations, Deaf people may drink to feel more confident, or because they find it hard to take part in the conversation.

People with severe and enduring mental illness may use drugs or alcohol to self-medicate, and this can worsen their illness.

A young Deaf woman became withdrawn and disturbed and was referred to mental health services. She was using cannabis and heroin and was referred to addiction services. She defaulted from appointments. Several months later, she was admitted urgently to the hospital deluded and hallucinated. Her symptoms improved after withdrawing from the drugs, but she had developed a schizophrenic illness and had been self-medicating the early symptoms.

Alcohol misuse can present as depression.

A 50-year-old Deaf man started drinking to excess after a painful divorce. He met a new partner who was also a heavy drinker. He became more withdrawn and missed work to the point of being suspended. When referred to mental health services, he had all the symptoms of a depressive illness. He was helped to withdraw from alcohol and his depressive symptoms resolved without the need for antidepressant treatment.

Some Deaf people turn to alcohol in an attempt to manage their symptoms of post-traumatic stress disorder following childhood abuse.

A 38-year-old Deaf woman was admitted to the hospital after an alcohol withdrawal fit. She had developed hallucinosis and was transferred to psychiatric care. During her admission, she was visited by her estranged parents and disclosed to them serious abuse while at her residential school. She had been drinking to cope with her ongoing distress from this experience.

Alcohol abuse can present with dementia.

A 60-year-old Deaf man became increasingly self-neglectful and would wander in the streets at night. He had a long history of heavy drinking and was often in conflict with his family. Despite hospital admissions for physical and mental health care, he continued to drink alcohol and died from liver failure.

Deaf people are sometimes protected by their families from the consequences of drug or alcohol misuse.

A 50-year-old Deaf man lost his factory job due to bad time-keeping after his alcohol consumption increased. He was bored and lonely and had poor communication with his family. He would drink at home, watching television in the evenings. His family asked the doctor to explain to him that he should only drink beer and not whisky as a way of containing the problem.

A 30-year-old Deaf man living with his parents felt very negative and angry about his deafness. He coped with this by drinking alcohol and would become violent toward his parents. However, they were convinced that he had a mental health problem that needed treatment and rejected advice to give him the responsibility to deal with his difficulties, which included crashing the family car while under the influence of alcohol.

A 35-year-old Deaf man had become increasingly isolated after leaving boarding school. He had made a few friends but they were heavy drug users and he had used cannabis regularly for 10 years when he was referred to mental health services. His behavior had deteriorated to the point that his mother, with whom he lived, had left the family home to live with a relative. He continued to use cannabis, and his mother returned every day to do his housework and cook him a meal.

PERSONALITY DISORDERS

There is no such thing as a "Deaf personality" (Lane, 1992). Older literature on "the personality of the deaf" makes painful reading. Hearing psychologists and psychiatrists surveyed the damage done to Deaf people by negative social attitudes and severe language deprivation and then built upon their observations to develop theories of a "Deaf personality." They failed to see that the characteristics they described were not due to deafness. Instead, the results of emotional and psychological abuse and neglect led Basilier (1964) to call this cluster of characteristics "surdophrenia," a term that is no longer used. Basilier did, however, go some way to recognize that this was the result of poor language development. "The hearing society and several of its pedagogical systems have tried to foster the young Deaf into our oral world without any ideas of the violence used against the nature of deafness by the enforced restriction of communication" (Basilier, 1964, p. 365). Lesser and Easser (1975), *Personality Differences in the Perceptually Handicapped*, expanded on the writings of Myklebust (1960) and Rainer and Altshuler (1967). Among the personality characteristics they attribute to Deaf people are egocentricity, rigidity, impulsivity without anxiety or guilt, lack of empathy, difficulty in understanding abstract processes and narcissistic character traits. Deaf people were also described as being obstinate, obsessive, and frustrated.

Chess and Fernandez (1980) put these ideas to the test by comparing levels of impulsivity, hyperactivity, rigidity, and suspiciousness between a group of Deaf children affected by rubella and a control group. Their findings indicated that deafness as the only byproduct of rubella did not have a significant effect on the personality of these children. Personality difficulties appeared only in those Deaf children who also had additional impairments. They concluded, on the basis of these findings, that the concept of a specific constellation of behavior symptoms in "the Deaf child" should be abandoned.

These past misconceptions have made it difficult to approach the subject of personality difficulties in individual Deaf people in an appropriate way. Many Deaf patients who have been considered to have personality disorders have turned out to be, for example, depressed or psychotic. Many Deaf people in recorded caseloads have been admitted because of behavior disorders (see Chapter 10) and these had often been attributed to personality problems, particularly in patients who are in the learning- and language-challenged group.

It could be argued that any effort at defining and diagnosing any particular personality disorder in a Deaf person is both unnecessary and counterproductive. A dimensional rather than categorical approach to personality disorders and increasing understanding of the disturbances in arousal, affect, and reality testing that have an impact on interpersonal and social functioning make the consideration of personality difficulties in Deaf people both more understandable and theoretically more treatable (Adshead & Sarkar, 2012). However, some diagnoses of specific personality disorders can be helpful in putting a person's long-term pattern of distress and behavior problems into perspective and enabling a constructive therapeutic approach.

> A Deaf 35-year-old woman had a long history of short-term relationships, alcohol abuse, and transient depression. She was difficult to engage in services. Her parents were alternatively rejecting and overprotective. A diagnosis of borderline personality disorder was made. The social work team, her family, and the mental health team worked together to provide her with a support network in a consistent way. She began to engage in services and accepted an alcohol treatment program.

Sometimes a Deaf person will have an ongoing dependent pattern of behavior. This can obviously arise from the way she has been treated throughout her life, but when this pattern is deeply engrained it can frustrate therapeutic work.

Paranoid personality traits and disorders are more usually associated with deafened people (see Chapter 16), but can also be found in people who are Deaf from early life.

> A 40-year-old Deaf man was permanently estranged from his family, as he was suspicious and angry toward them. Attempts were made to give him a trial of antipsychotic medication. They did not relieve his symptoms and he became angry because he thought the medication had caused people to persecute him. He continued to want help from mental health services to find a way to persuade other people to change their behavior toward him. His anger and aggressive attitude made people frightened of him in the Deaf community, which exacerbated his paranoid personality traits.

Psychopathic personality disorder is important in forensic settings. Difficulties in assessment can mean that Deaf people have been thought to have this personality disorder when in fact they have behavior and relationship difficulties that resulted in aggressive behavior. However, when a Deaf person truly has a psychopathic personality disorder, it is important that this is not missed, particularly if it is associated with violent offending.

SUMMARY

Deaf people have the same range of mental health disorders as the general population, but those with anxiety adjustment disorders, post-traumatic stress, substance abuse, and related problems may not present to services until a precipitating event occurs. The severity of these disorders may have been increased due to a prolonged period before help is sought or provided.

16 Deafened People

As described in Chapter 1, acquired deafness is extremely common and affects up to one in six of the general population and over 70% of people over 70 years old. Particularly in older people, it can be associated with other difficulties such as tinnitus, vertigo, reduced vision, other disabilities, and long-term health problems. These may or may not be linked with the cause of deafness (Action on Hearing Loss, 2011).

Profound acquired hearing loss in adults is qualitatively different from those who retain some residual hearing and can benefit from hearing aids. It is this profoundly deafened population that is the main subject of this chapter.

In the United Kingdom it is estimated that there are more than 85,000 people who have an acquired hearing loss in excess of 95 decibels (Davis, 1989). Etiology may include meningitis, industrial deafness, head injury, and genetic causes such as neurofibromatosis Type 2 (see Chapter 17). However, in the majority of cases there is no positive diagnosis, even after full investigation.

Different causes of acquired profound deafness lead to progressive or sudden hearing loss, and the age and speed of onset affects the mental health of people in different ways. Sudden complete deafness is the most traumatic (McCall, 1976). Jack Ashley (1922–2012), the British member of parliament who lost his hearing suddenly after an operation, wrote that deafness "destroys normal communication, robs people of their confidence and imprisons them in a cocoon of silence" (Ashley, 1992, p. 330).

Whether sudden or gradual, acquired profound deafness can have adverse effects on mental health. The "Hidden Lives" report by Link and the University of Greenwich (September 2005) described loneliness and frustration as major effects. The report also noted that the deafened person's family was affected as well. They felt frustrated and cut off from their relative. The deafened person tended to become dependent on one or two people to act as intermediaries, and this set up a pattern of dependency, poor confidence, withdrawing from social contacts, isolation, and depression.

Deafness can be regarded unsympathetically in society, and deafened people must endure negative attitudes.

> A deafened woman was trying to buy a train ticket. As her speech was unaffected, the ticket attendant did not accept that she couldn't understand what he was saying. He became irritated and asked her to wait until he had "served the normal people."

Employment can be adversely affected, with people changing jobs or taking early retirement. People may experience the stages of bereavement as they lose their hearing, moving from denial to anger, then from bargaining and depression toward acceptance. Auditory rehabilitation services encourage people to accept their deafness, giving them practical training and experience, usually in groups, to overcome not only communication difficulties but also their feelings of hopelessness. Deafened people need confidence and assertiveness to acknowledge their deafness to others and to establish effective communication. Lip reading, as one of the communicative methods that deafened people often try to acquire, is difficult and inexact. Even if they have attended classes, many deafened people still find it hard, especially with unfamiliar people or males with facial hair that blocks visual access to their lips.

Profoundly deafened people can benefit from many of the technological and environmental aids for people with more moderate forms of deafness (see Chapter 1). They cannot benefit from hearing aids, but cochlear implants can restore usable hearing, although these are not always suitable or effective. After surgery for acoustic neuromas, brainstem implants can sometimes be used. They are not usually able to give full speech perception, but they give some environmental sounds and are an aid to lip reading. It is hard for deafened people to monitor their own voices, and practice is needed for control of speech production, especially for volume and intonation. People with cochlear implants may be able to use loop systems and understand on the phone or hear the radio, but speech discrimination may not be sufficient without the visual clues from lip reading. Usually music is not usefully amplified, as the harmonies cannot be fully expressed by the limited number of electrodes, though familiar music may be recognized.

MENTAL HEALTH PROBLEMS IN DEAFENED PEOPLE

Depression and Anxiety

People who are deafened slowly over a number of years have time to adapt to their progressive loss, but there is a threshold when usable hearing for speech disappears, and this is a time of major adjustment. Deafened people often cling to their hearing identities and feel that they have lost everything. A fictional character in David Lodge's novel *Deaf Sentence* (2009, p. 19) sees his deafness "as a kind of pre-death, a drawn-out introduction to the long silence into which we will all eventually lapse." Famously, Beethoven wrote, "For me, there can be no relaxation in human society, no refined conversations and no mutual confidences. I must live quite alone and may creep into society only as often as sheer necessity demands; I must live like an outcast" (Heiligenstadt Testament, 1802, in Grant 1987, pp. 71–73).

It is ironic that those for whom hearing aids are no help and who do not wear them thus render their deafness invisible. They therefore can be thought to be rude, stupid, inattentive, or, if their speech is affected, to be loud or disturbed. Deafened people risk either asking people to repeat trivial statements, or missing important information. This can also be frustrating for the speaker, and Deafened people are constantly being told, "Oh, it doesn't matter," or, "I will tell you later." They can be unaware that somebody has even spoken to them. Deafened people need both confidence and concentration and both are affected by the constant effort of trying to lip read, and having to manage as if in a foreign country.

It is not surprising that anxiety and depression are common. The Link Report (2005) showed that depression was almost five times higher than the national average, and anxiety levels nearly two and a half times higher. Fellinger et al. (2005) studied a total of 373 members of a Hard of Hearing Association and found that oral deaf people showed greater levels of anxiety, depression, and interpersonal sensitivity than either hearing people or Deaf people who use sign language. Deafened people are cut off from their hearing culture, but usually do not identify with the Deaf community. Among its other effects, depression reduces the concentration that is needed for lip reading. Depression and anxiety make it harder for deafened people to deal with negative attitudes and the uncertainty of many social situations. Deafened people also have to cope with the consequences of misheard or missed information.

A 48-year-old deafened man with depression reported to his psychiatrist, in some distress, that he had been diagnosed with syphilis. He had in fact been tested for syphilis as part of the screening for the cause of his acquired deafness, but he did not have the disease.

A severely deaf 60-year-old woman who had numerous operations on her ears, the most recent about 10 years previously, thought she had been told that she should not fly to see her grandchildren in England. She was therefore very cut off from them as she could not face the long journey by road and ferry from Ireland. However, it transpired that she had been advised only to refrain from flying for a few weeks after her last operation and not permanently. She had missed this vital part of the advice given to her.

A 50-year-old deafened woman was criticized by her optician for having refused retinal photography at her previous appointment. She had been asked about this from behind in the darkened testing room and was unaware that the test had been offered.

Profound acquired deafness is especially hard to cope with if a person has never learned to read and write.

> A deafened man who had always done manual work and had never learned literacy became extremely isolated, and his speech became more difficult to understand. He was very sad at the loss of his hearing. He explained "that he used to be able to hear the grass grow."

DELUSIONAL DISORDER

It is commonly assumed by both psychiatrists and the general public that deafness is associated with paranoia in the sense of suspiciousness, persecutory ideas, and delusions. Kraepelin (1915) described "Der Verfolgungswahn der Schwerhörigen" (delusions of persecution of the hard of hearing). Zeckel, a psychoanalyst, stated, "the Deaf person is commonly believed to become peculiar in the course of time. It is assumed he easily becomes suspicious, irritable and seclusive" (Zeckel, 1950, p. 322). Although the circumstances of all forms of deafness mean that it is understandable that Deaf or deafened people might feel sensitive about others' attitudes toward them, there is no evidence that people profoundly Deaf from early life have a higher incidence of persecutory delusions than the general population. However, for acquired deafness, particularly in older adults, there are studies that show that these syndromes are indeed more common. Cooper (1976) summarized previous research and showed that a cohort of patients with delusional persecutory syndromes compared with those with affective disorder showed an over-representation of long-standing deafness. It is suggested that the psychological and social consequences of deafness and the interference of hearing loss with attention, perception, and communication could be modes of connection between deafness and delusional states. There has yet to be a prospective study looking at premorbid personality, progressive hearing loss, and development of delusional symptoms or illnesses.

> A 66-year-old woman with a 20-year history of severe deafness coped by controlling conversations. She could not lip read and gave up trying to do so. Her family increasingly ignored her monologue until she started accusing her husband of an affair with an elderly neighbor. Her accusations became increasingly bizarre. Eventually her delusional illness was diagnosed and treated.

Acquired deafness from head injury causing memory problems can increase the risk of persecutory symptoms.

> A 35-year-old doctor lost his hearing when he sustained a head injury in a traffic accident. He made a good recovery but never returned to practice as his memory was affected. He became increasingly suspicious and accused people of stealing things he had mislaid.

MUSICAL HALLUCINATIONS

Musical hallucinations have been reported in acquired deafness. Griffiths (2000) found spontaneous activity in a cortical module of the brain, which is usually involved in the normal perception of patterns in segmented sounds. Functional imaging data support the hypothesis that such a module is physically realized in a distributed cortical network distinct from the primary auditory areas of the brain.

> A 76-year-old deafened widow reported musical hallucinations after cochlear implantation. These occurred before her implant was switched on. She found them both pleasant and upsetting. She heard her late husband's favorite music, and this intensified her feelings of bereavement.
>
> A 60-year-old deafened woman described musical hallucinations after cochlear implantation. She could "request" choral music or opera. She also developed elaborate somatic hallucinations of touch and sexual assault and became increasingly deluded. She responded well to antipsychotic medication but the musical hallucinations persisted.

DEMENTIA

A prospective study (Lin et al., 2011) has shown that hearing loss is independently associated with dementia, including Alzheimer's, after adjustment for factors such as diabetes, smoking, and hypertension. The risk of all causes of dementia increased with the severity of the hearing loss in a cohort with recorded normal hearing and cognitive levels before the study began. The cohort was studied over 11 years, and the results showed that more than one-third of the risk of dementia in individuals older than 60 years of age was associated with hearing loss. As pure tone audiometry was used, it was not thought that the hearing loss was caused by higher levels of auditory cortical processing declining with the onset of the dementia. It was postulated that hearing loss might have been causally related to dementia through exhaustion of cognitive reserve in maintaining communication while hearing deteriorated, at the expense of other cognitive processes such as working memory. This apparent decline in cognitive reserve could expose earlier clinical expression of dementia. The other major mechanism could be through the hearing loss leading to social isolation in older adults. Decline in social networks is a known risk factor for dementia (Polidori et al., 2010), and as the environment is impoverished the dementia emerges. This raises the question of reducing these risks in deafened people by promoting proactive aural rehabilitation.

SUMMARY

People with acquired deafness, even if it is severe or profound, do not usually learn to sign or identify with the Deaf community. However, they may find it increasingly difficult to maintain their confidence in a hearing world and are at risk of social isolation, anxiety, and depression. Mental health problems may be missed, as they are attributed to the effect of the hearing loss.

17 Deafblind People

Deafblindness refers to the combination of deafness and visual impairment, which affects a person's communication, mobility, and information acquisition. There are widely varying degrees of deafblindness (Action on Hearing Loss, 2011). Some people have been deafblind from birth; others have acquired deafblindess in later life. Some people have congenital visual impairment and then their hearing declines. Others have been partially or profoundly Deaf from early life and then their vision declines. Other people have acquired both sight and hearing loss in adulthood or old age. A recent survey in the United Kingdom (Sense for Deafblind People, 2010) shows that the deafblind population has been significantly underestimated and is set to rise with an aging population. The present rate for people who have both visual and hearing loss in the United Kingdom is 572 per 100,000, a total of 356,000 in a population of about 60 million. Sixty-two percent of deafblind people are over 70 years of age and 6% are under 20. There are about 23,000 of this group in the United Kingdom who are totally deafblind.

Deafblind people have complex problems and risk having reduced access to services. People with visual impairment rely on their hearing, and Deaf people rely on their sight, so the difficulties of deafblind people are compounded. People who have acquired deafblindess experience disablement repeatedly as they reach thresholds with their sight and hearing and lose reading, music, independent travel, and face recognition.

People who have visual impairments are, like Deaf people, a heterogeneous group. This is captured by Kuusisto's account in the following narrative: "No two blind people are alike.... Blindness is often perceived by the sighted as an either/or condition: one sees or one does not see, but a blind person experiences a series of veils: I stare at the world through smeared and broken window panes" (Kuusisto, 1998, p. 5).

There are parallels in the history of blind people with deaf peoples' experience. Blind people were often in institutional care and their potential was underestimated. They were taught manual work. In parallel with the banning of sign language, the Braille library at the Paris school for the Blind was burned by the sighted director, Armand Dufau, in 1842, as he believed it made blind people too independent. Fortunately, the Braille method was preserved by the students of the school, who managed to save enough books.

Helen Keller (1880–1968) was deafblind from an early age due to meningitis. She became world famous for her academic achievements and inspiring life. She wrote, "I have found deafness to be a much greater handicap than blindness.... Deafness cheats many of their birthright to knowledge" (1948, in Grant, 1987, p. 37). The individual life journeys of deafblind people depend a great deal on the age and speed of onset of their deafness and blindness and on their communication. They need both acceptance and resilience.

CAUSES OF DEAFBLINDNESS

Deaf children have an increased risk of sight problems (Siatkowski et al., 1993). Many children who are deafblind to a significant degree from birth or early life also have other disabilities, including intellectual disabilities. There are rare genetic causes of early deafblindess, including CHARGE syndrome (which includes heart defects) (Kiani and Miller, 2010), but the main causes are prematurity, birth anoxia, and rubella.

If a mother is infected with rubella during the first 10 weeks of pregnancy, 90% of the babies can have effects, including deafness, sight problems, heart problems, and intellectual disability. If the infection takes place at 10 to 16 weeks of pregnancy, 33% of the babies are affected, generally just by deafness (Sense for Deafblind People, 2010). Other infections, such as cytomegalovirus, also cause early deafness with a risk of sight problems. The Sense website (www.sense.org.uk) gives details of many rarer causes.

USHER SYNDROME

For people who have been Deaf from early life, Usher syndrome is the most common cause of progressive sight loss (Picard, 2004). About 5% of people who are profoundly Deaf from early life have Usher syndrome Type 1 (Bloom et al., 1983). This is an autosomal recessive genetic condition that, in addition to early profound deafness, causes progressive retinitus pigmentosa (RP). This leads to night blindness, tunnel vision, and eventual severe or total blindness in middle age. There are also balance problems from early life. Usher Type 2, which accounts for 3–6% of hard of hearing children, refers to children who have a moderate to severe hearing loss and normal balance; visual problems start in teenage years and the hearing loss also progresses. People with Type 3 Usher have normal hearing at birth and sometimes develop balance problems later. Hearing loss and night blindness start in early adolescence and progress. Type 1 and Type 2 Usher account for 90–95% of cases; Type 3 is rare. Other syndromes associated with retinitis pigmentosa can also cause deafness (Mills & Calver, 1987).

NEUROFIBROMATOSIS TYPE 2

Neurofibromatosis Type 2 (NF2) is an autosomal dominant genetic condition affecting chromosome 22q, but over half the cases are due to new mutations. It occurs in about one in 35,000 people (The Neurofibromatosis Association, 2001). It is a disease of connective tissue that causes benign tumors on nerves, particularly the auditory nerve, and often the optic nerves, as well as in the spine and on peripheral nerves. Masses may also occur in the brain. People with NF2 can lose their hearing and their sight in step-wise fashion and also become physically disabled due to peripheral and spinal lesions.

DEAFBLINDNESS AND MENTAL HEALTH

The challenge to everyday life and the physical and mental well-being of deafblindness clearly presents risks to mental health. Deafblind people, even if the associated cause has also led to some intellectual disability, can, with appropriate assistance, lead satisfying lives, but sensory barriers and negative attitudes put many obstacles in their path (Hassinen, 2010). Much depends on the age and the speed of onset of the sensory losses. Communication is a key issue (White, 2001). People with Usher Type 1 often use sign language and identify themselves with the Deaf community. People with Usher Type 2 and 3 and with NF2 will have had useful hearing for speech, and as their hearing deteriorates, they can benefit from hearing aids and cochlear or brainstem implants. Like most deafened people, they rarely learn to sign or identify with the Deaf community (see Chapter 16). However, as their hearing and sight deteriorate, lip reading becomes more difficult and monitoring their own speech becomes harder. They are likely to have good literacy and can use enlarged print and Braille. For people who are signers whose sight then deteriorates, signing can be used in a progressively smaller frame as the tunnel vision develops, and then hands-on signing can be used, in which the deafblind person holds the signer's hands. Finger-spelling can also be used on the hand with the deafblind alphabet.

Visual environments should be adapted so that there is good contrast of edges and steps and clear lighting. Mobility training with a guide dog or a long cane is important. Communicator guides work with Deafblind people in ways that are individualized for each person.

However many medical, personal, and practical aids are provided, a person needs to have the concentration and confidence to use them, and deafblind people are at risk of anxiety, fear, panic, depression and social withdrawal. Communication can be slow, and other people may feel unskilled, frustrated, or impatient.

MENTAL HEALTH OF DEAFBLIND PEOPLE

Usher Type 1

Bailey and Miner (2010) have written about psychotherapy with deafblind clients, particularly people with Usher. They identify key issues: the effect on clients when they receive the diagnosis; the age at which the person becomes aware of his diagnosis; whether people receive accurate information; and whether they receive support from their family and other people with Usher syndrome. The authors also place a large significance on whether the people themselves had received the information at the same time as their parents or whether this information had been withheld from them. Family communication was of vital importance.

A young man with Usher was abusing alcohol. He felt lonely and frustrated as his sight deteriorated, but he did not have full information about what was happening to him. His mother did not want him to know the progressive nature of his sight loss as she felt he could not cope with it.

A Deaf teenage girl was being bullied at school and was losing her confidence. Her mother did not want to discuss the diagnosis of Usher with her, though she was fully aware of the implications herself. The mother told the doctor that she had told her daughter that she was going to go blind and her daughter had reacted by saying, "Don't be stupid." Neither of them was able to come to terms with or discuss between them what the diagnosis meant.

A 45-year-old woman lived with her elderly mother and attended a local intellectual disability day center where she mainly sat on her own and did craft work. Her sight continued to deteriorate. She had developed cataracts as well as retinitis pigmentosa. When the cataracts were removed, her sight improved sufficiently for her to start using sign language again in time to adapt to hands-on signing.

Many people with Usher lead full lives and give mentoring support to other affected family members or to other people with Usher who live in the community. However, in some families there is denial of the difficulties, and young people can be overwhelmed.

> A young girl with Usher was diagnosed while away at school. Her family never came to terms with the diagnosis, and she herself did not understand what was happening. She returned to the family home and became increasingly withdrawn. She lost her sign language and rarely left the house.

People with Usher can become depressed, particularly at thresholds with their sight loss such as becoming unable to read or follow sign language. Clinical depression can be missed as the low mood is seen as a natural reaction to the person's difficulties and can be attributed to bereavement.

> A middle-aged woman with Usher became depressed. She lived with her elderly mother, who was terminally ill. Her low mood was thought to be reactive due to the difficulties in her circumstances, but when she became suicidal she was admitted for treatment. Afterward her mood became hypomanic and it was clear she had bipolar disorder. After treatment she was able to return to the family home to care for her mother and coped well through her eventual bereavement.

A specific type of psychosis can occur in Usher (Hallgren, 1959). This may also be missed, either because of communication difficulties or because a person's distress is thought to be due to his or her sensory deprivation experiences or to an extreme reaction to the sensory loss.

> A man with Usher coped well with independent life, but when a close friend died he became deluded about the person's ashes, thinking that his friend was actually still alive in the urn. He was considerably distressed by this. He also was hallucinating neighbors making noises at night. He then started knocking on the walls himself, causing a complaint from them, which brought him to psychiatric attention. His psychotic breakdown was appropriately treated.
>
> A man with Usher became increasingly agitated and frightened of going out. He was previously quite independent with a guide dog. He had become deluded that the police radios were being picked up by his guide dog and therefore he could not trust the dog to take him out.

USHER TYPE 2

People with Type 2 Usher syndrome may not realize that their deafness and sight loss are connected and may have different explanations for each for them. The diagnosis may then be missed or delayed.

A middle-aged man with progressive deafness thought that he was losing his sight due to an accident. He attributed his hearing loss to infections as a child. He presented to psychiatric services deluded and hallucinated, living in an apartment on his own. He felt that the government was listening to him and he was also having somatic and visual hallucinations. After treatment of his illness, his sight and hearing were reassessed and it was apparent that he had retinitus pigmentosa. Type 2 Usher was diagnosed.

An elderly lady was widowed and was finding it very hard to cope. She had poor sight for some time, and then her hearing was markedly reduced. Usher Type 2 was diagnosed. She was admitted to residential care after treatment of her depression but continued to be very withdrawn. The visiting psychiatrist found that her own hearing aids were picking up interference in the home from electric appliances. This had meant that the elderly woman's residual hearing was of no help to her. She was moved to a part of the residence where her hearing aids worked more clearly and her confidence improved.

Sometimes because of the restricted opportunities of people with sight or hearing problems, the diagnosis of Usher Type 2 and the associated psychosis are missed.

A partially Deaf middle-aged man presented at the homeless outreach service. He had been living alone in poor circumstances for several years. He had been taken into care as a child when his mother was admitted to a psychiatric hospital, apparently with schizophrenia. His self-care deteriorated as his alcohol consumption increased, and he was referred for a cognitive assessment. He had incoherent speech. He was preoccupied with a perceived inability to breathe properly and believed that he needed an operation on his nose. He had delusional ideas about film stars coming to his apartment. On assessment, Usher syndrome Type 2 was diagnosed and his psychotic illness was treated. He no longer felt in need of an operation. His alcohol consumption stopped. He had normal intelligence.

NEUROFIBROMATOSIS TYPE 2 (NF2)

As described above, people with NF2 have an unpredictable course of illness and face sequential losses. Sometimes the tumors begin in the brain, and people will present with psychiatric symptoms before the diagnosis is made. Other people have understandable reactions of anxiety and depression and undergo a grief reaction as the illness progresses. Occasionally, the illness can be associated with psychotic symptoms, which are easily missed as they can be attributed to the accumulating sensory loss.

A young woman with NF2 had lost her hearing and was starting to lose her sight. She refused to go out. This was thought to be due to her difficulties in communication, which had made it hard for her to be with anybody except her immediate family. However it also transpired that she had complex hallucinations and delusions about people recording her thoughts and planning to attack her; when these were treated, she was able to take part in an active rehabilitation program and started to learn sign language.

SUMMARY

People who are deafblind are a heterogeneous group. Their deafness and sight loss may have occurred early or later in life, separately or together. Language and communication needs and preferences vary greatly among individuals. Mental health problems may be missed or misdiagnosed if clinicians do not take each person's subjective experience into account.

18 Mental Health of Older Deaf Adults

INTRODUCTION

Acquired deafness increases with age. Over 70% of people over 70 have some hearing loss (Action on Hearing Loss, 2011). It may be hidden, denied, or undetected. It may be combined with physical illness, sight, and mobility problems. This chapter is about older Deaf adults who have been profoundly Deaf from early life. For older people with acquired deafness, Chapter 16 should be consulted.

Deaf adults, as for hearing people, can continue to lead independent and satisfying lives into old age. However, older Deaf sign language users may be vulnerable and find it hard to have access to appropriate assessment, treatment, and care. They can be at risk of isolation. They may use older sign language, which is not easily understood by younger interpreters, or they may have always had limited sign due to past oralist educational policies. If isolated, their sign language may have fallen into disuse even without any mental health problems. Older Deaf signers may not have fluent written English, and this can be extremely deceptive if writing is used for communicating with them. Any sight problems added to the deafness will compound communication barriers (see Chapter 17). Mobility problems such as arthritis or Parkinsonism (Tyrone et al., 1999) will interfere with sign language production. A stroke in a Deaf person can not only produce motor problems, but can also result in a receptive or expressive sign dysphasia (Atkinson et al., 2005; Marshall et al., 2007).

The common mental health problems of old age all occur in Deaf older adults, and there are different client groups. Some are "graduates" from adult general or intellectual disability services, but most are newly presenting patients with confusional states, mood disorders, paranoid psychosis, or dementia. In addition, there are older Deaf people who have suffered long-term social isolation, either at home, living with families who do not sign, or in residential services where they are the only Deaf person. Some older Deaf adults have been in psychiatric hospitals without a diagnosis for years or even decades without access to sign language.

"GRADUATES"

Older Deaf signers who have been in mental health services from earlier life include those who have been in general adult services and in intellectual disability services. They may present with continuing illnesses such as schizophrenia or depression, or may go on to present with dementia in addition to their preexisting mental health problems. Some people present or re-present to services because of increased physical problems or changes in circumstances.

A 65-year-old Deaf woman had a long history of anxiety and depression. She relied heavily on her husband for support, and after his death she became increasingly reluctant to go out. She had not learned sign language as a child and was less confident in going to the Deaf Club on her own than she had been with her fluently signing husband.

A 70-year-old Deaf woman with mild intellectual disability had lived with her brother, but after his death she needed increasing levels of support. She was admitted to residential care after a fall at home.

A 60-year-old Deaf woman with mild intellectual disability had become increasingly isolated, as her Deaf husband did not like to mix with the Deaf community. Eventually, she was found in a distressed state in her house. Her husband was dead in bed, having died several days earlier.

DEPRESSION

Depression can present for the first time in old age.

A 65-year-old woman presented with a first episode of depression. She had recently disclosed serious abuse at her residential school, which she had felt unable to do while her elderly mother was still alive. She found it very difficult to cope with the emotions this disclosure had released and had become increasingly withdrawn, sleepless, and self-neglecting. She responded well to antidepressant medication and counseling. She was also helped to discuss her feelings with her family.

PSYCHOTIC ILLNESS

Older adults can present with psychotic illnesses, as the following cases illustrate.

A 75-year-old Deaf widow was tormented by hallucinated noises from her neighbor's house and had withdrawn into a single room in her house in an effort to avoid them. Her self-care deteriorated to the point that there were rats in the house, but she was unable to hear them. She received appropriate help after neighbors complained about the infestation.

A 65-year-old Deaf man had become deluded after his Deaf wife was killed in a traffic accident five years previously. He believed that aliens had taken her body. He withdrew from his deaf Club activities and spent a lot of time writing letters to newspapers about his wife's death. By the time he received treatment, his dog was dead and mummified. He kept it on the stairs in his house to protect him from the aliens.

A 60-year-old Deaf woman in residential care was referred to Deaf mental health services as she was refusing to eat. When she was assessed, she described seeing the ghosts of her parents. She then explained that she was also hearing them talk to her and they were telling her not to eat. When she was treated, she signed to the psychiatrist, "It's quiet now, I have peace, thank you."

INSTITUTIONALIZATION

Some older Deaf people have been in long-term institutional care.

An 80-year-old Deaf lady had been put in a psychiatric hospital by her mother at the age of 20 after her father had died, and had remained there ever since. The elderly lady explained that her father had been very fond of her, but her mother was ashamed of having a Deaf person in her family.

A 75-year-old Deaf woman had been admitted at the age of 60 to a long-stay psychiatric hospital when her Deaf husband died. When she was eventually visited, she was delighted to see people she could sign with. She had only occasional contact with sign for many years, and her receptive sign was better than her expressive sign. As the visitors left the ward, they turned to wave and they saw her signing to herself, weeping. She was later transferred to an old people's residence for Deaf people, where she was very happy and met old school friends.

DEMENTIA

Dementia in older Deaf people, as for all older people, may be of insidious onset and only present after, for example, bereavement. It may present with depression or agitation. It may be missed or misdiagnosed when an older Deaf person is not in a signing environment. The study *Dementia and Deafness* (Allan et al., 2005) explored these issues and gave the following example.

> One of the project workers visited a Deaf British sign language user in a residential service where no one could sign, and as she sat and signed to the client, one of the staff came in and told her they were amazed to see the person communicating. They did not realize he was profoundly Deaf and thought his seeming unresponsiveness and lack of engaging in communication with staff was a result of dementia.

OFFENDING

Older Deaf people can present to services because of offending behaviors. There may be historical offense disclosure, or the offending may be recent, often involving inappropriate behavior.

> A Deaf man with a long history of poor social functioning and alcohol abuse developed physical health problems when he was 65, and he was admitted to residential care where he was the only Deaf resident. He touched vulnerable female residents inappropriately. Their relatives reported him to the police. His behavior was attributed to a lack of knowledge of social norms and communication difficulties. When the problems persisted, he was transferred to a single-sex high-support residential service.

ASSESSMENT

In the history taking and clinical assessment of older Deaf people, it is important to pay close attention to the aspects of past history, personality, abilities, and medical history, which provide the baseline essential for diagnoses. For many older Deaf patients, past history may not be available, and a baseline of previous level of functioning may be deceptive. A person's education and general knowledge may have been restricted regardless of their level of intelligence. Limited communication from early language deprivation may affect the assessment process, as described in Chapter 11. A Deaf person living with relatives who can sign, such as grown children, is in a better position of being understood. However, a relative may find himself acting as both the interpreter and the informant, and serious difficulties can arise that involve conflict of roles. The relative's interpretation may be comfortable for the patient and ease communication, but the Deaf person may not want to upset her relative. At the same time, the son or daughter may be in a position of interpreting for the parent, yet having to explain to the doctor the difficulties that have arisen. The relative's interpretation may make the patient appear more confident, articulate, and capable than she is. The patient may not want to discuss problems in front of her relative, and the relative may be tempted to lead the patient. This can lead to dilution or confusion of information. If the diagnosis is either made or missed under these circumstances, it can create frustration and relationship difficulties for all concerned. Therefore, an independent interpreter should be used, even if the signing relative is a professional interpreter. Further details about mental health interpreting can be found in Chapter 10.

As for the general population, physical problems present with or instead of psychiatric symptoms in older people. A Deaf person may find it hard to go out because of mobility problems, but the Deaf Club may be the only opportunity they have to meet people and to sign. Older Deaf people travel a long way to visit Deaf Clubs. Other members may be unable to visit the older Deaf person at home and the individual then becomes extremely isolated quickly. When one partner of a Deaf married couple dies, the sudden isolation may be complete.

Deaf people can find it hard to see and communicate with their family doctor, and difficulties with medication can rapidly escalate. As for all older Deaf people, physical illness can be missed. Intoxication by prescribed drugs or polypharmacy can occur. Mistakes or confusion in medication adherence can rapidly lead to problems. Older Deaf people are at added risk of not understanding their medication if they have difficulty with written English. If they run out of medication or are over-medicating, it is hard for them to ask for help. Physical illness can be undetected or attributed to psychiatric problems in older Deaf people who have long-standing mental health problems and poor communication (see also Chapter 12).

Once the history has been taken as clearly as possible, the mental state examination will include a cognitive assessment. This issues surrounding cognitive assessment in Deaf sign language users have been discussed in Chapter 12. For elderly people, this can be even more complex. Because of the objective difficulties in establishing a baseline of functioning and general knowledge, identifying when these have deteriorated becomes challenging. Even Deaf people who have led full lives may not know common information, such as dates of wars or names of political leaders. In particular, the mini mental state examination (Folstein et al., 1975) is inappropriate for Deaf sign language users. If a older Deaf person does not read a newspaper or subtitles on television, either because of sight problems or because of poor literacy, he may not be in a position to know the exact day and date for a series of questions. He may have been brought to the appointment and not know where he is. He may have recently moved and may be unaware of his present address. The naming objects test involves the production of sign language handshapes, which in fact give some visual clues, and the person may gesture the shapes of the objects rather than producing their names. The spelling test is obviously misleading, and the English language tests are not applicable. To ask Deaf people to close their eyes is in fact quite threatening, as they rely on their sight for communication.

> A depressed 80-year-old Deaf lady who was hospitalized for physical reasons was asked to do the mini mental state examination. Despite the objections of the interpreter, she was then wrongly diagnosed with dementia.

TREATMENT

The assessment and treatment of older Deaf adults can be complex. Baseline information may be absent or misleading. Presentation may be delayed, and assessment can easily be inappropriate. Deaf older people can be subject to misunderstandings and negative attitudes.

One elderly Deaf signing man in a hospital asked for an interpreter, and a nurse responded by writing, "It's never too late to learn to lip read."

An elderly Deaf man was informed of his wife's death in the hospital by fax. He could not read it very well and he was uncertain what to do. He had long-standing mental health problems and happened to come the next day to a routine appointment. When the doctor asked about his wife, he signed, "I think she's dead, I am not sure."

An elderly Deaf lady with dementia was transferred to a nursing home. The staff reported that she was punching herself in the face. In fact, she was repeatedly using her regional sign (a closed fist, rested against the cheek) for "home," and she was saying "home, home, home!"

A Deaf lady with late onset schizophrenia was having intrusive auditory hallucinations. Her psycho-geriatrician had not treated these, as he thought it was normal for Deaf people to have these due to "sensory deprivation."

SUMMARY

Older Deaf adults who use sign can develop any of the mental health problems of late life. Careful assessment is vital. Appropriate treatment of older Deaf adults includes maximizing their communication and giving them appropriate social support. Deaf organizations and Deaf support workers can play a key role. For too long Deaf elders have been subject to "silent discrimination" (Eastwood, 2002).

19 Legal and Forensic Issues

INTRODUCTION

Deaf people can be at a serious disadvantage with regard to many aspects of the law. These include difficulties with informed/valid consent to medical procedures; capacity/competence with regard to property, wills, and place of residence; and in the criminal justice system as victims, witnesses, and offenders. In all these circumstances, mental health professionals may be invited to provide reports. When a Deaf person has restricted language, intellectual disability, or a mental health problem, or all of these, this task can be challenging.

CAPACITY/COMPETENCE

This is the underlying issue with regard to informed consent, undertaking legal transactions, and fitness to plead in the criminal justice system.

In each of these situations, the Deaf person must be able to understand relevant information, retain this information, assess benefits and adverse consequences related to each decision, and communicate his or her decision accordingly. There are many ways in which these procedures can break down. For Deaf people, in addition to the usual considerations of cognitive functioning and mental health, there are also all the factors associated with restricted communication, poor general knowledge, and vulnerability. Many Deaf people have been unused to making decisions, as they have been unduly protected by others and have not realized that they could have choices.

If, despite appropriate methods of communication and explanation, a Deaf person is found to lack capacity for informed consent or legal decisions, a formal assessment needs to be made. The Mental Capacity Act 2005 gives good guidance to this process in England and Wales (Church & Watts, 2007). There is an assumption of capacity unless demonstrated otherwise. A person must be enabled to have maximum autonomy. If the person is found not to have capacity, a decision should be made in his or her best interests with the least restrictive option. Capacity is assessed with regard to individual decisions, and it is decided on a balance of probabilities.

INFORMED CONSENT

Doctors have the legal and ethical responsibility to explain the options and the benefits and drawbacks of each procedure and any risks involved. The doctor also needs to listen to the patient's views and to share information in a way the patient can understand. However, many doctors believe that the written discussion with a Deaf person is sufficient, and they may not be aware that a sign language user has limited written English and would not understand many medical terms. Even if an interpreter is employed, the Deaf person's sign may be insufficient for technical information to be conveyed. Also, limitations in the Deaf person's education, knowledge, and experience may mean that concepts are unfamiliar. The best way to do this is to ask the Deaf person to explain back the information that he or she has been given. This often makes clear that the information needs to be represented in a more understandable form.

In 2003 Congress of the European Society for Mental Health and Deafness in Austria issued the Bad Ischl declaration calling on European governments to recognize the need for informed consent, particularly regarding mental health legislation (www.esmhd.org, 2003).

It must be clearly established that people with capacity have the right to refuse as well as to accept treatment. People can make decisions against their own best interest. But if they are assessed as having the capacity to make these decisions, their decisions have to be accepted.

An elderly Deaf lady developed closed angle glaucoma. She was losing her sight and was offered an operation. She refused to have surgery and her capacity was called into question. On examination, she understood that her sight was failing but she had an extreme fear of surgery and was refusing because of that. She understood and accepted the consequences of her decision. She did not have the operation, and her sight failed.

A Deaf man with schizophrenia that was hard to treat and was causing him great distress was started, with his consent, on Clozapine. However, this caused gastric bleeding, as he had a hiatus hernia, and the medication had to be stopped. Despite understanding that he could continue the medication that was helping him if he consented to surgical treatment of the hiatus hernia, he refused because of a fear of surgery. It was not possible to persuade him. The Clozapine was stopped and his schizophrenic illness relapsed.

Misunderstandings occur if there is a lack of clear communication.

A Deaf young man had broken his leg. He signed the consent form for an operation but then became very disturbed, as he believed his leg was going to be amputated.

A Deaf woman had a hysterectomy. When she was later asked what operation she had, she had no idea.

LEGAL TRANSACTIONS

If an attorney is asked to make a will or undertake other transactions as, for example, sale of property, it is his responsibility to ensure that the client understands any advice given. An interpreter must be used, and the interpreter should not be a relative. This does not always occur, and Deaf people have signed away their inheritance without full understanding of the implications of their actions. Making a will can be particularly problematic, and psychiatric advice is sought in cases of doubt.

To make a valid will, a Deaf person must understand what property he or she owns. She must understand who would have a reasonable claim to this property. Taking this into account, she must then identify independently the person(s) or organization to whom she would like to leave her property.

In fact, a Deaf person may not understand any of this because of a lack of knowledge, but can be capable of understanding if the facts are clearly explained in appropriate language. Some Deaf people may be unused to making independent choices and may feel that they are obliged to leave property as desired by relatives. This may be appropriate in some cases, but when relatives are in dispute and the Deaf person is vulnerable, the situation can become adversarial. The way forward is to ensure that the person has independent legal advice with suitable interpretation and that information is given in a way that the Deaf person can understand. A family tree can be given, with pictures of the people concerned, so that the Deaf person is enabled to discuss the merits of various choices. Even well-meaning relatives can influence a person's choice just by trying to help them to make the will. If a vulnerable Deaf person wants to leave property away from the family, perhaps to the church or Deaf Center, it can be necessary that the decision is documented as a valid one so that the will cannot be later contested.

A Deaf man wanted to make a will. He had several brothers, but he would not divide his property equally between them, as be believed that one brother had been guilty of a criminal offense. On examination, it was found that he had misunderstood the information conveyed to him, and he revised his decision.

A 55-year-old Deaf man with a long history of serious alcohol abuse became physically ill and was admitted to the hospital. Before admission, his family had found it increasingly difficult to cope. He would often be doubly incontinent in bed. Although his health improved in the hospital, he was unable to walk without assistance due to peripheral neurological damage. He insisted on going home, and an opinion was sought about his capacity. Assessment showed that he had no understanding of the level of help that he needed or of the consequences for himself and his family if he returned home. A decision was made in his best interest to go to a nursing home.

DEAF PEOPLE IN THE CRIMINAL JUSTICE SYSTEM

In everyday life, misunderstandings easily occur for Deaf people, either because of miscommunication or because the Deaf person is unaware of auditory cues or people speaking to them.

A Deaf woman had a hostile reaction in a supermarket when she did not realize that the two minute silence on Remembrance Day had been called and continued to pack her shopping.

The author has been forcibly ejected from a motorway service station by two security staff because she had left her hearing aid in her car and did not hear the fire alarm. She has also been led back into a shop by security staff because the magnet in her switched-off cochlear implant had set off the shoplifting alarm.

These are embarrassing and intimidating experiences that Deaf people are often subjected to, but others can lead to more serious consequences.

A young Deaf man was leaving a nightclub when there was a disturbance outside and a policeman told him to go back in. He did not hear and kept walking. The policeman grabbed him from behind. The Deaf man turned and tried to get the policeman at arm's length for lip reading. He was arrested for assaulting a policeman and waited overnight in the cells for an interpreter, even though he was not in fact a signer.

The police were called by neighbors to a house where a Deaf man and his wife were arguing. The man, who was not a signer, was shouting and his Deaf wife was signing silently back to him. As the neighbors just heard the man, they thought that he had attacked his wife.

A man with Usher syndrome (profoundly Deaf with tunnel vision) was unloading his shopping at the checkout in a supermarket. He failed to notice a few items at the back of the cart because of his restricted sight. He was asked whether he was going to pay for them. He did not answer as he did not hear the question. As he moved on past the checkout, security staff stopped him and called the police.

Two Deaf brothers were walking home one evening, signing to each other. They parted to let an elderly man walk between them. The man thought that their hand movements were threatening him, so he punched the younger brother. The older brother then punched him and they were all arrested.

Deaf people as victims of offenses are particularly vulnerable. One police station actually had a text phone, and a Deaf woman used it to report an intruder in her house. The police were just about to respond urgently when another message came MAN GONE NOT HERE. They therefore delayed their visit. The woman had in fact said MAN GONE NOT. HERE, but they misunderstood her limited English in sign word order.

A woman was being beaten by her husband. She had a number to text the police but was informed when she did so that she needed to register in order to use the number.

A Deaf man assaulted his Deaf girlfriend in their apartment and then pushed her out of the door and slammed it. She had in fact been stabbed, but the blood was not evident as she had a red sweater on. She collapsed but managed to crawl to the next apartment where she wrote "help" in blood after banging on the door.

A DEAF DEFENDANT IN A POLICE STATION

If a Deaf person has been arrested without an interpreter, he may not realize why he is being detained. An interpreter should be arranged as soon as possible, and the interview should be videotaped. Audio recording of the interpreter's voice is not sufficient. On a video there can be subsequent checking of the accuracy of the interpreting.

The written statement that is the transcription of the interview should be interpreted back to the client. This interpretation should also be videotaped.

The first requirement is for the Deaf person to understand the legal procedures of arrest and if this is not understood any information from the interview, including a confession is not valid. The Police and Criminal Evidence Act (PACE) in the United Kingdom (Ventress et al., 2008) and the Miranda Warning in the United States (Vernon et al., 1996) have a similar content. Detainees under PACE are told that they have the right to remain silent and that anything they do say may be given in evidence. The PACE warning goes on to explain that "it may harm your defence if you do not mention now something which you later rely on in Court." The Miranda Warning explains that the detainee has a right to a lawyer and can only be interviewed without one with his or her explicit agreement. A person who waives her right to a lawyer must sign a form consenting to be interviewed without one. Both these procedures need to be clearly understood and consented to before further questioning can proceed.

As well as communication, there are other factors that can affect a police interview with a Deaf person. There is the concept of mental vulnerability, which applies to anyone who may not understand the significance of what is said, either of the questions or their replies. It has wider scope than intellectual disability and can include factors like being emotionally aroused, just answering in order to end the interview, and feeling vulnerable or intimidated. According to O'Rourke and Reed (2007), Deaf people may be particularly suggestible and compliant. Deaf people may be acquiescent in that they will agree to contradictory statements as they are eager to please and unwilling to admit that they do not understand. They often feel like someone deciphering a foreign language and just getting some phrases. They will then give their response to a question that they had not fully understood. Deaf people may also be compliant in that they will say they agree when they really do not, as they want to end the questioning. Deaf people may also be more suggestible in that they will accept and agree with concepts put to them during questioning. This is more likely to happen when there is a power difference in an interview, which is of course very likely when the Deaf person is in a police station. Deaf people are also vulnerable if they lack knowledge to put the questions into context. Interpreting can inadvertently lead people. For example, there are few collective nouns in British Sign Language, so if a person is asked, "Did you have a weapon?" the interpreter is obliged to list things like knives, sticks, and guns. Listing the objects alters the question to "Did you have a knife or a gun, etc.? Which did you have?" which in effect may lead the witness. The person may in fact not have had a weapon at all.

Another difficulty can arise when the language structure in sign language obliges the user to become specific and provide more information than would be necessary in spoken language. For example, in the sign question "Did the man put his hand inside your pants?" the signer would have to indicate the direction by which the man has inserted his hand inside the pants. This potentially minor difference is significant for developing a shared and accurate understanding of the actions involved. A difference between "up" and "down" in the direction of the hand movement in sign could potentially lead to an inaccurate answer to the question.

A Deaf man who had stabbed his girlfriend was being interviewed in prison. He was asked in British Sign Language, "Did you stab your girlfriend?" indicating a downward movement. He denied this. When his statement admitting the attack was read back to him in sign, he said, "Oh yes, I stabbed her," indicating an upward movement.

A man was being interviewed about carrying drugs. The interpreter indicated an inside pocket and he denied this. Later he admitted that he had carried drugs, but in a different pocket.

Deaf people may nod when they want to convey they understand, but in reality they may not. They may also nod to mean that they are following what is being said.

A man being questioned in court about an assault nodded as he followed a long question that was put to him about his alleged actions. However, when the question was ended, he indicated no, he did not agree with what had been said. The impression was left that he was changing his mind or lying. (Tuema, R., personal communication, 2012)

FITNESS TO PLEAD

Fitness to plead is again a capacity/competence issue with regard to the criteria needed to have a fair trial. The British criteria for fitness to plead are derived from the case of Pritchard (1836), when a Deaf man was not able to plead guilty or not guilty on a charge of bestiality because of lack of language. At the time, he would have been subject to capital punishment had he been guilty, so it was an act of humanity to send him instead to a psychiatric hospital. It was established that a defendant must have the capacity to understand the charge, instruct a lawyer, challenge a juror, plead to the charge, and follow the evidence (Grubin, 1996). Fitness to plead cases usually involve intellectual disability, head injury, dementia, or people who are psychiatrically ill. However, Deaf people may be unfit to plead due to poverty of language alone. In Britain, until 1991 a person found unfit to plead had to go to a psychiatric hospital, and there was no alternative sentencing. This led not only to miscarriages of justice in cases when later alibi evidence emerged, but also to disproportionate use of the law. Glenn Pearson, a young Deaf man, was found unfit to plead for a minor theft and was committed to a high-security psychiatric hospital (Emmins, 1986). He was soon released by a tribunal, but the concern over this case led to a change in the law (Criminal Procedure Act, 1991; White, 1992). This Act meant that fitness to plead would be tried by the jury as before, but a separate jury would go on to hear a trial of the facts. The law also allowed a range of alternatives for the person found unfit to plead, so hospital admission was no longer compulsory.

FITNESS TO PLEAD FOR DEAF OFFENDERS

Young et al. (2001) reviewed a series of 30 people who were referred to a mental health and deafness service for assessment of fitness to plead. Forty-seven percent were assessed as unfit. In a study of all 295 people found unfit to plead in England and Wales in 1976–1998 (Grubin, 1996), seven people were Deaf, 2.4% of the total. For five of them, the communication problems were the primary reasons for unfitness. The other two also had intellectual disability. All assessments of Deaf offenders should include the consideration of fitness to plead.

PSYCHIATRIC REPORTS FOR DEAF OFFENDERS

Before a full history is taken, as described in Chapter 11, the psychiatrist must ensure that the Deaf person understands that the interview is not confidential in the usual way. Before even a casual conversation to put the person at his ease, and to establish that an appropriate language level can take place, the Deaf person must know that anything he says will be part of the assessment and can be presented in front of the court. This in itself can be difficult, as the person may not understand at the outset the purpose of the interview. He must also understand that he can refuse the interview but that this would probably be against his best interests. If there is any doubt, the attorney must be consulted before the interview proceeds, particularly as the Deaf person may see the psychiatrist as a signing person to whom he can confide information that will not go any further. It sometimes becomes apparent that the person has understood much less than has been realized.

> A Deaf remand prisoner was interviewed. His first request was to have the letters from his mother signed to him. He did not know where he was. He knew he was in prison but had no idea where. When shown the prison stationery, he couldn't read it.
>
> The transcript of a police interview showed that the defendant had been advised by his attorney to say "no comment" to questioning. However, he then answered every question, adding "no comment" at the end. He had therefore misunderstood his attorney's instructions, although they had been clearly conveyed with an interpreter.

With regard to the specific fitness to plead criteria, most Deaf people, even with limited language, do realize what they are accused of, even if they do not know the technical terms. It depends on the nature of the offense.

> A Deaf man was charged with not having a license for some gambling machines he had in his apartment. He was not able to understand the concept of a license. The same man was charged with stealing some cigarettes from a shop. He was able to understand this charge.

In the British courts, most Deaf people can understand that the solicitor is a person to help and give advice. However, they may not have the knowledge or understand the difference between a solicitor and a barrister. One man indicated "a man with a tie" to describe his solicitor, and this was taken to mean that he did not know who he really was. However, the regional sign for solicitor was exactly that, "a man with a tie."

> A Deaf man understood that the attorney who saw him in the police station was there to help him and give him advice. However, when later another attorney was involved, he had no idea who that person was.

Challenging a juror can be explained in ways like, "If you see a man on the jury and you know he doesn't like you, do you know you can tell your attorney?" Questions of this sort are usually fairly well understood, but the notion of objecting to a juror on the grounds of feeling that he would be prejudiced may not be possible. However, if the concept of objecting to a juror and the role of the jury can be explained and understood, the lack of previous knowledge of this is not relevant.

The person must be able to understand whether she admits to committing the act she is accused of or whether she denies it. It sometimes needs to be explained that this process has to happen.

> A Deaf man accused of a sexual assault wanted to write a note and give it to the judge in the court to say that he was sorry and would not do it again. He thought this would be sufficient to end the case.

Understanding the evidence and following the court proceedings is usually the most difficult aspect of the fitness to plead assessment for Deaf defendants. Many hearing people would not understand technical evidence or legal language, but their fitness to plead is not questioned. However, for Deaf people there are many factors that interact. First, the court will be conducted in spoken language, and they will have to follow it in sign, which has different linguistic rules and may not include technical terms. Second, Deaf defendants' own sign may be very restricted and limited. Third, Deaf people may have a mild intellectual disability from the cause of the deafness and/or additional mental health problems. None of these in themselves may render the person unfit to plead, but all combined could mean that the court case would be impossible to follow. Arrangements can be made through relay interpreters to maximize communication, but this is slow and laborious and also needs to be closely monitored.

In addition to diagnosing any intellectual disability or psychiatric illness, the assessment report needs to examine the index offense with regard to the defendant's state of mind, intent, and knowledge of consequences of actions, in the context of his or her life and circumstances. The person's level of understanding needs to be noted.

An elderly Deaf man who was accused of hitting children who came to his door thought when the police arrived that they were there to tell the children off and proceeded to complain to them about the children.

A young Deaf man was charged with robbing a post office at gunpoint. He had been caught, as he did not hear the alarm that was set off. He later felt that he should be let off as it was a replica gun and he didn't fire it. He was not able to see that his actions had terrified the staff.

Sometimes the defendant is not able to picture the consequences of his or her actions.

A Deaf woman took some gasoline and set fire to her ex-husband's house while he was away. Nobody was hurt, but there was a serious fire. She said she went to burn the family photos that he had kept as she was angry with him. She had no concept of the seriousness of her action.

SENTENCING OPTIONS

Deaf people who commit offenses are treated by the law in a very variable way. Sometimes sentences are unduly lenient.

> A Deaf man waited in his ex-girlfriend's house with an axe. When they quarreled on her return, he seriously injured her. He was given a short suspended sentence.

Other Deaf people have been given cautions or were not charged for repeat offenses, either out of misplaced sympathy, or because the police want to avoid the laborious process of charging a Deaf person. However, if eventually a more serious crime is committed, the offender is very taken aback because he does not understand why suddenly what was condoned before is now treated so seriously.

The psychiatric report should note any explanatory or mitigating circumstances. In the case of intellectual disability and psychiatric illness, there is a recommendation for care and treatment at an appropriate level of security.

DEAF PEOPLE IN PRISON

Prison sentences are usually particularly punitive for Deaf people. Deaf offenders in prison are potentially extremely isolated, especially if they are sign language users. Although there is some evidence that Deaf people are treated leniently as far as sentencing is concerned, Deaf offenders seem to be over-represented in the prison population (Gahir et al., 2011). This is no doubt an underestimate, as Deaf people do not identify themselves. Signers may not attempt to use their language in prison, and there is no routine screening for deafness of any kind.

For Deaf people in prison, there is lack of communication, as text phones are often not provided. Televisions often do not have subtitles, or if they do, other prisoners object to their use. Deaf people cannot hear fire alarms or other safety information, and they do not have equal access to educational programs or other activities. Their ability to have offense-related work in groups or individually is also severely curtailed, thus lengthening their sentences.

Deaf prisoners may be helped by other prisoners for communication and "interpreting." This is an unsafe situation and can lead to breaches of confidentiality.

DEAF PEOPLE IN SECURE MENTAL HEALTH FACILITIES

Until recently in Britain, there were only high security facilities available for Deaf mentally disordered offenders (Roberts, 1990). In the last 20 years, medium secure units have developed, so Deaf offenders with mental health problems can be diverted from the criminal justice system and can be treated in an appropriate level of security. The Royal College of Psychiatrists has recently issued standards for Deaf people in medium secure care (O'Rourke et al., 2011). It stipulates that the environment and amenities should be adapted for Deaf people and that care should be in a language that is appropriate for them. Procedures such as restraint should be carried out in an appropriate manner so that the person under restraint can see somebody signing at all times and their hands are released to sign themselves as much as possible.

The developments of these appropriate high security and medium secure services for mentally disordered Deaf offenders not only provide equality of access for Deaf people, they have also enabled the development of appropriate assessment and treatment programs for Deaf offenders (Gibbon & Doyle, 2011; O'Rourke & Grewer, 2005).

DEAF SEX OFFENDERS

Studies of Deaf sex offenders have shown that many have not received any sex education at school and many have been subject to sexual and or physical abuse as children (Iqbal et al., 2004). Many have suffered parental loss, and over a quarter have intellectual disabilities.

VIOLENT OFFENSES

Murders by Deaf people have been instrumental in moving deaf mental health issues up the agenda in the United Kingdom. Daniel Joseph killed his landlady in 1998 during a psychotic episode, and Al-Assaf killed his estranged wife's partner in 2004. Inquiries into both these cases exposed gaps in the mental health provision for Deaf people and the unavailability of interpreting, particularly in emergency situations.

In the United States, Vernon has reviewed aspects of the criminal justice system with regard to Deaf violent offenders (Vernon et al., 1999) and found that in this group there are low levels of literacy, reduced intellectual functioning, and limited sign language development.

SUMMARY

Deaf people, particularly those who are vulnerable due to language delay, can be treated inequitably under both civil and criminal law. Those who commit offenses can be isolated and at a disadvantage in both prisons and in secure mental health facilities. Appropriate assessment and care should be provided, not only in the interests of Deaf people themselves, but for the prevention of further offending.

20 Deaf Adults: Treatment

INTRODUCTION

Treatment in its wider sense for Deaf people with mental health problems should be delivered in a Deaf person's preferred language in a culturally appropriate way. Deaf people can feel disrespected, disempowered, and uninformed, and these feelings are compounded in the context of a mental health problem. The recovery model of a personal journey to self-empowerment and a meaningful life is especially applicable to Deaf people. For them it may include the extra dimension of building up a more positive identity, increased self-esteem, and more meaningful roles in society than they were able to achieve before the mental health problem developed. Griggs (2000) discusses the concept of "deaf wellness," which is defined as the achievement of a positive identity by Deaf people in a way that is meaningful and satisfying for themselves, not just in terms of the hearing society around them.

Care, treatment, and recovery programs for Deaf people need both a wide multidisciplinary approach and attention to detail (Glickman & Gulati, 2003). Deaf people may take time to present for help, and then may be lost to follow-up if they are not supported adequately.

A 30-year-old Deaf woman with a history of sexual abuse from a family member in her childhood became depressed. She found it difficult to cope. She kept moving between mental health catchment areas. She eventually was seen by a mainstream mental health team, and they wanted to give her cognitive behavioral therapy. The team felt unable to do this as she used sign language, so they gave her some written material instead, which she was unable to read. She moved again and was lost to follow-up for several years.

It must be ensured that the Deaf person really understands when and where to attend for appointments. She may not be able to use public transportation easily, may not be able to read a timetable or a map, may find it difficult to ask for help, and cannot hear travel announcements. Sending a letter that the patient may not be able to read clearly, with an appointment in an unfamiliar place, is therefore putting an intolerable burden on them. If it is not possible to ensure that the person is able to attend the first appointment, a home visit or a local appointment in a familiar place such as the doctor's office should be considered.

Once the initial assessment is complete, a multidisciplinary care plan should be drawn up, which could include other agencies, such as social workers with Deaf people, as appropriate, or resources in the voluntary sector (Mezzich et al., 2003).

Deaf people may present not just with a mental health problem but with long-standing difficulties in their physical health, in their relationships, in work, housing, and financial matters. All these should be addressed in detail as needed, as part of the package of care. People may have been poorly educated, particularly in literacy, and this may have had other effects on their lives. Deaf adults still living with their parents may lack many everyday practical skills, and this undermines both their confidence and their potential for independent living.

Sign language competence has been shown to correlate with improved outcomes (Horton, 2010). Many Deaf patients, particularly those in the language- and learning-challenged group, benefit from the opportunity to improve their sign language in a communicating environment.

Ideally, there should be a full range of treatment settings for Deaf people, including inpatient and day care. When admission is needed, a specialist Deaf mental health service acts as a therapeutic communicating environment, with Deaf staff and hearing staff who sign. This may be the first time, or the first time since leaving school, that the Deaf person is in an environment where he can communicate freely. This may at first be rather overwhelming, especially if he experiences a psychotic or depressed episode. Seeing professional Deaf staff can also be a culture shock for hearing families, and this usually has a very positive effect on their relationships with their adult Deaf children.

TREATMENT OF MENTAL HEALTH DISORDERS

Medication

Medication for psychiatric illness is indicated in the same way as with hearing patients, but as part of the treatment process, there are important ways in which extra care is needed. No medication should be prescribed without informed consent, but it is all too often the case that Deaf patients take medication for both physical and mental health problems without proper understanding of the reasons for the medication, the side effects, or any alternatives. It is not only ethically correct that patients understand their medication but it is also an important factor in compliance (Mitchell & Selmes, 2007). It is known that for all patients, poor literacy means poor compliance with health care (Parker, 2011), but at least hearing patients with literacy problems are more likely to have understood the initial spoken explanation. Even when the Deaf person understands, she is often not empowered to ask questions or ask for clarification.

For outpatients there are further barriers to treatment compliance. The patient may have to go the general practitioner to pick up the prescription and then to a pharmacy. These are all places where communication can break down. A Deaf person may not understand how frequently or for how long he has to take the medication, and can find it difficult to go back for renewed prescriptions between outpatient appointments. A medidose container or blister pack is very helpful, particularly if there is a complicated medication regime. It is also the doctor's responsibility to ensure that the psychotropic medication is compatible with other medication the patient is taking. Deaf patients may be particularly sensitive to side effects because of other health problems or neurological sensitivity, which could be related to the cause of deafness.

There may be a misunderstanding of side effects.

> A Deaf woman of 35, an outpatient, was on antidepressant medication that was helping her, but she had become quite constipated. She was given a small supply of laxatives. She could not read the packets and continued just to take the laxative. She came back to the outpatient facility complaining of diarrhea.

Medications may have different names, and this must be carefully explained. Quite reasonably, people may think they have been given the wrong medication, and in fact they sometimes have been. They may also be disconcerted by the different colors of tablets. Not being able to read the box, they have relied on the color to know which tablet was which, and as the dose changes, the color of the tablet may change. It is therefore important to ask patients to bring their medications to appointments, to check with their family doctor if there are any doubts, and to have a formulary with a description of the tablets to aid discussion, as misunderstandings can jeopardise treatment.

> A Deaf man, on a slow release mood stabilizer, refused to take it as he saw the word "retard" on the box. He became angry, saying that he was not retarded.

In Northern Ireland the days of the week are signed by what happened each day at the Deaf residential school. Wednesday is indicated by the sign of drinking soup, which is very similar to British Sign Language for breakfast.

> A Deaf man was asked to take his tablets with breakfast. He thought he just had to take them on a Wednesday.

It is important to take extra care with regard to side effects. These should be fully explained to patients, but there should also be careful monitoring.

A 35-year-old Deaf woman with schizophrenia maintained on Clozapine became short of breath at her residential home. She was seen by the general practitioner and was diagnosed with asthma. She had in fact developed heart failure due to a rare cardiomopathy associated with Clozapine treatment.

A 40-year-old Deaf woman who had a great deal of health anxiety was prescribed a small dose of Haloperidol at night. She collapsed in the street and was taken to the hospital, where she had frequently been seen without any physical illness being diagnosed. On this occasion she had developed neuroleptic malignant syndrome as a rare adverse reaction to Haloperidol.

COUNSELING AND PSYCHOTHERAPY

"The best therapy seems to me to lie in being understood, and in sharing with another human being our most unmanageable emotions" (Brampton, 2008, p. 196). For a Deaf person to feel understood, therapy must take place with a person they trust in a language they share, either directly or with an interpreter. In addition to the issues concerning interpreters discussed in Chapter 10, in a psychotherapeutic situation it is particularly important that the interpreter is acceptable to the Deaf person and is consistent throughout the therapy. The relationship between therapist and patient becomes a triad, and issues with confidentiality, transference, and counter-transference must be recognized. Preparations and debriefing by the interpreter and the clinician can address any difficulties or uncertainties, including those related to any limitations in the patient's language.

Hearing counselors may have unfounded assumptions about Deaf people (Corker, 1995). They may believe that all Deaf people are able to speak, or that they all use sign. Counselors must be vigilant about individual language and communication preferences. Counselors should not make prior assumptions about a Deaf person's feelings toward his or her deafness, whether positive or negative, as this is an issue for exploration in the therapy. Deaf people may also have other cultural identities, such as ethnic or gay, and these are also important (Leigh, 2010).

Therapy with Deaf people often involves some supportive educational and preparatory work. The concept of therapy may be unfamiliar to Deaf people and they may have mistaken assumptions. They may expect direct advice and for the therapist to fix their problems. The Deaf person may have long experience of powerlessness and limitation of choice and autonomy, and therapy should address these feelings. Trust in confidentiality is vital, especially as trust may have been broken in the past.

Therapists with Deaf people have identified issues of anger, identity, and attachment, as well as the consequences of emotional, physical, and sexual abuse (Carton, 2013). It may be the first time that the Deaf person has been able to discuss subjects that have seemed forbidden, and to be able to express themselves fully. Psychodynamic psychotherapy may enable the Deaf person to explore issues in the past and relate them to their present difficulties.

Cognitive behavioral therapy (CBT) can be particularly positive for Deaf people who wish to address their problems in a "here and now" way. Cognitive behavioral therapy can be adapted for use with Deaf people with language and learning challenges (Glickman, 2009).

Group therapy is a powerful tool and is used in mainstream settings, including for abuse work and also for sex offenders. However, for Deaf people, group work can be problematic, as in the small Deaf world, people are more likely to know or know of each other. This not only raises questions of confidentiality, it also inhibits open discussion within the group. More low-key group work, such as assertiveness training, anxiety management, or women's issues, is effective and not so intrusive on people's privacy.

Deaf therapists are well placed to provide counseling and psychotherapy to Deaf clients, but they may have to deal with boundary issues as well as the Deaf patient's raised or lowered expectations. Deaf therapists may be idealized as the Deaf parent the patient did not have, or may be perceived as less knowledgeable or powerful than a hearing therapist (Leigh & Lewis, 2010).

It is important that therapists, either Deaf or hearing, have access to appropriate peer support and clinical supervision.

As most Deaf people are born into hearing families, they make an emotional journey to discover their adult identity. This may or may not have been successful. People have described joining the Deaf community for the first time in their adult years as coming home.

OVERVIEW

Deaf people presenting with mental health problems, like all patients, rarely have just one area of difficulty. For Deaf people especially, the different areas of need or distress can compound each other over a long period of time. A complex presentation then needs to be assessed and treated in a detailed and interacting way. Even people with an obvious serious illness such as schizophrenia rarely have that as the sole difficulty. For Deaf people it is particularly important to take a whole person approach and not just concentrate on the presenting problem.

A Deaf person may have a previously unrecognized cause of deafness. This may then lead to further medical sight or neurological investigations with appropriate treatment as required.

The Deaf person's sign language may benefit from improvement with individual tuition and being in a signing environment. Literacy work may improve confidence and access to information and networking with e-mail and text. Assistive technology will improve independence.

When needed, practice in daily living skills, including independent travel and money management, improves confidence and self esteem.

Individually designed programs for understanding emotions and behavior, including anger management, improve relationships and quality of life.

The essence of treatment for Deaf people is threefold: appropriate and accessible language, acceptance and respect of their culture, and recognition of the obstacles they may have encountered in their lives. In this context, illnesses, distress, and maladaptive patterns of thoughts, feelings, and behavior can be understood and treated. For each patient this will mean a detailed assessment, treatment, and rehabilitation pathway.

SUMMARY

The recovery journey for a Deaf person can be much more than treatment of the presenting mental health disorder. Individual treatment plans in a communicating environment mean that Deaf people can be enabled to discover their optimal level of social, emotional, and psychological functioning, in a way which is most appropriate and meaningful for them. Provision of these services is far from universal. This will be considered further in the next chapter.

21 Service Development

Most mental health policies specifically state that access to services should be provided to everyone in an equitable and appropriate way and that there should not be discrimination against any group on grounds of age, gender, ethnicity, culture, or disability. Despite this, appropriate and accessible mental health services for deaf people, particularly sign language users, are only fully developed in some countries, and even then rarely on a national basis.

Historically, deaf people have been exposed to poor mental health care. Where specialized services have developed they have significantly improved deaf people's experience and outcomes. This has been documented in numerous papers (Briffa, 1999a). Sometimes it needs an adverse event, such as the Daniel Joseph tragedy (Mishcon, 2000), to give a stimulus to service development. In London, Daniel Joseph, a deaf man with schizophrenia, fell between services after his discharge from hospital. He discontinued his medication and killed his landlady when his illness relapsed. The inquiry after this murder led to consultation resulting in the England and Wales policy document, "Towards Equity and Access"

(Department of Health, 2005), a blueprint for mental health and deafness service development.

Deaf organizations and interested mental health professionals often campaign for appropriate mental health services for deaf people for many years before services are actually put in place. For example, a meeting in 1978 in Scotland (Montgomery, 1978) called for national Deaf services. The consultation document "Making the Case" was published thirty years later (Scottish Council on Deafness, 2008) and a pilot service was started in 2011. Similarly, in Northern Ireland and the Republic of Ireland, Deaf organizations and individual clinicians campaigned for services for many years before they were started in 2003 and 2005. The same pattern has occurred in many countries including Australia and New Zealand.

In the United States and the United Kingdom, pioneering services were started in the 1960s (Rainer & Altshuler, 1971) (Denmark & Warren, 1972). Similar initiatives have developed in many European countries. The European Society of Mental Health and Deafness (ESMHD) was established in 1986. This provided the unique opportunity and platform by which specialized mental health professionals from around the world met and exchanged their knowledge and expertise. Conferences across the world have raised awareness of the need to develop services for this historically neglected population. There have been European conferences on mental health and deafness since 1988, and following the first World Congress in Gallaudet University in 1998 there have been World Congresses in Europe, South Africa, Australia, and Mexico. Common themes have emerged. Deaf people who experience mental health problems face similar realities wherever they live.

When there is the political and financial will to set up a mental health service for deaf people, the first stage is often a needs assessment. This can pose difficulties, as deaf people may not come forward until a service actually starts.

In Northern Ireland there was an outreach clinic every two months from the Manchester Mental Health and Deafness Service until 2003, when a locally based service started, initially with a consulting psychiatrist two days a week and a community nurse specialist. In 2000–2003 there were 44 new referrals to the clinics held six times a year. In the first three years of the new local service (2003–2006) there were 125 new referrals (Rawlings, 2006).

Predictions of need can be made from knowledge of statistics in the population as a whole (Goldberg, 1995) and from estimates of mental health problems in the Deaf population (Fellinger et al., 2012). The Goldberg model describes about 250 people per thousand per year in the general population as developing a mental health problem. Of those, about 215 will present to primary care. Approximately 100 people will be diagnosed as having a mental health problem, about 25 will be referred to secondary services, and an average of 5 people will be admitted to a hospital. If these figures are transposed to the Deaf population, with the increased morbidity it could be predicted that a Deaf mental health service would receive in the region of 40 referrals per 1,000 Deaf people per year. However, the patterns of referral in the Deaf population are very different. Often, they bypass primary care and go straight to the Deaf mental health services if they are available. In addition, Deaf mental health services see a wider population than mainstream general adult services. They see patients who may otherwise go to adolescent services, older adult services, or intellectual disability services. As well as their core work with profoundly deaf people, one in a thousand of the population, Deaf mental health services may also see some partially deaf or deafened people and also deafblind people. Again, this makes prediction of referral rates a complex task.

As many deaf people have already had difficulties and delays in accessing Deaf mental health services, it is appropriate that the referral threshold is low for initial assessment. The referrer may not have had the opportunity to assess the deaf person's complex needs. In the design of services it is vital that the gate keeping is not done by the least experienced practitioners.

A 45-year-old deaf man was referred by his general practitioner at the request of a social worker with Deaf people to Deaf mental health services. He was being evicted from his rented property and was very distressed.

At that time the referral procedures were being changed to a tertiary referral pattern so that the deaf man had to be referred in the first instance to local mainstream mental health services. They felt that he did not reach the threshold for their services. When he was eventually seen by the Deaf service, it was clear that he was psychotic and that he was being evicted because his illness had caused disturbed behavior toward his neighbors.

Many mental health services for deaf people have started because individual clinicians or groups of clinicians have acted at catalysts. However the service is initiated, the aim should be the same—the development of an effective multidisciplinary team that includes culturally Deaf members. Deaf professional staff provide insight, skills, empathy, compassion, and role models that hearing staff cannot, however well they sign. More opportunities are becoming available for Deaf staff to train in professional roles (Cromwell, 2004), including mental health nursing (Sharples, 2001). The importance of Deaf staff in such teams is well described by Klein (2011). As well as their professional training and clinical supervision, Deaf staff should receive appropriate peer support as their overlapping roles in the Deaf community can give them ethical dilemmas (Gutman, 2005).

A fully functioning service should have all the components of inpatient beds, day services, outpatient services, peripheral clinics, and community-based care, which includes social work, nursing, and community support. Deaf community workers are especially important for culturally appropriate care and support. The team should include psychiatrists, psychologists, psychotherapists, nursing and care staff, occupational therapists, and social workers, with other therapies such as art therapy. There should be opportunities for sign language development and educational assessments, as well as access to medical, audiological, visual, and neurological assessment as required. The secretarial, administration, and domestic staff, who should all sign, need to be perceived as part of the therapeutic team. Interpreters are also part of the team, but they have a slightly different role, as their own codes of confidentiality do not allow them to share information they learn while interpreting.

Community psychiatric nurses and clinical nurse specialists attached to the Deaf mental health units, and clinical nurse specialists who work autonomously, are particularly vital members of Deaf mental health services. They are in a position to provide a locally based focus on mental health care for Deaf people and liaise closely with the area's primary care mental health provision, general mental health services, social work and voluntary services, and, most important, with local Deaf communities. These experienced nurses may be the first point of referral for deaf patients. They can provide services as part of, or in partnership with, the specialist Deaf mental health services to create a package of care appropriate for each individual (Horne & Pennington, 2010).

Because the Deaf team is usually generic, liaison and collaborative working have to be in place so that deaf people are not deprived of other specialist mental services such as mother and baby, intellectual disability, substance abuse, eating disorders, forensic, and older adult services.

Specialist Deaf mental health services are rarely able to provide crisis or out of hours coverage as they are thinly spread over large geographical areas. Local out of hours services, or crisis and home treatment teams, if available, are often hard for deaf people to contact, and the clinical staff may feel deskilled when working with a deaf patient. Despite these difficulties, robust arrangements must be made, so that patients know who to contact and how to do it, and mainstream mental health professionals know how to obtain out of hours interpreters.

Deaf patients need to move through the service appropriately so that the long inpatient stays of the past are avoided. Inpatient care will always be necessary for complex assessments and for people with serious mental health problems. Inpatient units also provide a therapeutic communicating environment in which recovery and rehabilitation can take place. A Deaf inpatient unit needs to be in a position to refer on to and to work in partnership with Deaf rehabilitation services.

In the past, Deaf residential and supported services ran the risk of taking people just because they were deaf, without the opportunity to offer people the specific service they needed. In the United Kingdom, large residential services for deaf people have been redesigned for a variety of specific needs, and more local services have also been developed. Deaf people can now be in rehabilitation, sheltered or supported accommodation, or a home for life, as appropriate. Community outreach services also enable people to live independently.

A scoping exercise with deaf patients and their families highlighted how deaf people with mental health needs want to live in their home areas and near their families (Northern Ireland Mental Health and Deafness Service, 2011). In this context, however, it is important to acknowledge that there may not be a critical mass of deaf people with the same needs for services to be provided as locally as people would wish, and there may always have to be some compromises.

The provision of mental health services for deaf people also includes liaison and teaching with mainstream services and close working with the Deaf community to raise mental health awareness.

SUMMARY

Wherever mental health services for deaf people have developed, they have grown in response to previously unmet needs. A multidisciplinary Deaf and hearing team can provide appropriate assessment and treatment, but cannot by itself give deaf people the range of locally based freely accessible services available to the general population. Deaf mental health services need to work closely with other service providers, and, vitally, with the Deaf community and its organizations in order to achieve "the right of every deaf person to have full and equal access to mental health services which can provide effective assessment and therapy to meet their needs" (Denmark, 1994, p. 126).

REFERENCES

Achenbach, T. M. (1991) *The Achenbach System of Empirically Based Assessment (ASEBA): Development, Findings, Theory, and Applications.* Burlington, VT: University of Vermont Research Center for Children, Youth and Families.

Action on Hearing Loss. (2011) "Deafblindness: The Facts." [online]. Available at: http//www.actiononhearingloss.org.uk.

Action on Hearing Loss. (2011) "Facts and Figures of Hearing Loss and Tinnitus: The Facts." [online]. Available at: http//www.actiononhearingloss.org.uk.

Adshead, G., and Sarkar, J. (2012) "The Nature of Personality Disorder," *Advances in Psychiatric Treatment*, 18, 162–172.

Agrawal, N., and Govender, S. (2011) "Epilepsy and Neuropsychiatric Comorbidities," *Advances in Psychiatric Treatment*, 17, 44–53.

Akamatsu, C. T., Mayer, C., and Hardy-Braz, S. (2008) "Why Considerations of Verbal Aptitude Are Important in Educating Deaf and Hard-Of-Hearing Students," in M. Marschark and P. C. Hauser (eds.), *Deaf Cognition: Foundations and Outcomes*, pp. 131–169. New York: Oxford University Press.

Allan, K., Stapleton, K., and McLean, F. (2005) "Dementia and Deafness: An Exploratory Study," University of Stirling. www.dementia.stir.ac.uk

Alloway, T. P. (2006). "How Does Memory Work in the Classroom?" *Educational Research and Reviews*, 1(4), 134–139.

Altshuler, K. Z. (1971) "Studies of the Deaf: Relevance to Psychiatric Theory," *American Journal of Psychiatry*, 127(11), 1521–1526.

American Academy of Pediatrics, (1999) "Newborn and Infant Hearing Loss: Detection and Intervention," *Pediatrics*, 103(2), 527–530.

American Psychiatric Association. (2000) *Diagnostic and Statistical Manual of Mental Disorders* (4th ed., text rev.). Washington, DC: Author.

Americans with Disabilities Act (1990) (as amended 2008) United States Code, Title 42, Chapter 126.

Appleby, L. (2012) "Suicide Prevention: The Evidence on Safer Clinical Care is now Good and Should be Adopted Internationally," *International Psychiatry*, 9(2), 27–29.

Appleford, J. (2003) "Clinical Activity Within a Specialist Mental Health Service for Deaf People: Comparison with a General Psychiatric Service," *Psychiatric Bulletin*, 27, 375–377.

Arnos, K. S., and Pandya, A. (2011) "Advances in the Genetics of Deafness," in *Oxford Handbook of Deaf Studies, Language and Education* (2nd ed.), pp. 412–424. New York: Oxford University Press.

Ashley, J. (1992) *Acts of Defiance*. London: Rheinhardt.

Atkinson, J. R. (2006) "The Perceptual Characteristics of Voice Hallucinations in Deaf People, Insights into the Nature of Subvocal Thought and Sensory Feedback Loops," *Schizophrenia Bulletin* 32(4), 701–708.

Atkinson, J., Marshall, J., Woll, B., and Thacker, A. (2005) "Testing Comprehension Abilities in Users of British Sign Language Following CVA," *Brain and Language*, 94, 233–248.

Atkinson, J. R., Gleeson, K., Cromwell, J. A., and O'Rourke, S. (2007) "Exploring the Perceptual Characteristics of Voice Hallucinations in Deaf People," *Journal of Cognitive Neuropsychiatry*, 12(4), 339–361.

Audiology Awareness. www.audiologyawareness.com

Austen, S., and Checinski, K. (2000) "Addictive Behaviours in Deafness," in P. Hindley and N. Kitson (eds.), *Mental Health and Deafness*, pp. 232-252. London: Whurr Publishers.

Austen, S., and McGrath, M. (2006) "Telemental Health Technology in Deaf and General Mental Health Services: Access and Use," *American Annals of the Deaf*, 151(3), 311–317.

Avery, C. B. (1948) "The Social Competence of Pre-School Acoustically Handicapped Children." *Journal of Exceptional Children*, 15, 71–73.

Bad Ischl Declaration. (2003) Congress of the European Society of Mental Health and Deafness, www.esmhd.org

Bailey, K., and Miner, I. (2010) "Psychotherapy for People with Usher Syndrome," in I. Leigh (ed.), *Psychotherapy with Deaf Clients from Diverse Groups*, pp. 136–158. Washington, DC: Gallaudet University Press.

Baines, D., Patterson, N., and Austen, S. (2010) "An Investigation into the Length of Hospital Stay for Deaf Mental Health Service Users," *Journal of Deaf Studies and Deaf Education*, 15(2), 179–184.

Baker, K., and Baker, F. (2011) "The Assessment of Intellectual Disability with Deaf Adults," *International Journal on Mental Health and Deafness*, 1(1), 23–36.

Barker, D. H., Quittner, A., Fink, N. E., Eisenberg, L. S., Tobey, E. A., and Niparko, J. K. (2009) "Predicting Behavior Problems in Deaf and Hearing Children: The Influences of Language, Attention, and Parent–Child Communication." *Developmental Psychopathology*, 21(2), 373–392. DOI: 10.1017/S0954579409000212.

Basilier, T. (1964) "Surdophrenia: The Psychic Consequences of Congenital or Early Acquired Deafness," *Acta Psychiatrica Scandinavica*, 40(180), 362–372.

Bat-Chava, Y. (1993) "Antecedents of Self-Esteem in Deaf People: A Meta-Analytic Review." *Rehabilitation Psychology*, 38, 221–234.

Bat-Chava, Y. (1994) "Group Identification and Self-Esteem of Deaf Adults." *Personality and Social Psychology Bulletin*, 20, 494–502.

Bat-Chava, Y. (2000) "Diversity of Deaf Identities." *American Annals of the Deaf*, 145, 420–427.

Bat-Chava, Y., and Martin, D. (2002) "Sibling Relationships of Deaf Children: The Impact of Child and Family Characteristics." *Rehabilitation Psychology*, 47, 73–91.

Bat-Chava, Y., and Martin, D. (2003) "Negotiating Deaf-Hearing Friendships: Coping Strategies of Deaf Boys and Girls in Mainstream Schools." *League for the Hard of Hearing*, 511–519.

Beethoven, L. van. (1802) "Heiligenstadt Testament". In Grant, B. *The Quiet Ear, Deafness in Literature*. 71–73, London: André Deutsch Ltd.

Beitchman, J. H., Wilson, B., Johnson, C. J., Atkinson, L., Young, A., Adalf, E., et al. (2001) "Fourteen-Year Follow-Up of Speech/Language-Impaired and Control Children: Psychiatric Outcome." *Journal of the American Academy of Child & Adolescent Psychiatry*, 40, 75–82.

Bell, A. G. (1883) *Memoir upon the Formation of a Deaf Variety of the Human Race*. New Haven, CT: National Academy of Science.

Bitner-Glindzicz, M. (2002) "Hereditary Deafness and Phenotyping in Humans," *British Medical Bulletin*, 63, 73–94.

Bitner-Glindzicz, M., and Rahman, S. (2007) "Ototoxicity Caused by Aminoglycosides," *British Medical Journal*, 335, 784–785.

Black, P. A., and Glickman, N. S. (2006) "Demographics, Psychiatric Diagnoses and Other Characteristics of North American Deaf and Hard of Hearing Inpatients," *Journal of Deaf Studies and Deaf Foundation*, 11(3), 303–320.

Bloom, T. D., Fishman, G. A., and Mafee, M. F. (1983) "Ushers Syndrome, CNS Defects Determined by Computed Tomography," *Retina*, 3, 108–113.

Bohlin, G., Hagekull, B., and Rydell, A.-M. (2000) "Attachment and Social Functioning: A Longitudinal Study from Infancy to Middle Childhood." *Social Development*, 9, 24–39.

Bolander, A. M., and Renning, A. N. (2000) *I Was #87: A Deaf Woman's Ordeal of Misdiagnosis, Institutionalization, and Abuse*. Washington, DC: Gallaudet University Press.

Boystown National Research Hospital. Retrieved January 2012 from http://www.babyhearing.org/hearingamplification/causes/genetics.asp.

Braden, J. P. (1992) "Intellectual Assessment of Deaf and Hard-of-Hearing People: A Quantitative and Qualitative Research Synthesis." *School Psychology* 21, 82–94.

Braden, J. (1994) *Deafness, Deprivation and I.Q.* London: Plenum Press.

Brampton, S. (2008) *Shoot the Damn Dog: A Memoir of Depression*. London: Bloomsbury Publishing.

Brelje, W. H. (1999) (ed.) *Global Perspectives on the Education of the Deaf in Selected Countries*. Hillsboro: Butte Publications.

Briffa, D. (1999a) "Deaf and Mentally Ill: Are Their Needs Being Met?" *Australian Psychiatry*, 7(1), 7–10.

Briffa, D. (1999b) "Hallucinations in Deaf People with a Mental Illness: Lessons From the Deaf Clients," *Australian Psychiatry* 7(2), 72–74.

British Deaf Association. (1975) *Gestuno: International Sign Language of the Deaf*. Carlisle, England: BDA.

Brown, A. S., Cohen, P., Greenwald, S., and Susser, E. (2000) "Nonaffective Psychosis After Prenatal Exposure to Rubella," *American Journal of Psychiatry*, 157(3), 438–443.

Bruffaerts, R., Demyttenaere, K., Borges, G., Haro, J. M., Chiu, W. T., Hwang, I., Karam, E. G., Kessler, R. C., Sampson, N., Alonso, J., Andrade, L. H., Angermeyer, M., Benjet, C., Bromet, E., de Girolamo, G., de Graaf, R., Florescu, S., Gureje, O., Horiguchi, I., Hu, C., Kovess, V., Levinson, D., Posada-Villa, J., Sagar, R., Scott, K., Tsang, A., Vassilev, M., Williams, D. R. and Nock, M. K. (2010) "Childhood Adversities as Risk Factors for Onset and Persistence of Suicidal Behaviour," *The British Journal of Psychiatry*, 197, 20–27.

Brunt, D., and Broadhead, G. D. (1982) "Motor Proficiency Traits of Deaf Children." *Research Quarterly for Exercise and Sport*, 53, 236–238.

Bubbico, L., Rosano, A. and Spagnolo, A. (2007) "Prevalence of Prelingual Deafness in Italy," *Acta Otorhinolaryngol Ital*, 27(1) 17–21.

Butterfield, S. A., Van der Mars, H., and Chase, J. (1993) "Fundamental Motor Skill Performance of Deaf and Hearing Children Ages 3–8." *Clinical Kinesiology*, 2–6.

Calderon, R. (2000) "Parental Involvement in Deaf Children's Educational Programs as a Predictor of Child's Language, Early Reading, and Social-Emotional Development." *Journal of Deaf Studies and Deaf Education*, 5(2), 140–148.

Cambridge, J., Singh, S. P., and Johnston, M. (2012) "The Need for Measurable Standards in Mental Health Interpreting: A Neglected Area," *The Psychiatrist*, 36, 121–124.

Canadian Association of the Deaf. (2007) Statistics on Deaf Canadians. Retrieved May 2012 from http://www.cad.ca/statistics_on_deaf_canadians.php.

Canadian Association of Speech-Language Pathologists and Audiologists. (2010) *CASLPA Position Paper on Universal Newborn Hearing Screening in Canada.* Ottawa: CASLPA.

Canadian Working Group on Childhood Hearing. (2005) *Early Hearing and Communication Development: Canadian Working Group on Childhood Hearing (CWGCH) Resource Document.* Ottawa.

Carton, C. (2013) Personal communication.

Carvill, S. (2008) "Sensory Impairments, Intellectual Disability and Psychiatry." *Journal of Intellectual Disability Research*, 45(6), 467–483. DOI: 10.1046j.1 365-2788.2001.00366x.

Cassady, G., Brown, K., Cohen, M., and DeMaria, W. (1965) "Hereditary Renal Dysfunction and Deafness," *Pediatrics* 35, 967–979. [Online.] Available at: http://pediatrics.aapublications.org/content/35/6/967

Centre for Addiction and Mental Health (CAMH) (2002) Mental Illness and Addiction Statistics. Retreived from http://www.camh.ca/en/hospital/about_camh/newsroom/for_reporters/Pages/addictionmentalhealthstatistics.aspx

Chatzidamianos, G. (2006) *Linguistic and Non-Linguistic Use of Gesture in Deaf Patients with Schizophrenia: Evidence for a Dissociation.* (M. Phil), Department of Experimental Psychology, University of Cambridge.

Chatzidamianos, G. (2013) *Language in Profoundly Deaf People with Schizophrenia*, PhD Thesis. University of Cambridge.

Chess, S., and Fernandez, P. (1980) "Do Deaf Children Have a Typical Personality?," *Journals of The American Academy of Child Psychiatry*, 19, 654–664.

Children's Mental Health Ontario. (2012) "Mental Health Disorders in Children and Youth." Retrieved from http://www.kidsmentalhealth.ca/parents/signs_disorders.php

Chovaz, C. J., Anderson, M., and Goldstein, G. M. (2011) *Autism Spectrum Disorder: A Resource for Parents, Teachers and Clinicians working with D/deaf and Hard of Hearing Children with ASD.* London, ON: Kings University College.

Chovaz McKinnon, Moran, and Pederson. (2004) "Attachment Representations of Deaf Adults," *Journal of Deaf Studies and Deaf Education,* 9(4), 366–386. DOI: 10.1093/deafed/enh043.

Chritchfield, A. B. (2002) "Cultural Diversity Series: Meeting the Mental Health Needs of Persons Who Are Deaf." *National Technical Assistance Center for State Mental Health Planning.*

Church, M., and Watts, S. (2007) "Assessment of Mental Capacity," *Psychiatric Bulletin,* 31, 304–307.

Collishaw, S., Maughan, B. and Pickles, A. (2004) "Affective Problems in Adults with Mild Learning Disability: The Role of Social Disadvantage and Ill Health," *British Journal of Psychiatry,* 185, 350–351.

Connolly, C. M., Rose, J. and Austen, S. (2006) "Identifying and Assessing Depression in Prelingually Deaf People: A Literature Review," *American Annals of the Deaf,* 151(1), 49–60.

Conrad, R. (1979) *The Deaf School Child: Language and Cognitive Function.* London: Harper and Row.

Cooper, A. F. (1976) "Deafness and Psychiatric Illness," *British Journal of Psychiatry,* 129, 216–226.

Cooper, A., Rose, J. and Mason, O. (2003) "Mental Health Professionals' Attitudes Towards People Who Are Deaf," *Journal of Community and Applied Social Psychology,* 13, 314–319.

Cooper, S., Smiley, E., Morrison, J., Williamson, A. and Allan, L. (2007) "Mental Ill-Health in Adults with Intellectual Disabilities: Prevalence and Associated Factors," *British Journal of Psychiatry,* 190, 27–35.

Corker, M. (1995) *Counselling—The Deaf Challenge.* London: Jessica Kingsley Publishers.

Corker, M. (1996) *Deaf Transitions: Images and Origins of Deaf Families, Deaf Communities, and Deaf Identities.* London: Jessica Kingsley Publishers.

Costello, E. J., Egger, H. L., and Angold, A. (2005) "The Developmental Epidemiology of Anxiety Disorders: Phenomenology, Prevalence, and Comorbidity." *Child and Adolescent Psychiatric Clinics of North America,* 14, 631–648.

Courtin, C. (2000) "The Impact of Sign Language on the Cognitive Development of Deaf Children." *Journal of Deaf Studies and Deaf Education*, 5(3), 266–276.

Criminal Procedure (Insanity and Unfitness to Plead) Act. (1991) United Kingdom Act of Parliament. www.legislation.gov.uk.

Critchley, E., Denmark, J. C., Warren, F. and Wilson, K. A. (1981) "Hallucinatory Experiences of Prelingually Profoundly Deaf Schizophrenics," *British Journal of Psychiatry*, 138, 30–32.

Cromwell, J. (2004) "Training Deaf Professionals," in S. Austen and S. Crocker (eds.), *Deafness in Mind: Working Psychologically with Deaf People Across the Lifespan*, 317-328. London: Whurr Publishers.

Crowe, T. V. (2003) "Self-Esteem Scores among Deaf College Students: An Examination of Gender and Parents' Hearing Status and Signing Ability." *Journal of Deaf Studies and Deaf Education*, 8, 199–206.

Crystal, D. (2010) *A Little Book of Language*. New Haven, CT: Yale University Press.

David, A., Malmberg, A., Lewis, G., Brandt, L., and Allebeck, P. (1995) "Are There Neurological and Sensory Risk Factors for Schizophrenia," *Schizophrenia Research*, 14, 247–251.

Davis, A. C. (1989) "The Prevalence of Hearing Impairment and Reported Hearing Disability Among Adults in Great Britain," *International Journal of Epidemiology*, 18, 911–917.

DeafHear.ie Services for Deaf and Hard of Hearing People, (undated) *Information on Deafness*, [available online] at://http.www.deafhear.ie.

de Bruin, E., and Brugmans, P. (2006) "The Psychotherapist and the Sign Language Interpreter," *Journal of Deaf Studies and Deaf Education*, 11(3), 360–368.

de Bruin, E., and de Graaf, R. (2005) "What Do We Know About Deaf Clients after Thirteen Years of Ambulatory Mental Health Care? An Analysis of the PsyDon Database, 1987–1999." *American Annals of the Deaf*, 149(5), 384–393.

Denmark, J. C. (1994) *Deafness and Mental Health*, London: Jessica Kingsley Publishers.

Denmark, J. C., and Eldridge, R. W. (1969) "Psychiatric Services for the Deaf," *Lancet* 22, 259–262

Denmark, J. C., and Warren, F. (1972) "A Psychiatric Unit for the Deaf," *British Journal of Psychiatry*, 120, 423–428.

Diamond, J. (2012) *The World Until Yesterday*, pp. 386–392. London: Allen Lane.

Dimmock, A. F. (1993) *Cruel Legacy: An Introduction to the Record of Deaf People in History*. Edinburgh: Scottish Workshop Publications.

du Feu, M. (2009) *Presentation at World Society of Mental Health and Deafness Meeting*, Brisbane. Unpublished.

du Feu, M. (2011) *Presentation at European Society of Mental Health and Deafness Meeting*, October 5–8, 2011. Tenerife.

du Feu, M., and McKenna, P. (1999) "Prelingually Profoundly Deaf Schizophrenic Patients who Hear Voices: A Phenomenological Analysis," *Acta Psychiatricia Scandinavica* 97, 1–9.

Dummer, G. M., Haubenstricker, J. L., and Stewart, D. A. (1996). "Motor Skill Performances of Children Who Are Deaf." *Adapted Physical Activity Quarterly*, 13, 400–414.

Dunst, C. (2000). "Revisiting 'Rethinking Early Intervention,'" *Topics in Early Childhood Special Education*, 20(2), 95-1-4. DOI: 10.1177/027112140002000 205.

Early Identification of Hearing Impairment in Infants and Young Children. (1993). National Institute of Health Consensus Statement. Online 11(1):1–24.

Eastwood, C. (2002) "Silent Discrimination," *Old Age Psychiatry*, 27, 4.

Edwards, L., and Crocker, S. (2008) *Psychological Processes in Deaf Children with Complex Needs*. London and Philadelphia: Jessica Kingsley Publishers.

Emerton, R. G. (1996). "Marginality, Biculturalism, and Social Identity of Deaf People," in I. Parasnis (ed.), *Cultural and Language Diversity and the Deaf Experience*, pp. 136–145. Cambridge: Cambridge University Press.

Emmins, C. (1986) "Unfitness to Plead: Thoughts Prompted by Glenn Pearson's Case," *Criminal Law Review*, Sept, 604-618

Emmorey, K. (2002) *Language, Cognition and the Brain: Insights from Sign Language Research*. Mahwah, NJ: Lawrence Erlbaum Associates.

Equality Act. (2010) United Kingdom Act Of Parliament. www.legislation.gov.uk

Eriksson, P. (1993) *The History of Deaf People: A Source Book*. Örebro: SIH Läromedel, The Learning Materials Division of the National Swedish Agency for Special Education.

European Society of Mental Health and Deafness (ESMHD) [available online] www.esmhd.org.

Evans, J., and Elliott, H. (1981) "Screening Criteria for the Diagnosis of Schizophrenia in Deaf Patients," *Archives of General Psychiatry*, 38, 787–790.

Ewing, A. W. G. (ed.) (1957) *Educational Guidance and the Deaf Child*. Manchester: Manchester University Press.

Farooq, S., and Fear, C. (2003) "Working Through Interpreters," *Advances in Psychiatric Treatment*, 9, 104–109.

Faye'herbe, K. and Teuma, R. (2010) "Interpreting for Indigenous Australian Deaf Clients in Far North Queensland within the Legal Context," in R. L. McKee and J. Davis (eds.) *Interpreting in Multilingual, Multicultural Contexts*, pp. 158–194. Washington, DC: Gallaudet University Press.

Fellinger, J., Hollzinger, D., Dobner, U., Gerich, J., Lehner, R., Lenz, G., and Goldberg, D. (2005) "Mental Distress and Quality of Life in a Deaf

Population," *Social Psychiatry and Psychiatric Epidemiology*, 40(9), 737–742.

Fellinger, J., Holzinger, D., and Pollard, R. (2012) "Mental Health of Deaf People," *The Lancet*, 379, 1037–1044.

Fellinger, J., Holzinger, D., Sattel, H., Laucht, M., and Goldberg, D. (2009) "Correlates of Mental Health Disorders among Children with Hearing Impairments." *Developmental Medicine and Child Neurology*, 51(8), 635–641.

Folstein, M. F., Folstein, S. E., and McHugh P. R. (1975) "Mini-Mental State: A Practical Method for Grading the Cognitive State of Patients for the Clinician," *Journal Psychiatry Research* 12, 196–198.

Foster, S. B. (1998). "Communication Experiences of Deaf People: An Ethnographic Account," in I. Parasnis (ed.), *Cultural and Language Diversity and the Deaf Experience*, pp. 117–135. NewYork: Cambridge University Press.

Gahir, M., O'Rourke, S., Monteiro, B., and Reed, R. (2011) "The Unmet Needs of Deaf Prisoners: A Survey of Prisons in England and Wales," *International Journal on Mental Health & Deafness*, 1(1), 58–63.

Garay, S. (2003) "Listening to the Voices of Deaf Students," *Exceptional Children*, 35(4), 44–48.

Garcia, J. (2005) *Complete Guide to Baby Signing*. London: Match Media Publishing.

Gehyson, F., Loots, G., and van Waelvelde, H. (2008) "Motor Development of Deaf Children with and without Cochlear Implants." *Journal of Deaf Studies and Deaf Education*, 13(2), 215–224. DOI: 10.1093/deafed/enm053.

Gentili, N., and Holwell, A. (2011) "Mental Health in Children with Severe Hearing Impairment," *Advances in Psychiatric Treatment*, 17, 54–62. DOI: 10.1192/apt.bp.109.006718.

Gibbon, S., and Doyle, S. (2011) "The Development and Future of Deaf Forensic Mental Health Services," *The British Journal of Forensic Practice*, 13(3), 191–196.

Glickman, N. S. (1996) "The Development of Culturally Deaf Identities," in N. S. Glickman and M. A. Harvey (eds.), *Culturally Affirmative Psychotherapy with Deaf Persons*, pp. 115–153. Mahwah, NJ: Lawrence Erlbaum Associates.

Glickman, N. (2009) *Cognitive Behavioural Therapy for Deaf and Hearing Persons with Language and Learning Challenges*. New York: Routledge, Taylor and Francis Group.

Glickman, N. S. (2013) *Deaf Mental Health Care*. New York: Routledge.

Glickman, N., and Gulati, S. (2003) *Mental Health Care of Deaf People: A Culturally Affirmative Approach*, Mahwah, NJ: Lawrence Erlbaum Associates.

Glickman, N. S., and Harvey, M.A. (1996). *Culturally Affirmative Psychotherapy with Deaf Persons*. Mahwah, NJ: Lawrence Erlbaum Associates.

Goldberg, D. (1995) "Epidemiology of Mental Health Disorders in Primary Care Settings," *Institute of Psychiatry*, 17(1), 182–190.

Goldberg, D., Benjamin, S., and Creed, F. (1994) *Psychiatry in Medical Practice* (2nd ed.). London: Routledge.

Greenberg, M., and Kusché, C. (1987) "Cognitive, Personal, and Social Development of Deaf Children and Adolescents," in M. C. Wang, M. C. Reynolds, and H. J. Walberg (eds.), *Handbook of Special Education: Research and Practice:* Vol. 3. *Low Incidence Conditions*, pp. 95–129. New York: Pergamon.

Gregory, S. (1976) *Deaf Children and Their Families*. Cambridge: Cambridge University Press.

Gregory, S., Bishop, J. and Sheldon, L. (1996) *Deaf Young People and Their Families*. Cambridge: Cambridge University Press.

Greville, A. (1996) "Identification of Hearing Loss In Infants," *New Zealand Medical Journal*, 109, 21–22.

Griffey, N. (1994) *From Silence to Speech: Fifty Years with the Deaf*. Dublin: Dominican Publications.

Griffiths, T. D. (2000) "Musical Hallucinosis in Acquired Deafness: Phenomenology and Brain Substrate," *Brain*, 123 (10), 2065–2076.

Griggs, M. (2000) "Deaf Wellness Explored," *Deaf Worlds*, 16(3), 74–80.

Groce, N. E. (1985) *Everyone Here Spoke Sign Language: Hereditary Deafness on Martha's Vineyard*. Cambridge, MA: Harvard University Press.

Grosjeàn, J. (1996) "Living with Two Languages and Two Cultures," in I. Parasnis (ed.), *Cultural and Language Diversity and the Deaf Experience*. 20-37. New York: Cambridge University Press.

Grubin, D. (1996) *Maudsley Monographs 38: Fitness to Plead in England and Wales*. Hove: Psychology Press.

Guthman, D., Sandberg, K., and Dickinson, J. (2010) "Chemical Dependency: An Application of a Treatment Model for Deaf People." In I. W. Leigh (ed.), *Psychotherapy with Deaf Clients from Diverse Groups* (2nd ed.), pp. 341–371. Washington, DC: Gallaudet University Press.

Gutman, V. (2005) "Ethical Reasoning and Mental Health Services with Deaf Clients," *Journal of Deaf Studies and Deaf Education*, 10(2), 171–183.

Hadadian, A., and Rose, S. (1991) "An Investigation of Parents' Attitudes and the Communication Skills of Their Deaf Children." *American Annals of the Deaf*, 136, 273–277.

Hale, W. W., III, Raaijmakers, Q., Muris, P., Van Hoof, A., and Meeus, W. (2008) Developmental Trajectories of Adolescent Anxiety Disorder Symptoms: A 5-Year Prospective Community Study.

Hallgren, B. (1959) "Retinitis Pigmentosa Combined with General Deafness; with Vestibulo-Cerebellar Ataxia and Mental Abnormality in a Proportion of Cases," *Acta Psychiatricia Scandinavica* 34, suppl. 138, 1–101.

Hamerdinger, S., and Hill, E. (2005) "Serving Severely Emotionally Disturbed Youth: A Statewide Program Model." *Journal of American Deafness and Rehabilitation Association*, 38(3), 1–30.

Harris, M. (2001) "It's All a Matter of Timing: Sign Visibility and Sign Reference in Deaf and Hearing Mothers." *Journal of Deaf Studies and Deaf Education*, 6, 177–185.

Harvey, M. A. (2003) *Psychotherapy with Deaf and Hard of Hearing Persons: A Systemic Model*. Mahwah, NJ: Lawrence Erlbaum Associates.

Haskins, B. (2000) "Serving and Assessing Deaf Patients: Implications for Psychiatry," *Psychiatric Times*, 17, 12.

Haskins, B. G. (2004) "Serving Deaf Adult Psychiatric Inpatients," *Psychiatric Services*, 55(4), 439–441.

Hassinen, L. (2010) *Sense of Life: The Life World, Psychological Problems, Psychosocial and Psychotherapeutic Rehabilitation of Deafblind Clients*, Offsetkolmio, Hämeenlinna: The MIELI Project, the Service Foundation for the Deaf.

Health Canada. (2002) A Report on Mental Illness in Canada. Retrieved from http://www.camh.net/news_events/key_camh_facts_for_media/addiction-mentalhealthstat istics.html.

Hindley, P. (2000). "Child and Adolescent Psychiatry," in *Mental Health and Deafness*, in P. Hindley and N. Kitson (eds.), pp. 42–74. London: Whurr Publishers.

Hindley, P. (2005) "Mental Health Problems in Deaf Children," *Current Pediatrics*, 15, 114–119.

Hindley, P., and Kroll, L. (1998) "Theoretical and Epidemiological Aspects of Attention Deficit and Overactivity in Deaf Children." *Journal of Deaf Studies and Deaf Education*, 3, 64–72.

Hindley, P. A., and Van Gent, T. (2002) "Psychiatric Aspects of Sensory Impairment." In M. Rutter and E. Taylor (eds.), *Child and Adolescent Psychiatry* (4th ed.), pp. 842–857. London: Blackwell.

Hinshaw, S. P., and Lee, S. S. (2003) "Conduct and Oppositional Defiant Disorders," in E. J. Mash and R. A. Barkley (eds.), *Child Psychopathology* (2nd ed.), pp. 144–199. New York: Guilford Press.

Hintermair, M. (2008) "Self-Esteem and Satisfaction with Life of Deaf and Hard of Hearing People: A Resource-Oriented Approach to Identity Work." *Journal of Deaf Studies and Deaf Education*, 13, 278–300.

Horne, N., and Pennington, J. (2010) "The Role of the Nurse Specialist in the Highly Specialized Field of Mental Health and Deafness," *Journal of Psychiatric and Mental Health Nursing*, 17, 355–358.

Horton, H. K. (2010) "Linguistic Ability and Mental Health Outcomes among Deaf People with Schizophrenia," *The Journal of Nervous and Mental Disease*, 198(9), 634–642.

Huxley, P., and Thornicroft, G. (2003) "Social Inclusion, Social Quality and Mental Illness," *British Journal of Psychiatry*, 182, 289–290.

Ianelli, V. (2009) Retrieved May 2012 from http://pediatrics.about.com/cs/mentalhealth/a/depression_stdy_2.htm

In the Land of the Deaf (Le Paye des Sourds). (1992) A Film by Nicholas Philibert, motion picture, www.secondrundvd.com.

Iqbal, S., Dolan, M. C., and Monteiro, B. (2004) "Characteristics of Deaf Sexual Offenders Referred to a Specialist Mental Health Unit in the UK," *Journal of Forensic Psychiatry and Psychology*, 15(3), 494–510.

Jaspers, K. (1912) Die Trugwahrnehmungen. Z. Neurol. Psychiat. Referate., 4, 289–354.

Jambor, E., and Elliott, M. (2005). "Self-Esteem and Coping Strategies among Deaf Students." *Journal of Deaf Studies and Deaf Education*, 10(1), 63–81. *Special Education*, 20(2), 95–104. DOI: 10.1177/027112140002000205.

Jenkins, J. M., and Astington, J. W. (1996) "Cognitive Factors and Family Structure Associated with Theory of Mind Development in Young Children." *Developmental Psychology*, 32, 70–78.

Joa, Inge, Johannessen, J. O., Auestad, B., Friis, S., McGlashan, T., Melle, I., Opjordsmoen, S., Simonsen, E., Valglum, P. and Larsen, T. K. (2008) "The Key to Reducing Duration of Untreated First Psychosis: Information Campaigns," *Schizophrenia Bulletin*, 34(3) 466–472.

Johnson, S. (1775) "A Journey to the Western Islands of Scotland," in B. Grant, 15, *The Quiet Ear, Deafness in Literature*. London: André Deutsch Ltd.

Joint Committee on Infant Hearing. (1990) "Position Statement," *American Speech/Language Hearing Association*, 33(Suppl. 5): 3–6.

Joint Committee on Infant Hearing (JCIH), American Academy of Audiology, American Academy of Pediatrics, American Speech-Language-Hearing Association, and Directors of Speech and Hearing Programs in State Health and Welfare Agencies. (2007). "Position Statement: Principles and Guidelines for Early Hearing Detection and Intervention Programs." *American Academy of Pediatrics*, 120, 898–921. Retrieved June 15, 2010 from http://pediatrics.aappublications.org/cgi/content/extract/120/4/898

Journal of Deaf Studies and Deaf Education jdsde.oxfordjournals.org

Kazvin, A. E., Kraemer, H. C., Kessler, R. C., Kupfer, D. J., and Offord, D. R. (1997) *Clinical Psychology Review*, 1'7(4), 375–406.

Keller, H. (1987) "Comparing Deafness and Blindness," in B. Grant, 34-37, *The Quiet Ear, Deafness in Literature*. London: André Deutsch Ltd.

Kessler, R. C., McLaughlin, K. A., Green, J. G., Gruber, M. J., Sampson, N. A., and Zaslavsky, A. M. (2010) "Childhood Adversities and Adult

Psychopathology in the WHO World Mental Health Surveys," *The British Journal of Psychiatry*, 197, 378–385.

Keyes, K. M., Eaton, N. R., Krueger, R. F., McLaughlin, K. A., Wall, M. M., Grant, B. F., and Hasin, D. S. (2012) "Childhood Maltreatment and the Structure of Common Psychiatric Disorders," *The British Journal of Psychiatry*, 200, 107–115.

Kiani, R., and Miller, H. (2010) "Sensory Impairment and Intellectual Disability," *Advances in Psychiatric Treatment*, 16, 228–235.

Klein, H. (2011) "Letter to the Editor: Breaking Barriers to Professional Achievement," *International Journal on Mental Health and Deafness*, 1(1), 64–67.

Knutson, J. F., Johnson, C. R., and Sullivan, P. M. (2004) "Disciplinary Choices of Mothers of Deaf Children and Mothers of Normally Hearing Children." *Child Abuse & Neglect*, 28, 925–937.

Kraepelin, E. (1915) Der Verfolgungswahn der Schwerhörigen. In *Psychiatrie*, Auflage 8 Band IV, p. 1441. Leipzig: Barth.

Kübler-Ross, E. (1969) *On Death and Dying*. New York: MacMillan.

Kuusisto, S. (1998) *Planet of the Blind*. London: Faber and Faber.

Kvam, M. H., Loeb, M., and Tambs, K. (2006) "Mental Health in Adults: Symptoms of Anxiety and Depression among Hearing and Deaf Individuals," *Journal of Deaf Studies and Deaf Education*, 12(1), 1–7.

Ladd, P. (1978) "Communication or Dummification: A Consumer ViewPoint," in G. Montgomery (ed.) *Of Sound and Mind: Papers on Deafness, Personality and Mental Health*. Edinburgh: Lindsay & Co Ltd.

Lane, H. (1984) *When the Mind Hears: A History of the Deaf*. Reprint. New York: Random House.

Lane H. (1991) "Why the Deaf Are Angry," in S. Gregory and G. M. Hartley (eds.) *Constructing Deafness*, pp. 117–120. London: The Open Univers

Lane, H. (1992) *The Mask of Benevolence: Disabling the Deaf Community*. New York: Alfred Knopf.

Lang, H. (2011) "Perspectives on the History of Deaf Education," in M. Marschark and P. E. Spencer (eds.), *The Oxford Handbook of Deaf Studies, Language, and Education* (2nd ed.), pp. 7–17. New York: Oxford University Press.

LaSasso, C. J., and Metzger, M. A. (1998) "An Alternate Route for Preparing Deaf Children for Bibi Programs: The Home Language as L1 and Cued Speech for Conveying Traditionally Spoken Languages." *Journal of Deaf Studies and Deaf Education*, 3(4), 265–289.

Leigh, I. W., and Lewis J. W. (2010) "Deaf Therapists and the Deaf Community-Issues to Consider," in I. W. Lewis (ed.) *Psychotherapy with Deaf Clients from Diverse Groups* (2nd ed.), pp. 39–61.Washington, DC: Gallaudet University Press.

Leigh, I. W., and Pollard, R. Q. Jr. (2011) "Mental Health and Deaf Adults," *The Oxford Handbook of Deaf Studies, Language and Education* (2nd ed.), p. 217. New York: Oxford University Press.

Lenneberg, E. H. (1967) *Biological Foundations of Language.* New York: Riley.

Lesser, S. R., and Easser, B. R. (1975) "Personality Differences in the Perceptually Handicapped," *Journal of the American Academy of Child Psychiatry*, 11, 458–466.

Lewis, B. A. (1992) *Kids with Courage: True Stories about Young People Making a Difference.* Minneapolis, MN: Free Spirit Publishing.

Lieberman, L. J., Volding, L., and Winnick, J. P. (2004) "Comparing Motor Development of Deaf Children of Deaf Parents and Deaf Children of Hearing Parents," *American Annals of the Deaf*, 149(3), 281–289.

Lieberman, M. B., Eisenberger, N. I., Crockett, M. J., Tom, S. M., Pfeifer, J. H., and Way, B. M. (2007) "Putting Feelings into Words: Affect Labeling Disrupts Amygdala Activity in Response to Affective Stimuli," *Psychological Science*, 18(5), 421–428.

Lin, F. R., Metter, E. J., O'Brien, R. J., Resnick, S. M., Zonderman, A. B. and Ferrucci, L. (2011) "Hearing Loss and Incident Dementia," *Arch Neurol* 68(2), 214–220.

LINK (2005) *Hidden Lives: The Psychological and Social Impact of Becoming Deafened in Adult Life.* Eastbourne: Link.

Lodge, D. (2009) *Deaf Sentence.* London: Penguin Books.

Luckner, J. L., and Velaski, A. (2004) "Healthy Families of Children Who Are Deaf." *American Annals of the Deaf*, 149(4), 324–335.

Lukomski, J. (2007) "Deaf College Students' Perceptions of Their Social Emotional Adjustment." *Journal of Deaf studies and Deaf Education*, 12(4), 486–494. DOI:10.1093/deafed/enm008.

Lundy, J. E. B. (2002) "Age and Language Skills of Deaf Children in Relation to Theory of Mind Development." *Journal of Deaf Studies and Education*, 7, 41–56.

Luterman, D. (1987) *Deafness in the Family.* Boston: College-Hill Press.

MacKay, S., and Trehub, S. (1993) *Communication Between Mothers and Their Deaf Adolescents.* National Health Research and Development Program, Ottawa, Ontario: Health Canada.

Maj, M. (2011) "When Does Depression Become a Mental Disorder?" *The British Journal of Psychiatry*, 199, 85–86.

Maller, S. J. (1997) "Deafness and WISC-III Item Difficulty: Invariance and Fit." *Journal of School Psychology*, 35, 299–314.

Maller, S. J., and Braden, J. P. (2011) "Intellectual Assessment of Deaf People: A Critical Review of Core Concepts and Issues," in M. Marschark and P. E. Spencer (eds.), *The Oxford Handbook of Deaf Studies, Language, and Education.* Vol. I (2nd ed.), pp. 473–485. Oxford: Oxford University Press.

Mandela, N. (2011) *Nelson Mandela by Himself.* Johannesburg: Pan Macmillan South Africa.

Markowitz, J. C., and Nininger, J. E. (1984) "A Case Report of Mania and Congenital Deafness," *American Journal of Psychiatry,* 141(7), 894–895.

Marschark, M. (2007) *Raising and Educating a Deaf Child: A Comprehensive Guide to the Choices, Controversies, and Decisions Faced by Parents and Educators,* (2nd ed.), New York: Oxford University Press.

Marschark, M., Lang, H., Albertini, J. (2002) *Educating Deaf Students: From Research to Practice.* New York: Oxford University Press.

Marschark, M., and Spencer, P. E. (2009) *Evidence of Best Practice Models and Outcomes in the Education of Deaf and Hard of Hearing Children: An International Review.* Tim, Co. Meath, Ireland: National Council for Special Education.

Marschark, M., and Wauters, L. (2011) "Cognitive Functioning in Deaf Adults and Children." In M. Marschark and P. E. Spencer (eds.), *Oxford Handbook of Deaf Studies, Language, and Education,* Vol. 1 (2nd ed.), pp. 486–499. New York: Oxford University Press.

Marshall, J., Atkinson, J., Smulovitch, E., Thacker, A. and Woll, B. (2007) "Aphasia in a User of British Sign Language: Dissociation Between Sign and Gesture," *Cognitive Neuropsychology,* 21(5), 537–554.

Mason, A., Mason, M., and Braxton E.T. (2004). Creating and strengthening the therapeutic system for treatment settings serving deaf children. JADARA, 37(2), 1-19

Mason, P., Rimmer, M., Richman, A., Garg, G., Johnson, J. and Mottram, G. (2008) "Middle-ear Disease and Schizophrenia: Case-Control Study," *The British Journal of Psychiatry,* 193, 192–196.

Mathos, K. K., and Broussard, E. R. (2005) "Outlining the Concerns of Children Who Have Hearing Loss and Their Families," *Journal of the American Academy of Child and Adolescent Psychiatry,* 44(1), 96–100.

Matthews, P. A. (1996) *The Irish Deaf Community: Survey Report, History of Education, Language and Culture,* Vol. 1. Dublin: The Linguistics Institute of Ireland.

Mayer, C. (2007) "What Really Matters in the Early Literacy Development of Deaf Children," *Journal of Deaf Studies and Deaf Education.* First published online: June 12, 2007. DOI: 10.1093/deafed/enm020.

McCall, R. F. (1976) "The Link Centre: A National Service for a Small Minority Group," *Proc. Roy. Soc. Med.* 69, 18–20.

McClelland, R., Chishlom, D., and Powell, S. (2001) "Mental Health and Deafness: An Investigation of Current Residential Services and Service Users Throughout the UK," *Journal of Mental Health*, 10(6), 627–636.

Meadow, K. P., Karchmer, M. A., Petersen, L. M., and Rudner, L. *Meadow/ Kendall social-emotional assessment inventory for deaf students: Manual.* Washington, D.C.: Gallaudet College, Pre-College Programs, 1980.

Meadow, K. (2005). "Early Manual Communication in Relation to the Deaf Child's Intellectual, Social, and Communicative Functioning," *Journal of Deaf Studies and Deaf Education*, 10(4), pp. 1–9. DOI: 10.1093/deafed/eni035.

Meadow-Orlans, K. P., Mertens, D., and Sass-Lehrer, M. (2003) *Parents and Their Deaf Children: The Early Years.* Washington, DC: Gallaudet University Press.

Mental Health Commission of Canada. (2012) "10-Year Research Update Review: The Epidemiology of Child and Adolescent Psychiatric Disorders: I. Methods and Public Health Burden." Retrieved from http://www.mentalhealthcommission.ca/english/pages/default.aspx.

Mezzich, J. E., Berganza, C. E., Von Cranach, M., Jorge, M. R., Kastrup, M. C., Murthy, R. S., Okasha, A., Pull, C., Sartorius, N., Skodol, A. and Zaudig, M. (eds.) (2003) "Essentials of the World Psychiatric Association's International Guidelines for Diagnostic Assessment (IGDA)," *The British Journal of Psychiatry*, 182(45), 37–66.

Middleton, A. (ed.) (2009) *Working with Deaf People: A Handbook for Healthcare Professionals.* Cambridge: Cambridge University Press.

Mills, R. P., and Calver, D. M. (1987) "Retinitis Pigmentosa and Deafness," *Journal of the Royal Society of Medicine*, 80(1), 17–20.

Mishcon, J. (Chair) (2000) "Report of the Independent Inquiry Team into the Care and Treatment of Daniel Joseph." Commissioned by: Merton Sutton and Wandsworth Health Authority and Lambeth Southwark and Lewisham Health Authority.

Mitchell, A. J., and Selmes, T. (2007) "Why Don't Patients take their Medicine? Reasons and Solutions in Psychiatry," *Advances in Psychiatric Treatment*, 13, 336–346.

Mitchell, R. E., and Karchmer, M. A. (2004) "Chasing the Mythical Ten Percent: Parental Hearing Status of Deaf and Hard of Hearing Students in the United States," *Sign Language Studies*, 4, 138–163.

Montgomery, G. (ed.) (1978) *Of Sound and Mind: Papers on Deafness, Personality and Mental Health.* Edinburgh: Lindsay & Co Ltd.

Moores, D. F. (1996) *Educating the Deaf: Psychology, Principles and Practices* (3rd ed.). Houghton Mifflin.

Morgan, C., Abdul-Al, R., Lappin, J. M., Jones, P., Fearon, P., Leese, M., Croudace, T., Morgan, K., Dazzan, P., Craig, T., Leff, J. and Murray, R. (2006) "Clinical and Social Determinants of Duration of Untreated Psychosis in the AESOP First-Episode Psychosis Study," *British Journal of Psychiatry*, 189, 446–452.

Munro, L., Philip, K., Lowe, R., and Biggs, H. (2005) "Counselling Deaf Clients: Politics, Practice and Process." In *Proceedings Australian Counselling and Supervision Conference*, Brisbane, Australia.

Muris, P., Merckelbach, H., Mayer, B., and Prins, E. (2000) "How Serious Are Common Childhood Fears?" *Behaviour Research and Therapy*, 38, 217–228.

Musselman, C., MacKay, S., Trehub, S. E., and Eagle, R. S. (1996) "Communication Competence and Psychosocial Development in Deaf Children and Adolescents," in J. Beitchman, N. Cohen, M. Konstantareas, and R. Tannock (eds.), *Language, Learning, and Behavior Disorders: Developmental, Biological, and Clinical Perspectives*, pp. 555–570. Cambridge: Cambridge University Press.

Myklebust, H. R. (1960) *The Psychology of Deafness*. New York and London: Grune and Stratton.

Myklebust, H., and Burchard, E. M. L. (1945) "A Study of the Effects of Congenital and Adventitious Deafness on Intelligence: Personality, and Social Maturity of School Children." *Journal of Educational Psychology*, 34, 321.

National Association of the Deaf. (2008) "Position Statement on Mental Health Services for Deaf Children." Retrieved May 2012 from http://www.nad.org/issues/health-care/mental-health-services/for-deaf-children

Neurofibromatosis Association, (2001) *The Neurofibromatosis Type 2: Information for Patients and Professionals*, Surrey: The Neurofibromatosis Association.

Newborn and Infant Hearing Screening: Current Issues and Guiding Principles for Action (2009). *Outcome of a World Health Organization Consultation*. Switzerland: World Health Organization.

Newschaffer, C. J., Croen, L. A., Daniels, J., Giarelli, E., Grether, J. K., Levy, S.E...Windham, G. C. (2007) "The Epidemiology of Autism Spectrum Disorders," *Annual Review of Public Health*, 28, 235–258.

Northern Ireland Mental Health and Deafness Service. (2011) *The Views of Our Service Users/Carers and Relevant Professionals*. Unpublished.

Oblako, M. N. (1987) "Profound Childhood Deafness in Nigeria: A Three Year Survey," *Department of Otolaryngology, College of Medicine*, 8(2), 74–77.

Øhre, B., Von Tetzchner, S. and Falkum, E. (2011) "Deaf Adults and Mental Health: A Review of Recent Research on the Prevalence and Distribution of Psychiatric Symptoms and Disorders in the Prelingually Deaf Adult Population," *International Journal of Mental Health and Deafness* 1(1), 3–22.

Ollendick, T. H., King, N. J., and Muris, P. (2002) "Fears and Phobias in Children: Phenomenology, Epidemiology and Aetiology." *Child and Adolescent Mental Health*, 7, 98–106.

O'Rourke, S., Gibbon, S., and Hough, W. (2011) "Standards for Deaf People in Medium Secure Care," *Forensic Quality Network for Forensic Mental Health Services*, London: Royal College of Psychiatrists.

O'Rourke, S., and Grewer, G. (2005) "Assessment of Deaf People in Forensic Setting: A Risky Business," *The Journal of Forensic Psychiatry and Psychology*, 16(4), 671–684.

O'Rourke, S., and Reed, R. (2007) "Deaf People and the Criminal Justice System," in Austen, S., and Jeffrey, D. (eds.), *Deafness and Challenging Behaviour: The 360° Perspective*. 257-274. Chichester: John Wiley and Sons Ltd.

Owen, M. J. (2012) "Intellectual Disability and Major Psychiatric Disorders: A Continuum of Neurodevelopment Causality," *The British Journal of Psychiatry*, 200, 268–269.

Oyebode, F. (2008) *Sims' Symptoms in the Mind: An Introduction to Descriptive Psychopathology* (4th ed.) USA, Saunders Elsevier.

Padden, C., and Humphries, T. (1988) *Deaf in America: Voices from a Culture*. Cambridge, MA: Harvard University Press.

Padden C., and Ramsey, C. (2000) "Language Acquisition by Eye." In C. Chamberlain, J. Morford, and R. Mayberry (eds.), *American Sign Language and Reading Ability in Deaf Children*. Mahwah, NJ: Lawrence Erlbaum Associates.

Paijmans, R., Cromwell, J., and Austen, S. (2006) "Do Profoundly Prelingually Deaf Patients with Psychosis Really Hear Voices?," *American Annals for the Deaf*, 151(1), 42–48.

Parker, B. (2011) "Poor Patient Literacy 'Hampers Healthcare,'" *BBC News Health*, www.bbc.co.uk/news/health-15478753.

Pederson, D. R., and Moran, G. (1995) "A Categorical Description of Infant-Mother Relationships in the Home and its Relation to Q-Sort Measures of Infant-Mother Interaction," in B. E. Vaughn, E. Waters, G. Posada, and K. Kondo-Ikemura (eds.), *Caregiving, Cultural, and Cognitive Perspectives on Secure-Base Behavior and Working Models: New Growing Point of Attachment Theory and Research. Monographs of the Society for Research in Child Development*, 60 (2–3, Serial No. 244), 111–145.

Peterson, C. C., and Siegal, M. (1995) "Deafness, Conversation and Theory of Mind." *Journal of Child Psychology and Psychiatry*, 36(3), 459–474.

Peterson, C. C., and Siegal, M. (2000) "Insights into Theory of Mind from Deafness and Autism." *Mind & Language*, 15, 123–145.

Petitto, L. A., Katerelos, M., Levy, B. G., Gauna, K., Tetreault, K. and Ferraro, V. (2001) "Bilingual Signed and Spoken Language Acquisition from

Birth: Implications for the Mechanism Underlying Early Bilingual Language Acquisition." *Journal of Child Language* 28, 453–496.

Petty, R. K. H., Harding, A. E., and Morgan-Hughes, J. A. (1986) "The Clinical Features of Mitochondrial Myopathy," *Brain*, 109, 915–938.

Piaget, J.-P. (1962) *Play, Dreams, and Imitation in Childhood*. New York: Norton.

Picard, M. (2004) "Children with Permanent Hearing Loss and Associated Disabilities: Revisiting Current Epidemiology Data and Causes of Deafness," *The Volta Review*, 104, 221–236.

Picchioni, M., and Murray, R. M. (2007) "Schizophrenia," *British Medical Journal*, 335(7), 91–95.

Pinker, S. (1994) *The Language Instinct: The New Language of Science and Mind*. London: Penguin.

Pinker, S. (2007) *The Stuff of Thought*. London: Penguin Books Ltd.

Poizner, H., Kilma, E. S. and Bellugi, U. (1987) *What the Hands Reveal about the Brain*. Cambridge, MA: Massachusetts Institute of Techology.

Polidori, M. C., Nelles, G. and Pientka, L. (2010) "Prevention of Dementia: Focus on Lifestyle," *Int J Alzheimers Dis*, pii: 393579.

Pollack, B. (1997) *Educating Children Who Are Deaf or Hard of Hearing: Additional Learning Problems*. Reston, VA: ERIC Clearinghouse on Disabilities and Gifted Education.

Pollard, R. (2006) *The Avenue: A History of Claremont Institution*. Dublin: Denzille Press.

Powell T., and Gallagher P. (1993) *Brothers and Sisters: A Special Part of Exceptional Families* (2nd ed.) Baltimore, MD: Brookes

Prieve, B. A., and Stevens, F. (2000) "The New York State Universal Newborn Hearing Screening Demonstration Projects: Introduction and Overview." *Ear & Hearing*, 21, 85–91.

Qin, P., Laursen, T.M., et al. (2005) "Epilepsy or a Family History of Epilepsy Increases the Risk of Schizophrenia or Schizophrenic Like Psychosis," *BMJ* 331, 23, DOI:10.1136/bmj.38488.462037.8F.

Rainer, J. D., and Altshuler, K. Z. (1971) "A Psychiatric Program for the Deaf: Experience and Implications," *American Journal of Psychiatry*, 127, 103–108.

Rainer, J. D., Altshuler, K. Z., Kallman, F. J., and Deming, W. E. (1963) *Family and Mental Health Problems in a Deaf Population*. New York: Columbia University Press.

Rainer, J. D., and Altshuler, K. Z. (eds.) (1967) *Psychiatry and the Deaf*. Washington, DC: Department of Health, Education and Welfare.

Rantakallio, P., Jones, P., Moring, J., and Von Wendt, L. (1997) "Association Between Central Nervous System Infections during Childhood and Adult Onset Schizophrenia and Other Psychoses: A Twenty Eight Year Follow-Up," *International Journal of Epidemiology*, 26(4), 837–843.

Raven, J. C. (1976) *Advanced Progressive Matrices, Set I*. Oxford: Oxford Psychologists Press.

Rawlings, B. (2006) *Deafness and Mental Health Audit*, Unpublished audit of Deaf and Mental Health in Northern Ireland.

Ree, J. (1999) *I See a Voice—Language Deafness and the Senses—A Philosophical History*. London: Harper Collins.

Remvig, J. (1969) "Deaf-Mutes with 'Auditory' Hallucinations," *Acta Psychiatrica Scandinavica Supplementum*, 210, 111–120.

Report of the Independent Inquiry into the Care and Treatment of Sarwat Al-Assaf. (2004) Commissioned by Gedling Primary Care Trust, Nottingham.

Rieffe, C. (2012) "Awareness and Regulation of Emotions in Deaf Children." *British Journal of Developmental Psychology*, 30, 477–492.

Rieffe, C., and Terwogt, M. M. (2006) "Anger Communication in Deaf Children." *Cognition and Emotion*. 20(8), 1261–1273.

Ritter-Brinton, K., and Stewart, D. (1992) "Hearing Parents and Deaf Children: Some Perspectives on Sign Communication and Service Delivery." *American Annals of the Deaf*, 125, 923–930.

Roberts, C., and Hindley, P. (1999). "Practitioner Review: The Assessment and Treatment of Deaf Children with Psychiatric Disorders." *Journal of Child Psychology and Psychiatry*, 40, 151–167.

Roberts, J. (1990) "A Deaf World in Rampton Hospital," *Psychiatric Bulletin*, 14, 279–281.

Royal National Institute for Deaf People. (1999) *Breaking the Sound Barrier, Can You Hear Us? Deaf People's Experience of Social Exclusion, Isolation and Prejudice*. London: RNID.

Royal National Institute for Deaf People. (2004) *A Simple Cure*. London: RNID.

Rutter, M. (2000). "Genetic Studies of Autism: From the 1970s into the Millennium." *Journal of Abnormal Child Psychology*, 28, 3–14.

Rutter, M. (2005) "How the Environment Affects Mental Health," *British Journal of Psychiatry*, 186, 4–6.

Sacks, O. (1991) *Seeing Voices: A Journey into the World of the Deaf*. London: Picador.

Sanghera, S. (2008) *The Boy with the Topknot*. London: Penguin Books Ltd.

Schatzlmayr, W. (2001) "A Special Preventative Medical Provision for Deaf People—An Absolute Necessity," in T. Hjortsø, L. Von Der Lieth, and C. Carlsen (eds.), *Mental Health Services for Deaf People a Worldwide Perspective Part I*, p. 247. Devon: European Society for Mental Health and Deafness.

Schlesinger, H. S. (1969) "Beyond the Range of Sound: The Non-Otological Aspects of Deafness," *California Medicine*, 110(3), 213–217.

Schlesinger, H. S. (2000) "A Developmental Model Applied to Problems of Deafness." *Journal of Deaf Studies and Deaf Education*, 5, 349–361.

Schlesinger, H. S., and Meadow, K. P. (1972) *Sound and Sign: Childhood Deafness and Mental Health*. Berkeley: University of California Press.

Schonauer, K., Achtergarde, D., Gotthardt, U. and Folkerts, H. W. (1998) "Hallucinatory Modalities in Prelingually Deaf Schizophrenic Patients: A Retrospective Analysis of Sixty Seven Cases," *Acta Psychiatrica Scandinavica*, 98(5), 377–383.

Scottish Council on Deafness. (2008) *Making the Case for Specialist Mental Health Services for Deaf People in Scotland*. Glasgow: ScoD.

Sense for Deafblind People. (2010) "A Sense of Urgency: The Deafblind Population Has Been Significantly Underestimated and Is Set to Rise Dramatically," www.sense.org.uk/urgency.

Sessa, B., and Sutherland, H. (2013) "Addressing Mental Health Needs of Deaf Children and Their Families: The National Deaf Child and Adolescent Mental Health Service." *The Psychiatrist Online* (May 2013) 37, 175–178; DOI:10.1192/pb.bp.112.038604

Shaffer, D. R., Wood, E., and Willoughby, T. (2002) *Developmental Psychology: Childhood and Adolescence, First Canadian Edition*. Toronto: Nelson.

Sharpe, M., Baldwin, D., and Walker, J. (2010) "Neurotic, Stress Related and Somatic Form Disorders," in E. C. Johnstone, D. C. Owens, S. M. Lawrie, A. M. McIntosh, and M. Sharpe (eds.), *Companion to Psychiatric Studies* (8th ed.), Edinburgh: Churchill Livingstone pp. 453–491.

Shapira, N. A., DelBello, M. P., Goldsmith, T. D., Rosenberger, B. M., and Keck, P. E. (1999) "Evaluation of Bipolar Disorder in Inpatients with Prelingual Deafness," *American Journal Psychiatry*, 156(8), 1267–1269.

Sharples, N. (2001) "Diversity in Nurse Education From Rhetoric to Action," in Hjortsø, T., Von Der Lieth, L. and Carlsen, C. (eds.) *Mental Health Services for Deaf People a Worldwide Perspective, Part II*. Devon: European Society for Mental Health and Deafness.

Sheridan, M. (2001) *Inner Lives of Deaf Children: Interviews and Analysis*. Washington, DC: Gallaudet University Press.

Sheridan, M. A. (2008) *Deaf Adolescents: Inner Lives and Lifeworld Development*. Washington, DC: Gallaudet University Press.

Siatkowski, R. M., Flynn, J. T., Hodges, A. V. and Balkany, T. J. (1993) "Visual Function in Children with Congenital Sensorineural Deafness," *Transactions of the American Ophthalmological Society*, 91(1), 309–323.

Sinkkonen, J. (1994) *Hearing Impairment, Communication and Personality Development*. PhD thesis. Department of Child Psychiatry, University of Helsinki. Cited in Gentili, N. and Holwell, A. (2011) "Mental Health in Children with Severe Hearing Impairment," *Advances in Psychiatric Treatment*, 17, 54–62.

Sinkkonen J. (1994) "Hearing Impairment, Communication and Personality Development: Depression in Hearing-Impaired Children." *International Journal of Pediatric Otorhinolaryngology* (October 2011), 75(10), 1313–1317.

Smith, D. J., Griffiths, E., Kelly, M., Hood, K., Craddock, N., and Simpson, S. A. (2011) "Unrecognised Bipolar Disorder in Primary Care Patients with Depression," *The British Journal of Psychiatry*, 199, 49–56.

Solomon, A. (2010) *Far from the Tree: Parents, Children and the Search for Identity.* New York: Scribner.

Spencer, P. E., and Marschark, M. (2010) *Evidence-Based Practice in Educating Deaf and Hard of Hearing Students.* New York: Oxford University Press.

Sroufe, L. A., Egeland, B., Carlson, E. A., and Collins, W. A. (2005) *The Development of the Person.* New York: Guilford Press.

Steinberg, A. (1991) Issues in Providing Mental Health Services to Hearing Impaired Persons. *Hospital and Community Psychiatry*, 42(4), 380–389.

Stinson, M. (1994) "Affective and Social Development." In R. C. Nowell and L. E. Marschark (eds.), *Understanding Deafness and the Rehabilitation Process,* pp. 81-82. Boston: Allyn & Bacon.

Stokoe, W. C., Casterline, D. C., and Croneberg, C. G. (1976) *A Dictionary of American Sign Language on Linguistic Principles* (rev. ed.). Silver Spring, MD: Linstok Press.

Streng, A., and Kirk, S. A. (1938). "The Social Competence of Deaf and Hard-of-Hearing Children in a Public Day School." *American Annals of the Deaf,* 83, 244–254.

Strong, M. and Prinz, P. M. (1997) "A Study of the Relationship Between American Sign Language and English Literacy." *Journal of Deaf Studies and Deaf Education,* 2(1), 37–46.

Sullivan, P., Brookhouser, P., and Scanlan, M. (2000) "Maltreatment of Deaf and Hard of Hearing Children," in P. Hindley, and N. Kitson (eds.), *Mental Health and Deafness,* pp. 149–184. London: Whurr Publishers Ltd.

Sullivan, P. M., and Montoya, L. A. (1997) "Factor Analysis of the WISC-III with Deaf and Hard-of-Hearing Children." *Psychological Assessment,* 9, 317–321.

Sussman, A. E., and Brauer, B. A. (1999) "On Being a Psychotherapist with Deaf Clients." In I. W. Leigh (ed.), *Psychotherapy with Deaf Clients from Diverse Groups,* pp. 3–22. Washington, DC: Gallaudet University Press.

Symington, B., and Carberry, J. (2006) *British and Irish Sign Languages: The Long Road to Recognition.* Belfast: The Linen Hall Library.

Szymanski, C., and Brice, P. (2008) "When Autism and Deafness Coexist in Children: What Do We Know Now." *New Directions in Deaf Education: Odyssey*, 9, 10–15.

Teuma, R. (2012) Personal communication.

Thacker, A. J. (1994) "Formal Communication Disorder: Sign Language in Deaf People with Schizophrenia," *British Journal of Psychiatry*, 165, 818–823.

Theunissen, S. C., Rieffe, C., Kouwenberg, M., Soede, W., Briare, J. J., Frijns, J. H. (2011) "Depression in Hearing-Impaired Children." *International Journal of Pediatric Otorhinolaryngology*, 75(10), 1313–1317.

Thomson, N. R., Kennedy, E. A., and Kuebli, J. E. (2011) "Attachment Formation Between Deaf Infants and Their Primary Caregivers: Is Being Deaf a Risk Factor for Insecure Attachment?" in D. H. Zand and K. J. Pierce (eds.), *Resilience in Deaf Children: Adaptation Through 27 Emerging Adulthood*, pp. 27–64. DOI: 10.1007/978-1-4419-7796-0_2, © Springer Science+Business Media, LLC 2011.

The Times, (2012) "Review on Richard Griffiths Career," 25th April, pp. 10–11.

Timmermans, L. (1989) "Research Project," *European Society for Mental Health and Deafness European Congress*, Utrecht 1989 Conference Proceedings, pp. 87–89.

Timmermans, N. (2005) *The Status of Sign Languages in Europe*, Strasbourg:Council of Europe Publishing.

Towards Equity and Access Report, Department of Health. (2005) "Mental Health and Deafness: Towards Equity and Access," Department of Health, London.

Traxler, C. (2000) "The Stanford Achievement Test, 9th Edition: National Norming and Performance Standards for Deaf and Hard of Hearing Students." *Journal of Deaf Studies and Deaf Education* 5, 337–348.

Trumbetta, S., Bonvillian, J., Siedlecki, T., and Haskins, B. (2001) "Language-related Symptoms in Persons with Schizophrenia and How Deaf Persons May Manifest these Symptoms," *Sign Language Studies*, 1, 228–253.

Turnbull, H. R., Turnbull, A., and Wehmeyer, M. (2010). *Exceptional Lives: Special Education in Today's Schools* (6th ed.). Upper Saddle River, NJ: Merrill/Prentice Hall.

Tyrone, M. E., Kegl, J., and Poinzer, H. (1999) "Interarticulator Co-Ordination in Deaf Signers with Parkinson's Disease," *Neuro Psychologia*, 37, 1271–1283.

United Nations Convention on the Rights of Persons with Disabilities (2006). www.un.org/disabilities.

US Department of Health and Human Services. (1999). *Mental Health: A Report of the Surgeon General*. Washington, DC: Author. Available: http://www.surgeongeneral.gov/library/mentalhealth.

Vaccari, C., and Marschark, M. (1997) "Communication between Parents and Deaf Children: Implications for Social-emotional Development." *Journal of Child Psychology and Psychiatry*, 38, 793–801. DOI: 10.1111/j.1469-7610.1997. tb01597.x.

Van Eldik, T. (2005) "Mental Health Problems of Dutch Youth with Hearing Loss as Shown on the Youth Self Report," *American Annals of the Deaf*, 150(1), 11–16.

Van Eldik, T., Treffers, P. D. A., Veerman, J. W., and Verhulst, F. C. (2004) "Mental Health Problems of Deaf Dutch Children as Indicated by Parents' Responses to the Child Behavior Checklist." *American Annals of the Deaf*, 148(5), 390–396.

van Gent, T., Goedhart A. W., Hindley, P. A, and Treffers, P. D. (2007) "Prevalence and Correlates of Psychopathology in a Sample of Deaf Adolescents." *Journal of Child Psychology and Psychiatry* 48, 950–958.

van Ijzendoorn, M. H., and Sagi-Schwartz, A. (2008) "Cross-Cultural Patterns of Attachment: Universal and Contextual Dimensions," in J. Cassidy and P. R. Shaver (eds.), *Handbook of Attachment: Theory, Research and Clinical Applications*, pp. 880–905. New York and London: Guilford Press.

Ventress, M. A., Rix, K. J. B., and Kent, J. H. (2008) "Keeping PACE: Fitness to be Interviewed by the Police," *Advances in Psychiatric Treatment*, 14, 369–381.

Vernon, M., and Miller, K. (2005) "Obstacles Faced by Deaf People in the Criminal Justice System," *American Annals of the Deaf*, 150(3), 283–291.

Vernon, M., and Daigle-King, B. (1999) "Historical Overview of Inpatient Care of Mental Health Patients Who Are Deaf," *American Annals of the Deaf*, 144(1), 51–61.

Vernon, M., and Miller, K. (2001) "Interpreting in Mental Health Settings: Issues and Concerns," *American Annals of the Deaf*, 146(5), 420–434.

Vernon, M., Steinberg, A. G., and Montoya, A. (1999) "Deaf Murderers: Clinical and Forensic Issues," *Behavioural Sciences and the Law*, 17, 495–516.

Vernon, M., Raifman, L., and Greenberg, S. (1996) "The Miranda Warnings and the Deaf Suspect," *Behavioural Sciences and the Law*, 14, 121–135.

Vogel-Walcutt, J. J., Schatschneider, C., and Bowers, C. (2011). "Social-Emotional Functioning of Elementary-Age Deaf Children: A Profile Analysis." *American Annals of the Deaf*, 156(1), 6–22.

Vostanis, P., Hayes, M., Du Feu, M., Warren, J. (1997) "Detection of Behavioral and Emotional Problems in Deaf Children and Adolescents: Comparison of Two Rating Scales." *Child: Care, Health and Development*, 23, 233–246.

Waddell, C., McEwan, K., Shepherd, C. A., Offord, D. R., and Hua J. M. (2005) "A Public Health Strategy to Improve the Mental Health of Canadian Children." *Canadian Journal of Psychiatry*, 50, 226–233.

Waddington, J. L., Brown, A. S., Lane, A., Schaefer, C. A., Goetz, R. R., Bresnahan, M. and Susser, E. S. (2008) "Congenital Anomalies and Early Functional Impairments in a Prospective Birth Cohort: Risk of Schizophrenia-Spectrum Disorder in Adulthood," *The British Journal of Psychiatry*, 192, 264–267.

Wallis, D., Musselman, C., and MacKay, S. (2004) "Hearing Mothers and Their Deaf Children: The Relationship Between Early, Ongoing Mode Match and Subsequent Mental Health Functioning in Adolescence." *Journal of Deaf Studies and Deaf Education*, 9(1), 2–13. DOI: 10.1093/deafed/enh014.

Watson, L. M., Hardie, T., Archbold, S. M., and Wheeler, A. (2008) "Parents Views on Changing Communication After Cochlear Implant," *Journal of Deaf Studies and Deaf Education*, 13,104-116.

Wechsler, D. (2010) "Testing Examinees Who Are Deaf or Hard of Hearing," Administration and Scoring Manual, *Wechsler Adult Intelligence Scale (WAIS IV)*, Ed. 4, Oxford: Pearson. pp. 12–19.

Weinberg, N., and Sterritt, M. (1986) "Disability and Identity: A Study of Identity Patterns in Adolescents with Hearing Impairments." *Rehabilitation Psychology*, 31(2), 95–102.

Western Interstate Commission for Higher Education. (2006) "Information Gaps on the Deaf and Hard of Hearing Population: A Background Paper," *WICHE*, pp. 1–38.

White, P. J. (2001) *The Deafblind Helpbook*. Peterborough: Deafblind UK.

White, S. (1992) Criminal Procedure (Insanity and Unfitness to Plead) Act 1991. *Criminal Law Review*, 1992, Jan, 4–14.

Wiegersma, P. H., and Van der Velde, A. (1983) "Motor Development of Deaf Children." *Journal of Child Psychology and Psychiatry*, 24(1), 3–111.

Williams, C. L. (2004) "Emergent Literacy of Deaf Children." *Journal of Deaf Studies and Deaf Education*, 9, 352–365.

Willis, W. G., and Vernon, M. (2002) "Residential Psychiatric Treatment of Emotionally Disturbed Deaf Youth." *American Annals of the Deaf*, 147(1), 31–38.

World Health Organization. (1992) *ICD-10 Classifications of Mental and Behavioural Disorder: Clinical Descriptions and Diagnostic Guidelines*. Geneva: World Health Organization.

World Health Organization. (2001) *The world health report 2001–Mental Health: New Understanding, New Hope*. Geneva: World Health Organization.

World Health Organization. (2012) Retrieved from http://www.who.int/whr/2001/en/. The Epidemiology of Autism Spectrum Disorders* *Annual Review of Public Health*, 28, 235–258.

World Health Organization. (2013) Deafness and Hearing Impaired Fact Sheet No. 300.

World Health Organization and World Bank. (2011) Disabilities and Rehabilitation Report.

Young, A., Howarth, P., Ridgeway, S. and Monteiro, B. (2001) "Forensic Referrals to the Three Specialist Psychiatric Units for Deaf People in the UK," *Journal of Forensic Psychiatry*, 12(1), 19–35.

Young, A., and Tattersall, H. (2005) "Parents of Deaf Children's Evaluative Accounts of the Process and Practices of Universal Newborn Hearing Screening." *Journal of Deaf Studies and Deaf Education*, 10, 134–145.

Young, A., and Tattersall, H. (2007) "Universal Newborn Hearing Screening and Early Identification of Deafness: Parents' Responses to Knowing Early and Their Expectations of Child Communication Development." *Journal of Deaf Studies and Deaf Education*, 12(2), 209–220. DOI: 10.1093/deafed/enl033.

Youngblade, L. M., and Dunn, J. (1995) "Individual Differences in Young Children's Pretend Play with Mother and Sibling: Links to Relationships and Understanding of Other People's Feelings and Beliefs." *Child Development*, 66(5), 1472–1492. DOI: 10.1111/j.1467-8624.1995.tb00946.

Zeckel, A. (1950) "Psychopathological Aspects of Deafness," *J Nerv and Ment Dis*, 112, 322–346.

INDEX

Page numbers followed by *t* and *f* indicate tables and figures, respectively.